T0361374

Information Privacy in the Evolving Healthcare Environment

SECOND EDITION

Edited by

Linda Koontz, CIPP/US, CIPPG

CRC Press is an imprint of the
Taylor & Francis Group, an **informa** business

A PRODUCTIVITY PRESS BOOK

The author's affiliation with The MITRE Corporation is provided for identification purposes only, and is not intended to convey or imply MITRE's concurrence with, or support for, the positions, opinions, or viewpoints expressed by the author.

Mission Statement

To lead healthcare transformation through effective use of health information technology.

CRC Press
Taylor & Francis Group
6000 Broken Sound Parkway NW, Suite 300
Boca Raton, FL 33487-2742

First issued in paperback 2021

© 2017 by Healthcare Information and Management Systems Society (HIMSS).
CRC Press is an imprint of Taylor & Francis Group, an Informa business

No claim to original U.S. Government works

ISBN 13: 978-1-03-209710-7 (pbk)
ISBN 13: 978-1-138-19612-4 (hbk)

Library of Congress Cataloging-in-Publication Data

Names: Koontz, Linda D., editor.
Title: Information privacy in the evolving healthcare environment / [edited by] Linda Koontz.
Description: [2nd edition]. | Boca Raton, FL : CRC Press, 2017. | Includes bibliographical references and index.
Identifiers: LCCN 2016050104| ISBN 9781138196124 (hardback : alk. paper) | ISBN 9781315303635 (eBook)
Subjects: | MESH: Medical Records | Confidentiality | Records as Topic | Security Measures | United States
Classification: LCC R864 | NLM WX 173 | DDC 610.285--dc23
LC record available at https://lccn.loc.gov/2016050104

**Visit the Taylor & Francis Web site at
http://www.taylorandfrancis.com**

**and the CRC Press Web site at
http://www.crcpress.com**

Contents

Editor

Linda Koontz, CIPP/US/G, is a Senior Principal for Privacy and Strategy at MITRE, a not-for-profit corporation chartered to work solely in the public interest, where she advises senior-level staff at federal agencies on strategic approaches to building privacy into their organizations, processes, and systems. Drawing from her more than 30 years' experience in information systems and technology, she has provided privacy advice and support at the Office of the National Coordinator, the Centers for Medicare and Medicaid, the Department of Homeland Security (DHS), and Centers for Disease Control and Prevention. She is also a former member of DHS's Data Protection and Integrity Advisory Committee (DPIAC) and the Health Information Management Systems Society (HIMSS) Privacy and Security Committee.

Before joining MITRE, Ms. Koontz served as the Director, Information Management, for the U.S. Government Accountability Office (GAO). In that role, she directed a broad portfolio of congressionally requested studies, producing numerous reports on privacy, information access and dissemination, information collection, and records management. Ms. Koontz also testified numerous times before congressional committees as an expert witness on these issues.

She holds a BA in Accounting from Michigan State University and is a Certified Information Privacy Professional. She also is an Executive Coach and a graduate of Georgetown University's Leadership Coaching Program.

Contributors

Robert Belfort, JD, is Partner at the law firm Manatt, Phelps & Phillips, LLP. He advises hospitals, community health centers, medical groups, managed care plans, and other healthcare stakeholders on regulatory and transactional matters. He assists clients with managing health information in compliance with HIPAA and state confidentiality laws and advises on Stark law, anti-kickback, and other fraud and abuse matters.

Linda Dimitropoulos, PhD, is Vice President of eHealth, Quality and Analytics at RTI International. Dr. Dimitropoulos is a social psychologist with expertise in attitude change and persuasive communications applied to consumer behavior and decision-making. She has led major projects focused on privacy and security of health information exchange, including Privacy and Security Solutions for Interoperable Health Information Exchange and the Health Information Security and Privacy Collaboration (HISPC), and she served as Senior Advisor to the State Health Policy Consortium project. Dr. Dimitropoulos has served on numerous expert committees and panels, including the Health IT Safety Committee for the National Quality Forum and the expert panel on Health IT and Mental Health: the Path Forward, sponsored by AHRQ and the National Institute of Mental Health.

Leslie Francis, PhD, JD, is Director of the Center for Law & Biomedical Sciences, Alfred C. Emery Distinguished Professor of Law, and Distinguished Professor of Philosophy at the University of Utah, Salt Lake City, Utah. She also holds adjunct appointments in the Departments of Internal Medicine (Medical Ethics), Political Science, and Family and Preventive Medicine (Public Health). Dr. Francis is past co-chair of the subcommittee on Privacy, Confidentiality, and Security, U.S. National Committee on Vital and Health Statistics (NCVHS advises HHS and CDC on issues of health data and population statistics) and was elected president of the Pacific Division of the American Philosophical Association in 2015. With John G. Francis, she is the author of *Privacy: What Everyone Needs to Know*, to be published by Oxford University Press in 2017.

Kimberly S. Gray, Esq., CIPP/US, is an attorney and is the chief privacy officer of QuintilesIMS, a leading global company that delivers integrated information and technology solutions to drive healthcare forward. She is responsible for the company's privacy and data protection strategy. Gray serves on the Advisory Board of the Future of Privacy Forum, the Centre for Information Policy Leadership (CIPL), the Ethics Committee of the European Pharmaceutical Market Research Association (EphMRA), the Confidentiality Coalition of the Healthcare Leadership Council, the Information Accountability Foundation (IAF), and the Executive Council of HITRUST. She has served on the Board of Directors of the International Association of Privacy Professionals (IAPP) and continues to be actively involved with IAPP. Gray earned a Juris Doctor degree from The Dickinson School of Law of the Pennsylvania State University. She lectures frequently on privacy and data protection issues.

Susan Ingargiola, MA, is Director at Manatt Health Solutions. She provides strategic business, regulatory, and reimbursement advice to healthcare providers, nonprofit organizations, and pharmaceutical/biotechnology companies. She specializes in health information privacy and confidentiality laws and health information technology.

John Mattison, MD, is privileged to follow in the path of Dr. Sidney Garfield, visionary founder of the Kaiser Permanente model of integrated value-based caring. John led the largest integrated EHR deployment in the United States and, as CMIO in KP SCAL, oversees all healthcare technology solutions and leads various national virtual care implementations. His work outside KP includes teaching at Singularity University (and others), chairing the eHealth Workgroup of the Global Alliance for Genomics and Health (GA4GH), and supporting Vint Cerf's global initiatives for Innovation for Jobs (i4j) and People Centered Internet (PCI). He chairs and keynotes conferences nationally and internationally on a wide variety of health, health policy, and technology topics and consults and writes internationally on those topics.

Julie S. McEwen, CISSP, PMP, FIP, CIPP/G, CIPP/US, CIPT, CIPM, is a Principal Privacy and Cybersecurity Engineer and leads the privacy engineering capability at the Cybersecurity and Privacy Technical Center at MITRE. She has worked on privacy research in the healthcare area and is currently supporting the U.S. Department of Health and Human Services. Prior to joining MITRE, she managed privacy and cybersecurity programs and advised organizations on policy and technology issues while at the U.S. Department of Defense, Deloitte, IIT Research Institute, the Logistics Management Institute, and T. Rowe Price. She is a contributor to the second edition of *U.S. Government Privacy: Essential Policies and Practices for Privacy Professionals*.

Kris Miller, JD, LLM, MPA, CIPP/US, CIPP/G, CIPP/E, SMP, is a Principal Business and Privacy Strategist at the MITRE Corporation. Mr. Miller's practice focuses on strategic management, privacy compliance, and policy development. He has been a trusted advisor to senior executives at the Department of Defense, the Department of Health and Human Services, the Administrative Office of the U.S. Courts, the Veterans Administration, and the Department of Homeland Security. Mr. Miller is licensed to practice law in both Connecticut and New York.

Larry Ozeran, MD, is a surgeon and software developer. He programmed an inpatient EHR in 1989, using DOS, FoxPro, and Turbo Pascal, programmatically connecting to disparate lab and transcription systems by dial-up modem, and screen-scraping to collect the data. He has served on public policy committees for AMIA and HIMSS, has read and responded to many NPRMs, and has testified before state and national officials. As President of Clinical Informatics, he supports healthcare organizations, software vendors, and government on public policy, strategic planning, provider engagement, and clinician training. As President of Informed Health Technologies, he leads a development team advancing a patient-centric, collaborative care platform that enables patients to obtain, manage, and securely share all of their health data to optimize their health status and support the Triple Aim.

Acknowledgments

I would like to thank the chapter authors once again for providing your brilliant updates in this second edition of our book on health information privacy. I appreciate your contributions more than I can fully express.

Also, thank you to HIMSS for making the book part of its series; I consider it an honor. And of course, special thanks to Kris Mednansky, our editor, and Alex Gryder, our editorial assistant, for all your help along the way and for answering all of my questions. It was a pleasure to work with both of you.

Finally, I would like to acknowledge my husband, Dan, who sticks by me no matter how many projects I take on.

Linda Koontz, CIPP/US/G

Introduction

There is clearly a tension in the healthcare domain between individual privacy and the goal of transforming our healthcare system. According to the Centers for Medicare and Medicaid, total U.S. healthcare spending reached $3 trillion in 2014[1] and expenditures are expected to grow by an average of 5.8 percent per year between 2015 and 2025.[2] Despite spending more than other industrialized nations, the United States continues to lag behind in quality and was ranked last among 11 wealthy nations in efficiency, equity, and outcomes.[3] These developments make it clear that we must continue to look for ways to improve patient care and the healthcare system itself using a variety of means, including through the adoption of health information technology (health IT). However, the ability to successfully leverage the potential of health IT depends to a large degree on the public trusting that their information will be kept private and secure. Greater adoption of health IT and electronic health records will also produce vast amounts of data which, if aggregated and analyzed via "Big Data" initiatives, holds promise for advancing our ability to understand disease, providing personalized medicine, improving the quality of care, detecting and even preventing healthcare fraud, enhancing patient safety, and achieving other important outcomes. However, this data is among the most sensitive and innately personal that exists. It has been reported that hackers now find this information more valuable than financial information. For these reasons, privacy must be considered as a vital component of the nation's efforts to improve our healthcare system.

As is fitting for a book about privacy in an evolving environment, this second edition expands on the ideas presented in the first edition, recognizing the significant policy, technological, and social developments that have occurred over the last 4 years. It is divided into three parts. The first four chapters lay the foundation by exploring the meaning of privacy, including an overview of the most pressing privacy issues facing the health domain, the relationship between privacy and medical ethics, the synergy that exists between information privacy and security, and the complex legal landscape governing health information privacy. The middle of the book, Chapters 5 through 8, explore some of the most significant privacy challenges faced by the healthcare community as it seeks to transform itself. The topics span the gamut from health information exchange to secondary use to transparency. The final chapter looks to the past and present of healthcare privacy, and then to the future, providing a view of the changes we might expect to see.

The expert authors of the various chapters in this book represent a diversity of disciplines as well as thought. Among them are physicians, researchers, policy analysts, lawyers, privacy practitioners, and privacy advocates. Given this diversity, however, the reader may note that there are differences in how the various authors describe privacy and in the solutions they are proposing to the challenges that face us. These are not contradictions as much as a reflection of the reality of the multiple meanings of privacy and that, in many ways, we are still at the beginning of a very long discussion on this subject. My hope is that the reader will walk away with a greater understanding of privacy, the issues in healthcare, and an appreciation of the range of viewpoints and options that exist.

Linda Koontz, CIPP/US/G

Notes

1. Office of the Chief Actuary, Centers for Medicare & Medicaid Services (CMS). National Health Expenditures 2014 Highlights; 2015. Available at: http://www.cms.gov/Research-Statistics-Data-and-Systems/Statistics-Trends-and-Reports/NationalHealthExpendData/Downloads/highlights.pdf.
2. Office of the Chief Actuary, Centers for Medicare & Medicaid Services (CMS). National Health Expenditure Projections 2015–2025; 2015. Available at: http://www.cms.gov/Research-Statistics-Data-and-Systems/Statistics-Trends-and-Reports/NationalHealthExpendData/Downloads/Proj2015.pdf.

3. Davis K, Schoen C, Squires, D, Stremikis K. Mirror, Mirror on the Wall: How the Performance of the U.S. Health Care System Compares Internationally, 2014 Update, The Commonwealth Fund; June 2010. Available at: http://www.commonwealthfund.org/publications/fund-reports/2014/jun/mirror-mirror.

Chapter 1

What Is Privacy?

By Linda Koontz, CIPP/US/G

Contents

Many experts have written about the difficulties of defining privacy. As legal theorist Robert Post once said, "Privacy is a value so complex, so entangled in competing and contradictory dimensions, so engorged with various and distinct meanings, that I sometimes despair whether it can be usefully addressed at all."[1] Daniel Solove, an internationally known expert in privacy law, has pointed out that privacy has been interpreted to mean many things, ranging from freedom of thought to solitude in one's home to protection from unlawful searches and seizures. He concludes that privacy is a "concept in disarray" and that "nobody can articulate what it means."[2] Helen Nissenbaum, Professor of Media, Culture, and Communication and Computer Science at New York University, sums it up nicely when she writes that, in considering the vast landscape of the theoretical work on privacy, "One point on which there seems to be near-unanimous agreement is that privacy is a messy and complex subject."[3]

Although complex, information privacy has never been more important than it is today, especially in the healthcare domain. The nation's healthcare community, facilitated by numerous federal and state government initiatives, is rapidly moving toward digitizing medical information and enabling greater sharing of this information for purposes of improving patient care and the healthcare system itself. Electronic health records (EHR) are intended to provide physicians with an accurate and complete picture of a patient's health, enabling providers to diagnose health problems sooner, reduce medical errors, and provide safer care at a lower cost. These records should also facilitate coordination of patient care among multiple providers and provide the means to securely share information with patients and their caregivers, allowing them to more fully participate in their own healthcare. With widespread implementation of health information technology (IT), the goal is to make the healthcare system more efficient, reduce paperwork for patients and doctors, and expand access to affordable care.

In addition to health information exchange, the healthcare environment is experiencing many other changes. As seen in other areas, such as finance and other commercial domains, the use of IT can allow the aggregation and manipulation of information for novel uses that were not anticipated at the time the information was originally collected, and that may not be consistent with the public's expectations about the use of their data. For example, concerns about communications to patients encouraging them to purchase or use a healthcare-related product or service led Congress to expand limitations on the sale of medical information to third parties for marketing purposes. Policymakers also recognize the tremendous potential of the Internet of Things (referring to the increasing number of devices and sensors ["things"] connected to the Internet that collect data) and of Big Data (analysis of large, aggregated datasets from a variety of sources) to improve healthcare, but have also cautioned against potential dangers to privacy and security.[4,5] In addition, the more that medical information is aggregated, the more serious the consequences of a data breach. One needs only to examine the U.S. Department of Health & Human Services' (HHS) website, on which data breaches affecting more than 500 individuals are reported, to see that thousands or even millions of data records can be exposed in a single breach.[6]

Despite frequent declarations that "privacy is dead," research has consistently shown that while the public sees the potential value of health IT, they remain gravely concerned about the privacy of their sensitive health information. For example, an April 2010 survey, *Consumers and Health Information Technology*, reported that 68 percent of the respondents were concerned about the privacy and security of their health information.[7] More recently, the Office of the National Coordinator for Health IT (ONC), reported, based on national consumer surveys conducted in 2012 and 2013, that 72 percent of individuals in 2013 had concerns about the privacy of their medical records while 77 percent had concerns about security. These studies also signaled support for health IT, despite concerns about privacy and security. The studies indicated that in 2013, 76 percent of individuals wanted their providers to use an electronic health record and 70 percent wanted their medical records shared with other providers treating them. The ONC noted that these attitudes did not change significantly between 2012 and 2013, even though EHR adoption had increased.[8]

The goal of this chapter is to shed light on the meaning of privacy. To accomplish this, the chapter will highlight key writings, frameworks, and conceptual models that have been developed over the years and use them as the basis for describing the attributes of information privacy in the modern healthcare domain. Finally, the chapter highlights and summarizes key issues and trends that are providing challenges for ensuring individual privacy.

The Right to Privacy

Most discussions of privacy in the United States begin with an article entitled "The Right to Privacy," published in the *Harvard Law Review* in 1890.[9] This article, written by Samuel Warren and Louis Brandeis, who had practiced law together in the 1880s, discussed a new, evolving right in the common law known as privacy, or the right "to be let alone."[10] Interestingly, Warren and Brandeis cited changes in technology—the introduction of a portable camera allowing "instantaneous" photography that could be done outside of a formal studio setting and the unauthorized circulation of portraits of individuals being prime examples—as reasons for concern.[11] They also complained of the ill effects of the so-called "Yellow Press," a type of journalism that was increasingly reporting on gossip and scandal.[12,13] Warren and Brandeis underscored the importance of privacy protections when they wrote: "Of the desirability—indeed of the necessity—of some such protection, there can, it is believed, be no doubt."[14]

In particular, the article's descriptions of the press are particularly unflattering. For example:

> The press is overstepping in every direction the obvious bounds of propriety and of decency. Gossip is no longer the resource of the idle and of the vicious, but has become a trade, which is pursued with industry as well as effrontery. To satisfy a prurient taste the details of sexual relations are spread broadcast in the columns of the daily papers. To occupy the indolent, column upon column is filled with idle gossip, which can only be procured by intrusion upon the domestic circle.[15]

Some have theorized that the motivation for writing this article was Warren's personal experience with the press: Warren was married to the daughter of Thomas Bayard, a senator from Delaware, former candidate for president, and, eventually, the Secretary of State under Grover Cleveland. There was press coverage of the Bayard family, including the Warrens' marriage, the deaths of Mrs. Warren's sister and mother within a 15-day period, and her relationship with President Cleveland's young wife.[16]

Years later, in a letter to Warren, Brandeis wrote that he recalled, ". . . it was a specific suggestion of yours [Warren's], as well as your deep-seated [sic] abhorrence of the invasions of social privacy, which led to our taking up the inquiry." Warren replied, "You are of course right about the genesis of the article." Although it is not known for certain whether or which specific press coverage may have influenced Warren's interest, at least one scholar has concluded that it was quite likely that the article might not have been written had Warren not had this experience with the press.[17]

In their article, Warren and Brandeis stated that the common law has always evolved to meet the changing needs of society and provide new protections. As an example, they explained how the common law evolved from protecting individuals from bodily harm to also protecting them from intangible injury. The authors reviewed a number of legal cases involving copyright laws, breach of confidence, and trade secrets. They concluded that the principle that protected personal writings and other products of the intellect or the emotions was not the principle of property law, but instead a right to privacy, and that this protection extended to the personal appearance, sayings, acts, and to personal relations. The authors stated that if the common law did not allow the reproduction of a woman's face photographically without her consent, ". . . how much less should be tolerated the reproduction of her face, her form, and her actions, by graphic descriptions colored to suit a gross and depraved imagination?"[18] Finally, the authors suggested that individuals' privacy should also be protected by criminal law, but noted that legislation would be needed to accomplish that change.[19]

Despite their strong feelings about the need for protections, Warren and Brandeis did not think that the right to privacy was absolute and noted important limitations. For example, a right to privacy did not prohibit disclosure of information considered to be in the public or general interest. Further, individuals' right to privacy ends when they consent to the publication of information about themselves. The authors also noted that neither a lack of malice on the part of the individual disclosing personal information nor the truthfulness of what is disclosed could be used as a defense for invasion of privacy.[20]

Many have noted that although the article had little immediate effect, the public and both state and federal courts eventually began to endorse and expand the right to privacy. This article has been characterized as establishing the field of privacy law. For this reason, it is commonly regarded as the most influential (and one of the most frequently cited) of all law review articles.[21]

Privacy and Freedom

Let us fast-forward to 1967 and the publication of Alan Westin's historic book, *Privacy and Freedom*.[22] In this book, Westin provided what many believe represents the modern version of the meaning of information privacy: "Privacy is generally defined as the claim of individuals to determine for themselves when, how, and to what extent information about them is communicated to others."[23] He further described privacy as the temporary withdrawal from society to solitude or smaller groups. He added that privacy is not an absolute and that, because participation in society is an equally strong desire, individuals are continuously balancing their desire for privacy with their desire for communications and disclosure to others.

Westin's book provided a study of the conflict between privacy and surveillance in society at that time. Westin highlighted the increase in surveillance after World War II and described a growing trend of the many technological innovations that enabled this increase, including the development of radio-signal transmitters that could be hidden on a person; eavesdropping devices such as tiny microphones; closed-circuit television; powerful binoculars; and telephoto lenses. He also described psychological surveillance, which uses polygraphs and personality tests. He argued that the increase in surveillance was due to two important trends strikingly similar to today's environment: (1) the increased availability of electronic devices at a low cost; and (2) the increased willingness of individuals to divulge information about themselves, as well as curiosity about public figures.[24,25]

Of particular interest to this discussion of privacy and health IT, Westin described the dangers associated with what he calls data surveillance, enabled by the growth in computerized record-keeping. He warned that as individuals are forced to leave behind "documentary fingerprints and footprints" each day and these are put into computer-retrievable storage systems, the government may acquire an unprecedented position of power. Westin predicted that the future would raise even broader privacy concerns. For example, according to Westin's book, a medical data bank, containing the medical case histories of all Americans, was under consideration at the time by the federal government. While Westin acknowledged the benefits to public health and for treating individuals away from home, he noted the damage that could be caused by such sensitive information falling into the wrong hands. He asked, "Who will be permitted to push the button, and for what purpose? An employer? A Congressional Committee? The White House?"[26] As many in healthcare explore the value of data aggregation for diverse purposes, including quality assurance, research, and commercial uses, the questions of who will ultimately have access and for what purpose persist today.

Westin noted that technological advances resulted from research intended to solve important problems, including space travel, medical research, and communications. It was only after these technologies were deployed that they were used for surveillance purposes.[27] Such unanticipated uses of technology—along with novel uses of personal information mentioned earlier—help create a complex landscape of privacy issues.

Overall, Westin advocated "restoring the balance of privacy in America," prohibiting surveillance but allowing limited use in cases of national security and major crimes.[28] He believed that there was a need for legislation in certain areas to safeguard privacy rights, but also supported the use of other measures. For example, he concluded that the actions of private entities to protect privacy rights might have more impact than legislation. These entities could, for example, raise moral consciousness about "invasion of privacy issues," develop technological counter-measures to combat surveillance devices, set rules in private sector organizations (including privacy protections in contractual agreements), and expand ethical codes already in professional standards.[29]

The Fair Information Practices

About 5 years after the publication of Westin's book, Eliot Richardson, then Secretary of Health, Education, and Welfare, commissioned an advisory committee to examine to what extent limitations should be placed on the application of computer technology to keep records on the American public. This was largely in response to the growing concern about the harmful consequences that computerized data systems could have on the privacy of personal information. The committee's final report proposed a set of five principles for protecting the privacy and security of personal information, known as the Fair Information Practices (FIPs).[30] These practices were intended to address what the committee termed a poor level of protection afforded to privacy under existing law:

- There must be no personal data record-keeping systems whose very existence is secret.
- There must be a way for an individual to find out what information about him or her is in a record and how it is used.
- There must be a way for an individual to prevent his or her information to be obtained for one purpose from being used or made available for other purposes without his or her consent.
- There must be a way for individuals to correct or amend a record of identifiable information about them.
- Any organization creating, maintaining, using, or disseminating records of identifiable personal data must assure the reliability of the data for their intended use and must take reasonable precautions to prevent misuse of the data.[31]

These principles underlie the major provisions of the 1974 Privacy Act, which was enacted in the wake of the Watergate scandal and other government abuses of personal information. The Privacy Act was the first comprehensive legislation placing limits on the federal government's collection, use, and dissemination of personal information.[32]

A revised version of the FIPs, developed by the Organisation for Economic Cooperation and Development (OECD) in 1980, has been widely adopted.[33] This version of these principles was reaffirmed by OECD ministers in a 1998 declaration and further endorsed in a 2006 OECD report,[34] demonstrating that these principles have truly stood the test of time. The eight FIPs in the OECD version are summarized in Table 1.1.

The FIPs are, with some variation, the basis of privacy laws and related policies in many countries, including the United States, Germany, Sweden, Australia, and New Zealand, as well as the European Union.[35] HHS relied upon FIPs in issuing the Privacy Rule, regulations implementing the requirements of the Health Insurance Portability and Accountability Act (HIPAA). In adopting the rule, HHS did not restate these principles, but stated, "This final rule establishes, for the first time, a set of basic national privacy standards and fair information practices that provides all Americans with a basic level of protection and peace of mind that is essential to their full participation in their care."[36,37]

At an organizational level, FIPs provide a framework that can be used to evaluate privacy issues and questions, and as a foundational element for an entity's privacy program. FIPs represent a holistic approach to privacy; all the principles are important and should be considered in any program, initiative, or business process that involves the collection and use of personal information. (See Chapter 6 for a more complete discussion of this approach.)

Application of FIPs to the Healthcare Environment

As a set of principles, FIPs lend themselves to application in a variety of domains, including healthcare, finance, government, and the commercial environments. The principles are, by design, high level and do not represent by any means a precise recipe for protecting privacy. However, they do provide a useful blueprint for understanding many aspects of privacy. The following paragraphs explore in more detail the essential components of each principle, and how they apply to the healthcare domain.

The *Collection Limitation* principle established that the collection of personal information should be limited, should be obtained by lawful and fair means, and, where appropriate, should be with the knowledge or

Table 1.1 The Fair Information Practices

Principle	Description
Collection Limitation	The collection of personal information should be limited, should be obtained by lawful and fair means, and, where appropriate, with the knowledge or consent of the individual.
Data Quality	Personal information should be relevant to the purpose for which it is collected, and should be accurate, complete, and current as needed for that purpose.
Purpose Specification	The purposes for the collection of personal information should be disclosed before collection and upon any change to that purpose, and its use should be limited to those purposes and compatible purposes.
Use Limitation	Personal information should not be disclosed or otherwise used for other than a specified purpose without consent of the individual or legal authority.
Security Safeguards	Personal information should be protected with reasonable security safeguards against risks such as loss or unauthorized access, destruction, use, modification, or disclosure.
Openness	The public should be informed about privacy policies and practices, and individuals should have ready means of learning about the use of personal information.
Individual Participation	Individuals should have the following rights: to know about the collection of personal information, to access that information, to request correction, and to challenge the denial of those rights.
Accountability	Individuals controlling the collection or use of personal information should be accountable for taking steps to ensure the implementation of these principles.

Source: Organisation for Economic Cooperation and Development.

consent of the individual.[38] The collection limitation principle also suggests that organizations could limit collection to the minimum amount of data necessary to accomplish a function. This limitation is specifically reflected in the HIPAA Privacy Rule, which applies to protected health information (PHI), defined as individually identifiable health information (including demographics and information about the individual's health conditions, the care provided, and payment for that care) held or transmitted by a covered entity or its business associate (an entity performing functions on behalf of the covered entity), whether electronic, paper, or oral.[39] The rule's *minimum necessary standard* establishes that PHI should not be used or disclosed when it is not necessary to satisfy a particular purpose or carry out a function. The implementation specifications for this provision require a covered entity to develop and implement policies and procedures for determining the minimum necessary data appropriate for its own organization to disclose, reflecting the entity's business practices and workforce and the purpose of the requestor.[40] This principle also introduces the concept of individual consent, but constrains its use to "as appropriate." Chapters 5 and 6 provide an extensive discussion of consent and its importance in protecting individual privacy rights.

The *Data Quality* principle states that personal information should be relevant to the purpose for which it was collected, and should be accurate, complete, and current as needed for that purpose.[41] This principle recognizes that personal information is frequently used to make decisions about the individual and, thus, must be accurate and complete. However, the level of accuracy, completeness, and currency is contextual; the information must be accurate enough for the purpose for which it is to be used. Personal information needed, for example, to facilitate communication with an individual via email or postal mail may not need to meet the same accuracy level as the data that indicates on which leg a surgeon is to operate. The data quality principle is also related to the security concept of data integrity, which involves preventing unauthorized modification or deletion of information.[42] Typical mechanisms to ensure data integrity include controls ensuring that only authorized users are permitted to change data and protections against threats—such as viruses—intended to corrupt data.

The *Purpose Specification* principle states that the purposes for the collection of personal information should be disclosed before collection, and upon any change to that purpose, and its use should be limited to those purposes and those compatible.[43] This means that entities must establish a specific purpose or purposes for collecting personal information and must notify individuals of this purpose before collecting. This, in theory, permits the individual to decide whether to provide the information or not. (However, this is often a bit of a technicality; as a practical matter, individuals often must provide information to obtain a desired service.) Of course, another practical challenge in implementing this principle has been defining the bounds of such compatible purposes.

Use Limitation states that personal information should not be disclosed or otherwise used for anything other than the specified purpose without consent of the individual or legal authority.[44] Once entities establish a specific purpose, any use or sharing of the information must be for that specific purpose only; any other purpose requires the consent of the individual. However, privacy laws may specifically authorize use of the information without consent. For example, HIPAA allows many disclosures of PHI without authorization (consent) for certain public health, law enforcement, research, and other purposes.

The *Security Safeguards* principle establishes that personal information should be protected with reasonable security safeguards against certain risks, such as loss or unauthorized access, destruction, use, modification, or disclosure.[45] Keeping personal information from unauthorized access and disclosure is an important aspect of ensuring privacy. The HIPAA Security Rule, one of the regulations that implement the provisions of HIPAA, establishes the specific physical, administrative, and technical controls that must be implemented to protect personal health information.

It is worth noting here that the concept of *security* is often confused with *privacy*. However, such safeguards are only one aspect of the holistic approach to privacy (as discussed in Chapter 6) represented by the FIPs. A more complete discussion of the differences between privacy and security, as well as the symbiotic relationship between them, will be discussed in Chapter 3.

The *Openness* principle provides that the public should be informed about privacy policies and practices, and individuals should have ready means of learning about the use of personal information.[46] In other words, entities have to tell the individual what information is being collected from them and how it will be used. This is most often accomplished through a written notice made available to the individual. Entities covered under HIPAA are required, for example, to provide individuals with a Notice of Privacy Practices (NPP). The NPP is intended to inform individuals of how an entity covered under HIPAA may use and disclose their PHI, the individuals' rights with respect to that information, as well as the covered entity's obligations to protect the information.[47] Notices should be complete and accurate, and written at an appropriate reading level for the intended audience.

Individual Participation states that individuals should have the following rights: to know about the collection of personal information; to access that information; to request correction; and to challenge the denial of those rights.[48] This principle provides additional information about what the privacy notice should typically contain: what information is collected, how it is to be used, and how it is protected. In addition, individuals should have the ability to find out what personal information that a particular entity holds about them and have the ability to challenge its accuracy. The HIPAA Privacy Rule, for example, provides individuals with the right to request a copy of their records, to contest the accuracy of those records, and to obtain an "accounting of disclosures" recounting how their information was shared.[49] In one case, the Office of Civil Rights (OCR), which enforces the HIPAA Privacy and Security Rules, fined a provider organization $4.3 million for failing to provide 41 patients with copies of their medical records, and for failing to respond to requests for information related to the complaints.[50] The subjects of openness and transparency will be covered in more detail in Chapter 7.

Accountability provides that individuals controlling the collection or use of personal information should be accountable for taking steps to ensure the implementation of these principles.[51] Entities need to have privacy policies, procedures, and training in place to guide their employees' actions. Further, they need to hold themselves and their employees accountable for following these principles. Privacy laws may provide civil and criminal penalties as an additional means of ensuring accountability. For example, HIPAA does not provide an individual right of action for violations; therefore, individuals cannot bring suit against entities that violate their privacy. However, the Office for Civil Rights within HHS is charged with enforcing HIPAA and can levy fines and other penalties against those who violate its provisions.[52] In addition, the Health Information Technology for Economic and Clinical Health (HITECH) Act provides that individuals who are harmed by HIPAA violations may now be able to share in any civil monetary penalties or settlements collected as a result of those violations. The Secretary of HHS has up to 3 years to issue a regulation establishing a methodology by which the monetary penalties or settlements will be shared.[53]

FIPs for Electronic Health Information

FIPs have continued to evolve and there are now many versions, often now referred to by the authoring entities as Fair Information Practice Principles (FIPPs). Many government agencies, including the Department of Homeland

Security, the Defense Advanced Research Projects Agency, and the Internal Revenue Service, have adopted their own versions of FIPs as a way of articulating the value they place on privacy in the context of their own operations. In 2008, HHS published its *Nationwide Privacy and Security Framework for Electronic Exchange of Individually Identifiable Health Information.*[54] This framework described the privacy and security principles modeled on FIPs, and was intended to establish a single, consistent approach to address the privacy and security challenges related to electronic health information exchange through a network for all persons, regardless of the legal framework that may apply to a particular organization. These FIPPs are summarized in Table 1.2.

This framework embodies many of the principles in the OECD version of FIPs. There are, however, several important differences. Specifically, the framework places additional emphasis on "individual choice," or consent, by elevating the concept to the level of a principle. Also, with regard to the accountability principle, the framework not only emphasizes the importance of implementing the principles, but also specifies that the entity should use monitoring and other methods to ensure compliance. Additionally, this principle calls out the need to report both non-adherence and breaches as a means of achieving accountability.

The Consumer Bill of Rights

In February 2012, the White House issued a report entitled "A Framework for Protecting Privacy and Promoting Innovation in the Global Digital Economy."[55] The White House framework consists of:

- A Consumer Privacy Bill of Rights, based on FIPs and adapted to the dynamic environment of the commercial Internet.
- A process for convening stakeholders in a deliberative process to develop enforceable codes of conduct for various industry sectors.
- A proposal to strengthen Federal Trade Commission's (FTC)—responsible for consumer protection regulation—enforcement over these codes of conduct; and engaging with other countries to increase interoperability in privacy laws.[56]

The report urges Congress to pass legislation adopting the Consumer Privacy Bill of Rights, which would set a baseline of privacy rights

Table 1.2 HHS Fair Information Practice Principles

Principle	Description
Individual Access	Individuals should be provided with a simple and timely means to access and obtain their individually identifiable health information in a readable form and format.
Correction	Individuals should be provided with a timely means to dispute the accuracy or integrity of their individually identifiable health information, and to have erroneous information corrected or to have a dispute documented if their requests are denied.
Openness and Transparency	There should be openness and transparency about policies, procedures, and technologies that directly affect individuals and/or their individually identifiable health information.
Individual Choice	Individuals should be provided a reasonable opportunity and capability to make informed decisions about the collection, use, and disclosure of their individually identifiable health information.
Collection, Use, and Disclosure Limitation	Individually identifiable health information should be collected, used, and/or disclosed only to the extent necessary to accomplish a specified purpose(s) and never to discriminate inappropriately.
Data Quality and Integrity	Persons and entities should take reasonable steps to ensure that individually identifiable health information is complete, accurate, and up-to-date to the extent necessary for the person's or entity's intended purposes and has not been altered or destroyed in an unauthorized manner.
Safeguards	Individually identifiable health information should be protected with reasonable administrative, technical, and physical safeguards to ensure its confidentiality, integrity, and availability and to prevent unauthorized or inappropriate access, use, or disclosure.
Accountability	These principles should be implemented, and adherence assured, through appropriate monitoring and other means, and methods should be in place to report and mitigate non-adherence and breaches.

Source: Office of the National Coordinator, Department of Health & Human Services.

throughout the commercial sector. The White House's intention was to avoid putting in place duplicative regulatory regimes; the report also states that it supports exempting companies from consumer data privacy legislation to the extent that their activities are subject to existing federal data privacy laws.[57] Thus, the Bill of Rights would not apply to healthcare entities when conducting activities already subject to HIPAA and its implementing regulations. However, it would apply whenever healthcare entities are performing activities not currently covered by law. For example, HIPAA may not apply to certain specialized providers (such as therapists and drug stores) that conduct business online and do not accept insurance; however, the Bill of Rights may eventually require these providers to implement baseline privacy protections.

The Consumer Privacy Bill of Rights aims to give consumers more control over the commercial uses of their personal data, which the Privacy Report defines as any data, including aggregations of data, which are "linkable to a specific individual."[58] The Bill of Rights is summarized in Table 1.3.

The Consumer Bill of Rights is focused on the private sector and on consumers. Many of its aspects are similar to both the HHS FIPPs and the OECD FIPs. The Bill of Rights, like the HHS FIPPs, places additional emphasis on choice (consent), as well as the ability of individuals to control how companies collect information and how it is used and shared. The document establishes a new principle of "Respect for Context," in which companies should use personal information in ways that closely match customer expectations.

For example, consumers would likely expect that personal medical information provided to their doctors would be used for the purposes of treating them and for facilitating payment for that treatment. However, patients might not expect that their information would be aggregated and sold for marketing purposes. Finally, the Bill of Rights calls out in its Focused Collection principle that not only should companies limit their collection of personal information, but that they should securely dispose of the information that is collected when it is no longer needed.

Privacy Models

Many scholars have developed conceptual models of privacy. Here, two of these models are discussed in greater detail: Daniel Solove's taxonomy of potentially harmful activities and Helen Nissenbaum's concept of "contextual

Table 1.3   Consumer Privacy Bill of Rights

Right	Description
Individual Control	To enable consumers' control over commercial use of their personal data, companies should present simple and prominent choices for personal data use and disclosure. In addition, consumers would have a right to control how companies collect and use personal data, and what personal data companies share with others. The administration encourages consumer-facing companies to "act as stewards of personal data that they and their business partners collect from consumers."
Transparency	Companies should present consumers with easily understandable and accessible information about the relevant privacy and security risks.
Respect for Context	Companies should use and disclose personal data only in ways that a consumer would expect based on the context in which the data were provided. This idea that a consumer's expectations about privacy are guided by the nature of their interaction with a business is a central element of the administration's approach.
Security	Companies should assess and maintain reasonable privacy and security safeguards to control unauthorized access or other harm to personal data.
Access and Accuracy	Companies should allow consumers reasonable access to the personal data collected and provide methods to correct inaccurate data and allow requests that data be deleted. In addition, companies should ensure the reasonable accuracy of the personal data they keep.
Focused Collection	In conjunction with the "Respect for Context" consumer right, the administration recommends that companies should collect only the personal data needed for the specified purpose. And unless under independent legal obligations to retain the data, companies should also securely dispose of personal data when no longer needed.
Accountability	Companies and their employees should be accountable to enforcement authorities and consumers, conduct full audits of their privacy policies, and ensure that disclosure of data to third parties is subject to contractual provisions adhering to the Consumer Privacy Bill of Rights.

Source: The White House. Consumer Data Privacy in a Networked World; February 2012.

integrity." Both of these models introduce insights useful to readers' understanding of privacy.

Solove's Taxonomy

In his book entitled *Understanding Privacy*,[59] Solove proposes a taxonomy
of four classes of potentially harmful activities that could give rise to privacy
issues or problems. These four classes are:

- Information collection: Various entities—people, businesses, govern-
  ment—collect information
- Information processing: Use, storage, and manipulation of data
- Information dissemination: Information is transferred or disclosed to
  other people or entities
- Invasion: Impacts directly on the individual[60]

In doing so, Solove stresses his desire to "shift the conversation from
elucidating the inherent meaning of privacy to discussing the nature of
certain privacy-related problems" from a bottom-up perspective.[61]

This taxonomy is meant to describe the types of privacy problems
that can occur. Thus, some of these activities—such as surveillance and
interrogation—may be less applicable to the healthcare environment than
other domains, such as intelligence and law enforcement. However, the
categories of information processing and dissemination identify a number of
activities that are clearly germane to the healthcare domain.

What is most helpful to this discussion of privacy, however, is Solove's
comprehensive discussion of the harm to the individual that can result from
these activities. For example:

- *Exclusion:* Defined as the lack of sufficient openness with individuals
  that can "create a sense of vulnerability and uncertainty." Individuals
  may feel powerless because they are unable to influence the collection and use of their information. This feeling of powerlessness may be
  exacerbated when individuals' information is used to make decisions
  about them.
- *Aggregation:* Solove argues that at its core, this practice—although not
  new—flies in the face of individuals' expectations about the information they are giving away about themselves. They give away pieces of
  information in a variety of contexts, never thinking that a dossier on

them can be assembled which reveals much more about them than they intended to reveal. He also concludes that aggregation can increase the power that others have over individuals by facilitating judgments about them.

■ *Secondary Use:* In the healthcare domain, there are many examples of the benefits of secondary use, including research, public health, and even law enforcement under certain conditions. In recognition of such "public benefit" purposes, the HIPAA Privacy Rule permits the disclosure of PHI for many of these purposes without the specific, written authorization of the individual. Solove, however, cautions that secondary use may not always be consistent with individuals' expectations and can create unease over how information is to be used in the future. He adds that data originally collected for one purpose may not be so appropriate for another purpose, especially if it is used for decision-making about the individual.[62] (For a more complete discussion of secondary use, see Chapter 8.)

Contextual Integrity

Helen Nissenbaum provides yet another theoretical model of the meaning of privacy. She argues that privacy is neither a right to secrecy nor a right to control, but a right to the *appropriate* flow of personal information. She proposes a framework of "contextual integrity," for understanding and predicting reactions to changes in information practices, particularly those caused by the introduction of information technology.[63]

Nissenbaum disputes the notion that privacy is perceived to be many things to many people. She acknowledges that there is "great complexity and variability in the privacy constraints that people expect to hold over the flow of information." However, she believes that these expectations are not arbitrary, but are deeply rooted in what she calls *context-relative informational norms.*[64] Norms are accepted standards or patterns of social behavior.[65] According to Nissenbaum, information norms or rules govern the flow of information; context-relative informational norms govern this flow within distinct social contexts (e.g., education, healthcare, and politics).[66]

In greatly simplified terms, following are the parameters of such context-specific information norms and the key questions that could be asked in evaluating the potential impact of a new practice or the introduction of information technology:

- *Context*: Contexts are the backdrop for informational norms. Nissenbaum defines contexts as structured social settings characterized by the activities, roles, relationships, power structures, norms or (rules), and internal values (goals, ends, purposes). Examples of contexts include healthcare, education, employment, and the commercial marketplace.
  Key Question: What is the prevailing social context?
- *Actors*: These include the individual or organization that receives information (recipient), the individual that the information is about (subject), and the individual/organization that transmits the information (sender).
  Key Question: Does the new practice or technology change who receives the information, who it is about, or who transmits the information?
- *Attributes*: This refers to the type or nature of information.
  Key Question: Does the practice or technology change affect the types of information transmitted from senders to receivers?
- *Principles of Transmission*: A transmission principle is a constraint on the flow (distribution, dissemination, and transmission) of information among entities. An example of a transmission principle is stating that an entity receiving information cannot further share it. Conversely, a transmission principle could encourage further sharing for particular purposes.
  Key Question: Does the practice or technology change entail a revision in the principles governing the transmission of information from one party to another?[67]

Nissenbaum concludes that if the new practice or technology causes changes in actors, attributes, or transmission principles, it produces a "red flag" indicating that the change would appear to violate information norms and the concept of contextual integrity. However, this does not mean that the new practice or technology should automatically be abandoned. Instead, the new practice/technology's effectiveness should be weighed against the effectiveness of the status quo. If the new approach is more effective, Nissenbaum concludes this could provide a justification for making the change. She uses as an example the increased scrutiny that air travelers have faced since 9/11. On its face, the increased information flows—new information attributes flowing to new actors—that result from this scrutiny may appear to be a violation of contextual integrity. However, Nissenbaum points out that with further analysis, one might find that the new practices are more effective in achieving goals like safety and security that are important in the context of transportation.[68]

Key principles in Nissenbaum's argument help to explain the meaning of privacy. First, privacy is affected by the environment and context. Individuals might be very comfortable sharing huge amounts of personal information with their physicians in the context of a doctor's appointment, with the expectation that it will be used to care for them. They might not be so willing to share if the same information would be used to market a new drug to them or for other advertising or commercial purposes. Second, changes in information practices and flows and the introduction of new technology may produce a dynamic that is inconsistent with patients' expectations about the appropriate use of their information. Such changes need to be carefully considered, and asking the questions that Nissenbaum poses about changes in who has access to information, the effect on information types, and on the assumptions around how the information is to be used, may be a useful way to start such a discussion.

Privacy Challenges in the Healthcare Environment

Now that we have discussed the various meanings of privacy, the following summarizes some of the key privacy trends and issues that exist in the healthcare environment today. Many of these will be discussed in more detail throughout this book.

Electronic Health Records and Health Information Exchange

One of the most important technological trends in healthcare is the movement toward electronic health records (EHR) and health information exchange. Largely fueled by government incentive programs, healthcare providers—including individual physicians, other healthcare professionals, and hospitals—are increasingly storing patient records electronically in EHR systems. The creation of these digitized records will, in turn, enable electronic sharing among providers to show a more complete picture of an individual's health. The goal is that this information will be shared with researchers more quickly and aggregated, analyzed, and turned into actionable knowledge to improve the overall quality of healthcare in this country. However, these trends also mean that an individual's health records may be resident in multiple entities' systems and accessible to many more individuals than would have been the case with paper records. This is further compounded by the fact that the individuals to whom this sensitive information applies may have little knowledge of who has their information and how it is used and protected. Chapter 5 provides a more detailed exploration of privacy and health information exchange.

De-Identified Data

As discussed in Chapter 4, HIPAA provides for the creation of de-identified data, which has been anonymized to protect the individual's identity. The HIPAA privacy regulation prescribes two ways of de-identifying health information. One relies on the removal of specified direct and indirect identifiers (referred to as the Safe Harbor method), the other on the opinion of a qualified statistical expert that the chance of re-identification of individuals is very low (the expert determination method).[69] Once data are properly de-identified, they are no longer governed by HIPAA or its regulations and may be freely used, shared, and published. De-identification provides the means to provide researchers, for example, with meaningful data without the privacy risks associated with identifiable data.

Over the years, there has been intense debate on de-identification and the related regulations, including how well it protects individuals' identities. (And, in fact, these regulations were developed because of concerns about the ability to identify individuals in aggregated data with only a few data points.)[70] Researchers have demonstrated how individuals can be re-identified from de-identified data using other data sets available to them.[71] Others have argued that de-identification was never intended to be absolute and that existing standards provide an appropriate balance between privacy and use of the data for research and other worthwhile purposes.[72] Chapters 8 and 9 provide additional perspective on the issues associated with de-identified health data.

Big Data Analytics

"Big Data" has promise to provide benefits to many sectors of our economy, including healthcare. In May 2014, the White House published its report entitled, "Big Data: Seizing Opportunities, Preserving Values,"[73] which explores the use of Big Data in health, education, homeland security, and law enforcement. The report notes that big data sets are "large, diverse, complex, longitudinal, and/or distributed datasets generated from instruments, sensors, Internet transactions, email, video, click streams, and/or all other digital sources available today and in the future." The amount of data being collected from a variety of sources is growing rapidly. Big Data analysis can identify lifestyle factors that could prevent people from having to visit a doctor, evaluate the efficacy of various clinical treatments and drugs, and ensure providers are reimbursed on the quality of patient outcomes, rather than the quantity of care delivered. The report characterizes "predictive medicine" as the ultimate application, i.e., the ability to fuse large amounts of information on an individual and their genetic makeup to predict whether they will develop disease. While recognizing the current and potential benefits of big data in healthcare, the report also notes that the current privacy framework for health may not be adequate to protect individual privacy. Noting the complexity of the various laws involved, as well as the number of organizations handling this information, the report states that healthcare leaders have voiced the need for a trust framework that protects all health information, regardless of its source. See Chapters 8 and 9 for more discussion of this subject.

Consumer Health Devices and Applications

Recent years have seen an explosion in the growth of consumer-oriented health and fitness apps and wearable devices, which collect information for use by the individual, their families, and care team.[74] According to a 2016 survey, 49 percent of respondents owned at least one wearable device (up from 21 percent in 2014), while 36 percent owned more than one.[75] Gartner Research has predicted that by 2018, 2 million individuals—primarily in dangerous or physical jobs like emergency response—will be required by their employee to wear fitness tracking devices.[76]

While the information is identifiable and health related, device manufacturers and application developers are not covered by HIPAA or by HHS implementing regulations. (An exception is when these devices and related services are offered on behalf of an entity covered by HIPAA, such as a healthcare provider. In this case, the data would be protected by HIPAA.)[77] However, the Federal Trade Commission (FTC), the federal agencies that is charged with protecting consumers from unfair and deceptive trade practices, has emphasized that health information is highly sensitive and communicated its concern over how consumer-generated health data will be protected. And there is some reason for concern. In a May 2014 "snapshot" study, the FTC found that 12 health and fitness apps were sharing information with 76 third parties. Among the information being shared was device and consumer-specific identifiers and information about consumers' exercise and eating habits. The FTC concluded that there were significant privacy implications where information might be aggregated using these identifiers.[78]

A related issue involves whether and how such patient-generated health data (PGHD) generated by devices or other means should or could be added to a patient's electronic medical record. According to the ONC, PGHD is defined as health-related data created, recorded, or gathered by or from the patient. A unique aspect of PGHD is that the responsibility for gathering the data rests with the patient who also has control over its use. While the use of PGHD, which provides continuous longitudinal data outside the clinical setting, could be useful to both patient care and research, there are a number of concerns, including data overload due to the potentially large amount of data involved, the quality and accuracy of the data itself, and provider liability issues related to PGHD use. In response to these concerns, the ONC started a 2-year effort in 2015 to develop a framework for the use of PGHD that identifies best practices, gaps, and opportunities for progress in the collection and use of PGHD for research and care delivery through 2024. As part of the 2-year project, ONC will conduct pilots to test implementation of and further refine the topics identified in the policy framework. The policy framework will consider how PGHD can be collected in a way that protects the patient and the integrity of the patient record, maximizes the provider–patient relationship, builds confidence among providers and researchers to use these data, and encourages individuals to donate their health data for research.[79]

Internet of Things

In view of the increasing number of devices or "things" that are connected to the Internet—25 billion in 2015 and expected to be 50 billion by 2020—the FTC issued a report in 2015 summarizing the results of a 2014 workshop and making recommendations.[80] According to the FTC, the Internet of Things (IoT) refers "to 'things' such as devices or sensors – other than computers, smartphones, or tablets – that connect, communicate or transmit information with or between each other through the Internet."[81] The FTC's focus, consistent with its mission, was on consumer devices, including medical devices.

In addition to a number of security risks, including that of unauthorized access to information, the report identified privacy risks associated with the collection of personal data from individuals and the possible misuse of this information for such things as credit and employment decisions. The Commission staff agreed that companies should adopt policies and procedures that place reasonable limits on the collection and retention of personal data. In addition, the report states that both notice and choice in the IoT environment are important, but emphasized that companies should not have to seek consent for intended uses that are consistent with the transaction, that is, reasonably expected by the consumer. However, companies should seek consent for those uses *not* reasonably expected by the consumer. The report notes the difficulties associated with providing choice when there is no direct consumer interaction, but identified alternative means such as providing choice at the point of sale and using product codes (such as bar codes) to point the consumer to relevant materials.[82]

Given the early stage of development of the IoT, the report declined to recommend legislation to regulate the IoT, although it did point out that self-regulatory programs could encourage adoption of good privacy and security practices. FTC, however, reiterated its recommendations from 2012 that Congress enact broad-based, technology-neutral, (1) security legislation to strengthen security enforcement and provide for notification to consumers of data breaches and (2) privacy legislation to establish baseline privacy standards.[83]

Health Information Breaches

The health sector is increasingly experiencing data breaches. While health information breaches are caused by failures in security, the result of these breaches have implications for individuals' privacy. For 2015, OCR, responsible for enforcing HIPAA and its implementing regulations, reported 269 significant breaches of health information affecting approximately 113 million individuals, including a much-publicized breach at Anthem, Inc., affecting about 79 million individuals.[84] According to the 2015 annual Ponemon Institute study on privacy and security of healthcare data, criminal attacks were, for the second year in a row, the number one cause of data breaches in the sector, citing that healthcare records are particularly attractive to criminals because they provide personal information, credit information, and medical information all in one place. In addition, 38 percent of covered entities and 26 of business associates surveyed reported that they were aware of medical identity theft (occurring when an individual's medical identity is stolen and used to procure healthcare services) affecting their patients and customers.[85] Chapter 3 contains a more detailed discussion of information security in healthcare and how privacy and security professionals can work together to protect personal medical information.

Conclusion

Privacy is a complex concept which is best understood as the embodiment of fair information principles. Individuals should have the right to have control of their own information, transparency as to uses and sharing, access the information held by various entities, and challenge its accuracy. There must also be meaningful limits on the collection of personal health information and its use. Moreover, entities that collect and use this information must be accountable for implementing privacy principles.

The rapid changes in the healthcare system are creating challenges for ensuring individual privacy. These challenges demonstrate the tensions that often exist between privacy and other societal and personal goals, and the difficult balancing that must be done to accommodate both. Privacy matters in the healthcare environment—just as it does in many information-rich domains—and we need to continue the struggle to understand the concept and carefully consider it as we deploy new information practices and technology.

Notes

1. Post RC. Three Concepts of Privacy. *Faculty Scholarship Series*. 2001, Paper 185. Available at: http://digitalcommons.law.yale.edu/fss_papers/185.
2. Solove D. *Understanding Privacy*. Cambridge, MA: Harvard University Press; 2008.
3. Nissenbaum H. *Privacy in Context: Technology, Policy, and the Integrity of Social Life*. Stanford, CA: Stanford Law Books; 2010.
4. Federal Trade Commission. 2015. Internet of Things: Privacy and Security in a Connected World. Available at: https://www.ftc.gov/system/files/documents/reports/federal-trade-commission-staff-report-november-2013-workshop-entitled-internet-things-privacy/150127iotrpt.pdf.
5. Executive Office of the President. 2014. Big Data: Seizing Opportunities, Preserving Values. Available at: https://www.whitehouse.gov/sites/default/files/docs/big_data_privacy_report_may_1_2014.pdf, pp. 22–24.
6. See https://ocrportal.hhs.gov/ocr/breach_report.jst.
7. California HealthCare Foundation. *Consumers and Health Information Technology: A National Survey*. CHCF: Oakland, CA; 2010. Available

at: http://www.chcf.org/~/media/MEDIA%20LIBRARY%20Files/PDF/PDF%20C/
PDF%20ConsumersHealthInfoTechnologyNationalSurvey.pdf.

8. Patel V et al. Individuals' Perceptions of the Privacy and Security of Medical Records. *ONC Data Brief*. June 2015. No.27. Available at: https://www.healthit. gov/sites/default/files/briefs/oncdatabrief27june2015privacyandsecurity.pdf.

9. Warren SD, Brandeis LD. The Right to Privacy. *Harvard Law Review*. 1890; IV:5.

10. Ibid.

11. Ibid.

12. Richards NM. The Puzzle of Brandeis, Privacy, and Speech. *Vanderbilt Law Review*. 2010; 63:5:1295–1352.

13. Freidman LM. *Guarding Life's Dark Secrets: Legal and Social Controls over Reputation, Propriety, and Privacy*. Palo Alto, CA: Stanford University Press; 2007.

14. Warren, op. cit.

15. Ibid.

16. Gajda A. What If Samuel D. Warren Hadn't Married a Senator's Daughter?: Uncovering the Press Coverage That Led to The Right to Privacy. *Illinois Public Law and Legal Theory Research Papers Series*. 2007; 7(06).

17. Ibid.

18. Warren, op. cit.

19. Ibid.

20. Ibid.

21. Shapiro FR, Pearse M. The Most-Cited Law Review Articles of All Time. *Michigan Law Review*. June, 2012; 110:1483. Available at: http://repository.law. umich.edu/cgi/viewcontent.cgi?article=1084&context=mlr.

22. Westin AF. *Privacy and Freedom*. New York: Antheneum; 1968.

23. Ibid.

24. Ibid.

25. Bland RL. Book Notes: Privacy and Freedom. *Washington and Lee Law Review*. March 1968; 25:1:20.

26. Westin, op. cit.

27. Ibid.

28. Bland, op. cit.

29. Westin, op. cit.

30. U.S. Department of Health, Education & Welfare. Records, Computers, and the Rights of Citizens: Report of the Secretary's Advisory Committee on Automated Personal Data Systems. Washington, DC; 1973.

31. Ibid.

32. U.S. Government Accountability Office. Privacy: Alternatives Exist for Enhancing Protection of Personally Identifiable Information. GAO-08-536. Washington, DC: 2008.

33. Organisation for Economic Co-operation and Development. Guidelines on the Protection of Privacy and Transborder Flow of Personal Data. 1980.

34. Organisation for Economic Co-operation and Development. Making Privacy Notices Simple: An OECD Report and Recommendations. 2006.

35. European Union Data Protection Directive: Directive 95/46/EC of the European Parliament and of the Council of 24 October 1995 on the Protection of Individuals with Regard to the Processing of Personal Data and the Free Movement of Such Data. 1995.

36. Gellman R. Fair Information Practices: A Basic History. Version 1.89, April 25, 2012. Available at: http://bobgellman.com/rg-docs/rg-FIPShistory.pdf.

37. *Standards for Privacy of Individually Identifiable Information; Final Rule*. 65 FR 250 (December 28, 2000) p. 82464. Available at: http://www.hhs.gov/ocr/privacy/hipaa/administrative/privacyrule/index.html.

38. Organisation for Economic Co-operation and Development, op. cit.

39. U.S. Department of Health & Human Services, Summary of the HIPAA Privacy Rule, op. cit.

40. U.S. Department of Health & Human Services. Health Information Privacy. Posted December 3, 2002, Revised April 4, 2003. Available at: http://www.hhs.gov/ocr/privacy/hipaa/understanding/coveredentities/minimumnecessary.html.

41. Organisation for Economic Co-operation and Development, op. cit.

42. U.S. Department of Health & Human Services, Office for Civil Rights. HIPAA Administrative Simplification: Regulation Text. Available at: http://www.hhs.gov/sites/default/files/hipaa-simplification-201303.pdf.

43. OECD, op. cit.

44. OECD, op. cit.

45. OECD, op. cit.

46. OECD, op. cit.

47. Department of Health & Human Services, Office of the National Coordinator. The HIPAA Privacy Rule and Electronic Health Information Exchange in a Networked Environment: Openness and Transparency. Available at: http://www.hhs.gov/sites/default/files/ocr/privacy/hipaa/understanding/special/healthit/opennesstransparency.pdf.

48. OECD, op. cit.

49. U.S. Department of Health & Human Services. HIPAA Administrative Simplification: Regulation Text, op. cit.

50. http://www.hhs.gov/hipaa/for-professionals/compliance-enforcement/examples/cignet-health/.

51. OECD, op. cit.

52. U.S. Department of Health & Human Services. How OCR Enforces the HIPAA Privacy Rule. Available at: http://www.hhs.gov/ocr/privacy/hipaa/enforcement/process/howocrenforces.html.

53. Health Information Technology for Economic and Clinical Health Act § 13410(c), 42 U.S.C. § 17939(c).

54. U.S. Department of Health & Human Services, Office of the National Coordinator. The Nationwide Privacy and Security Framework for Electronic Exchange of Individually Identifiable Health Information. December 15, 2008.

Available at: https://www.healthit.gov/sites/default/files/nationwide-ps-frame-work-5.pdf.

55. The White House. Consumer Data Privacy in a Networked World: A Framework for Protecting Privacy and Promoting Innovation in the Global Digital Economy. February 2012. Available at: https://www.whitehouse.gov/sites/default/files/privacy-final.pdf.
56. The White House, op. cit.
57. The White House, op. cit.
58. The White House, op. cit.
59. Solove, op. cit.
60. Solove, op. cit.
61. Solove, op. cit.
62. Solove, op. cit.
63. Nissenbaum, op. cit.
64. Nissenbaum, op. cit.
65. *The New Oxford American Dictionary. Second Edition.* Oxford University Press. 2005.
66. Nissenbaum, op. cit.
67. Nissenbaum, op. cit.
68. Nissenbaum, op. cit.
69. U.S. Department of Health and Human Services. Office for Civil Rights. Guidance Regarding Methods for De-identification of Protected Health Information in Accordance with the Health Insurance Portability and Accountability Act (HIPAA) Privacy Rule Available at: http://www.hhs.gov/sites/default/files/ocr/privacy/hipaa/understanding/coveredentities/De-identification/hhs_deid_guidance.pdf.
70. Barth-Jones D. 2012. The Debate Over 'Re-Identification' of Health Information: What Do We Risk? Health Affairs Blog. Available at: http://healthaffairs.org/blog/2012/08/10/the-debate-over-re-identification-of-health-information-what-do-we-risk/.
71. Sweeney L. Simple Demographics Often Identify People Uniquely. Carnegie Mellon University, Data Privacy Working Paper 3. Pittsburgh 2000. Available at: http://dataprivacylab.org/projects/identifiability/paper1.pdf.
72. Barth-Jones D. 2012. The Debate Over 'Re-Identification' of Health Information: What Do We Risk? Health Affairs Blog. Available at: http://healthaffairs.org/blog/2012/08/10/the-debate-over-re-identification-of-health-information-what-do-we-risk/.
73. Executive Office of the President. 2014. Big Data: Seizing Opportunities, Preserving Values. Available at: https://www.whitehouse.gov/sites/default/files/docs/big_data_privacy_report_may_1_2014.pdf.
74. Agency for Healthcare Research and Quality (AHRQ). 2014. Data for Individual Health. Available at: http://healthit.ahrq.gov/sites/default/files/docs/publication/2014-jason-data-for-individual-health.pdf.
75. PwC. 2016. The Wearable Life 2.0: Connected living in a wearable world. Available at: http://www.pwc.com/us/en/industry/entertainment-media/assets/pwc-cis-wearables.pdf.

76. Gartner Research. 2015. Available at: http://www.gartner.com/newsroom/id/3143718.
77. HIMSS 16 Conference & Exhibition. 2016. Navigating Health in a Data-Driven World. Available at: http://www.himssconference.org/sites/himssconference/files/pdf/201.pdf.
78. Federal Trade Commission. 2014. Federal Trade Commission Spring Privacy Series: Consumer Generated and Controlled Health Data. Available at: www.ftc.gov/system/files/documents/public_events/195411/2014_05_07_consumer-generated-controlled-health-data-final-transcript.pdf.
79. U.S. Department of Health and Human Services, Office of the National Coordinator. Patient-Generated Health Data. Available at: https://www.healthit.gov/policy-researchers-implementers/patient-generated-health-data.
80. Federal Trade Commission. 2015. Internet of Things: Privacy and Security in a Connected World. Available at: https://www.ftc.gov/system/files/documents/reports/federal-trade-commission-staff-report-november-2013-workshop-entitled-internet-things-privacy/150127iotrpt.pdf.
81. Ibid.
82. Ibid.
83. Ibid.
84. U.S. Department of Health and Human Services. Office for Civil Rights. Breaches Affecting More Than 500 Individuals. Available at: https://ocrportal.hhs.gov/ocr/breach/breach_report.jsf;jsessionid=DA88923DA6C9C2E116E17301B716263E.
85. Ponemon Institute. 2016. Sixth Annual Benchmark Study on Privacy and Security of Healthcare Data. Available at: https://www2.idexpertscorp.com/sixth-annual-ponemon-benchmark-study-on-privacy-security-of-health-care-data-incidents.

Chapter 2

Considering Ethics in Privacy

By Larry Ozeran, MD

Contents

This chapter is intended to be used like a workbook, enabling organizations to define ethics in a practical way for local benefit. It begins with definitions, offers sample principles, describes ethical dilemmas intended to promote internal paradigm shifts, and describes a process for developing organizational policies to support an organization's ethical standards.

What are ethics? One common definition is that ethics are the principles of conduct governing an individual or a group.[1] Another definition is similar to the golden rule: treat others in the way that you (personally) would wish to be treated, with honesty, consistency, and respect. Ethics drive how we treat each other, how we value people, their property, their participation, their ideas, and describe our ideals.

There are differences of opinion about how strictly to define ethics (i.e., whether the circumstances of a situation should be open to interpretation or whether the parameters of the situation can more easily determine the calculus of what is ethical). For example, how might one define the ethical management of a pregnant teenager who wants to keep this information, legally, from her parents. Should policies stay silent on this issue except to the legal requirements, i.e., the institution has no specific ethics in this matter? Should there be no leeway for the clinician's evaluation of the teen's psychological state? If so, is "unless the teen appears emotionally unable to decide" sufficient? This leaves much of the ethics open to individual interpretation. Is it better to say something like "unless the licensed, treating clinician documents why it is in the interest of the teen to reject her request?" The former addresses only one parameter in the determination and leaves key parameters out: licensure, active management, documentation, what is in the teen's interest. Under the first exclusion, any staff member with access to the chart could say the teen emotionally needed the support of her parents. It is this author's opinion that organizations that value consistency in management of patients, families, visitors, and staff should leave as little open to interpretation as possible.

In this chapter, we will inspect the confluence of medical ethics and privacy, with the medical ethics component providing the necessary context for the privacy discussion. In some cases, the privacy issues will predominate. In other cases, the general medical ethics issues predominate and the privacy component is subsequently dissected from them.

This chapter offers a context for evaluating ethics within your organization. As a foundation upon which to build that context, we begin with definitions and a few sample principles. We describe how principles may need to be balanced when they conflict. We end with a suggestion for how you might implement a process to identify the ethics in your organization as they exist or as you would like them to exist. The remainder of the chapter offers a dozen sample questions intended to prod your thinking, both personally and within your organization. There are examples, but no definitive answers. There is a process for developing policies, but no policies for your organization to simply adopt.

Both within and beyond this chapter, there are no *right* answers, though there are answers that will make it easier or harder to meet the needs of patients, comply with laws, and minimize lawsuits. This chapter offers sample situations, sample principles, and a description of a process that is intended to help your organization develop its own principles and ethical policies based upon your organizational mission and goals.

One of the challenges in medicine, as in life, is our desire to compartmentalize issues that cross boundaries. Dissecting complex problems into component issues allows for simpler solutions, but sometimes we simplify too much, ignoring significant interaction among multiple components of a problem. In the case of this chapter, much of what we discuss will look like discussions of general medical ethics. Medical ethics for treatment may not differ significantly from medical ethics for billing, medical ethics for informatics, or medical ethics for privacy or security. The challenge in identifying ethical conundrums that have purely privacy considerations is that the privacy implications often impact our ability to provide the best medical care or how we are paid. As a result, the ethical and privacy issues are naturally intertwined with the other components of the issue. We are unable to isolate the ethical issues in medical privacy from other aspects of healthcare and must therefore discuss them in the context of a larger discussion of medical ethics.

Setting Principles

Principles are basic truths, laws, or standards, especially of good behavior, indicating what is desirable and positive for a person, group, organization, or community, which help it to determine the moral view of its actions (right or wrong).[2] Principles are more basic than either policies or objectives, and are meant to govern both. Principles are foundational. Each individual has an implicit knowledge of his or her own principles, yet few of us take the time to explicitly enumerate them. It can be a time-consuming process, yet enriching in understanding of one's self. Organizations do not have the luxury of implicit principles. When organizational principles are unstated, many staff will not know what those principles are. Most healthcare organizations expend significant resources to identify mission and vision statements, develop strategic plans and key objectives, and periodically revisit them, but defining an organization's principles is not done routinely. Perhaps it should be.

To help organizations start the process, an annotated list of principles that an organization might use as a starting point is included. The principles listed may be accepted, modified, or rejected, and the discussion leading to those decisions might assist your organization in identifying principles that fit better with your organizational mission and goals. It should be noted that some of these principles share concepts with the privacy frameworks discussed in Chapter 1, including the HHS Privacy and Security Framework,[3] which was intended to establish a consistent approach to privacy and security challenges related to health information exchange. For example, one sample principle—a competent patient should have the absolute right to limit the sharing of his or her personal clinical data—is similar to the principle of *Individual Choice* from Chapter 1 (see Table 1.2), which establishes that individuals should be provided reasonable opportunities to make decisions about the collection, use, and disclosure of their identifiable health information.

This list of sample principles described in this chapter is far from exhaustive and is presented in no particular order. Even if your organization adopted each of the principles in this chapter, how your organization prioritizes one principle versus another should have nothing to do with the order in this chapter and everything to do with the mission of your organization. This list is merely intended to jumpstart your organization's conversation to determine its principles.

Parallel to the discussion of general medical ethics versus medical privacy ethics, it is important to note that few of your organizational principles will be laser focused on privacy. It is valuable to define all of your organization's principles as they may apply to all aspects of behavior and operations in your organization and not focus on privacy in isolation. As with ethics, privacy cannot be addressed in your organizational principles in a vacuum that is free of both competing and complementary issues.

Sample Principles

Organizations Should Treat Everyone according to the Same Ethical Principles

Does this need to be said? Isn't it *obvious*? What is the alternative? An organization could treat different people according to different principles. If a murderer is admitted to the hospital from the jail, having been stabbed by another inmate, should different principles apply to him or be applied in a different way than they might apply to a newborn infant with a delivery-related injury? What would the laws of your state say about different treatment under otherwise similar circumstances based on a patient's ideology, race, gender, or ability to pay? This principle of equal treatment applies similarly to privacy ethics, general medical ethics, and most other ethical questions. It warrants explicit consideration with examples that demonstrate why it is important.

Everyone Now Living Will Die Someday

Anyone who doubts the truth of this principle should consider whether anyone has lived to be 140 years old. The importance of this principle should not be undervalued. It is important in each of the following fictional scenarios (that are based on real events):

■ A woman with terminal cancer has lost 50 pounds and her family does not want her to be told that she is dying. Is this a reasonable option to even consider? Patients so often already know or are highly suspicious that death may be coming quickly, even if no family members want to talk about it. Honoring the family's request may preclude the woman from fulfilling her final wishes while she still has the strength to do so. It may preclude her from saying goodbye to friends and loved ones, making plans, and so much more. Will the patient's outcome (death) be changed based on your organization's decision about whether to honor the family's request? Will it (negatively) impact her quality of remaining life? Is it a privacy issue to keep someone's diagnosis a secret from them? Is it a privacy violation to withhold information from a patient? What if the patient was 8 years old? Is this something that should be decided by the treating physician? What if the staff disagree; how should that disagreement be managed?

■ A 20-year-old woman has been shot in the neck and is brain-dead. She is 22 weeks pregnant. Her family wants the woman kept on life support so that her baby can be delivered at a reasonable gestational age. (As a side note, do your organization's ethics depend on whether a) the patient's family is wealthy and agrees to pay; b) the patient has insurance that will cover all costs; or c) the patient is uninsured or has insurance that will pay the hospital less than the cost of providing her care?) Is it ethical either to inform the woman's priest that she is dead while she is in the hospital or instead to provide the hospital's chaplain as an acceptable alternative to breaching the patient's privacy? If the patient has no specific written request to inform her priest, can your organization assume that she would want your staff to talk to her priest? If the woman's family thinks that the woman's priest is the father of the baby (whether or not this belief is accurate) and they do not want your staff to talk to him, what would you personally or your organization collectively do or say? Who should have the authority to grant or deny permission for anyone to speak to the priest? You learn that the woman was shot by her ex-boyfriend, who also fathered the child. He is in jail. Should he be permitted to have a say in what information is released about the woman or about his unborn child and to whom?

Quality of Life Has a Higher Value than Quantity of Life

A 95-year-old man with progressive Alzheimer's disease for 5 years is admitted unresponsive to the intensive care unit (ICU) with pneumonia. He has chronic renal failure requiring dialysis three times weekly. His family asks that his treating physicians "do everything" to save their father and grandfather. When is treatment an unreasonable prolongation of life? When is life no longer being lived? Should the providers talk with the members of the family about the inevitability of death and encourage them to either reconsider the intensity of care offered a) during this episode of care or b) for future events? What are the privacy implications in this situation? How much does your staff tell the family about the patient's condition so that they can make an informed decision? Should a provider's personal ethics be permitted to impact how much information is given?

For the purposes of further evaluating this principle, but not this scenario, would a short duration of poor quality of life be worth markedly extending life (i.e., how absolute is this principle)? Would tolerating significant pain and multiple procedures for a year to recover from a major burn be worthwhile? What is the privacy aspect in each case?

Human Life and Limb Hold Very High Value

Most of us intuitively agree with this principle. We value a human life more than we value an insect's. And yet, without pollinating insects, we would be unable to grow many food items that are important to support human life. Would we be willing to kill off all global bee populations because some humans are deathly allergic to bee stings? When a limb has been irreparably damaged in an accident, how far are we willing to go to try to save it? The privacy implications may relate to how a patient feels about what will become a visible sign of his or her illness, limb loss. Should we routinely ask how patients feel about this loss of privacy? Do we routinely consider that limb loss, whether due to trauma, cancer, or any other reason, is deeply personal and also publicized to everyone around the patient? Is there a way to manage this privacy issue, or is it something that the patient must manage on his or her own? How much does privacy impact a) our desire to preserve the limb; and b) our desire to find a suitable prosthesis when limb salvage has failed? How can we assist patients in the management of their privacy when their clinical information may be easily observed by others? Do we have a duty to support patients emotionally and with resources?

Human Life Is More Valuable than a Human Limb

Most of us would be willing to lose a limb to save our life, like the hiker who amputated his own limb to save his life when stuck in a mountain crevice. We support his value of life over limb. In fact, most appreciate his bravery for being able to manage the situation on his own. Yet, some patients value life and limb equally. The author once treated a patient who refused limb amputation despite untreatable chronic infection. Diabetes had caused neuropathy and small vessel disease that could not be treated. Once the patient refused amputation, the next best option was antibiotics and periodic drainage of recurring abscesses. The patient died within 6 months specifically due to refusal to amputate the foot. Should the patient's request that family not be informed about the diagnosis and treatment options be honored? If a provider thinks that the patient's family might help the patient to accept an amputation, should your staff violate the request for privacy in order to value life over limb? At what point does maintaining privacy harm the patient more than it helps? Is it acceptable to be paternalistic and pre-sume that the patient doesn't know what they are doing, so violating privacy is a responsibility?

A Patient's Personal Principles Should Be Valued Higher than Organizational Principles When Applied to That Individual Patient's Care

In some cases, patients may have a belief that they should not receive blood or blood products. They may believe that violating this principle will keep them from a higher reward after their death. Is it appropriate for them to be given blood against their principles? Do any of us have evidence to prove that these patients are wrong? The author has treated many patients who refused blood. The real question often becomes: how strongly do they believe this principle and how do they balance it with their other principles as the risk of death increases? When investigating patient principles, it is important to understand the value of the patient's principles, as it may relate to other principles. That is why full informed consent is so important. None of us will know the patient's other principles, including those pertaining to privacy. Some patients use multiple identities in order to keep certain infor-mation from being aggregated about their health. This action may be seen among patients who are celebrities or patients with mental illness who may be embarrassed to have their primary providers aware of their condition. It may occur when a patient needs a pregnancy or HIV test. Providers should recognize that patients may not always share complete information or every component of their decision-making process; this may negatively impact a provider's view of the full picture of a patient's health. This suggests that providers should therefore give great deference to the patient's stated prin-ciples and wishes on privacy and other medical issues.

A Patient's Personal Principles and Choices Should Not Be Permitted to Violate the Rights or Principles of Another Person

Your organization must balance the common space among all patients and visitors. This principle may come into play if a patient wants to smoke cigarettes, proselytize religious or political ideas, or yell obscenities in the hospital or medical office. The impact on others should be considered and a solution developed to resolve the violation. If a patient wants someone to know something, what does your organization do if the person identified does not want to know? If a married couple had an all-out physical fight causing major injury, what if one injured spouse wants the spouse who caused their injury to see the extent of the damage, but the spouse who is responsible does not want to see? Is it a privacy issue to not share information that the patient wants to share, but the intended recipient does not want to receive? The converse tends to be easier: one spouse wants to see the damage they inflicted, but the injured spouse wants them to stay away. Most organizations would agree that the patient's right trumps the spouse's interest.

Among the more unusual, what if a patient wants to know where to get a live chicken for a ceremonial sacrifice? How do you respond? While you might personally be more focused on the logistics and technique, and perhaps how it offends you, how might this ceremony impact the privacy of other patients? What if the patient shares a room with a vegetarian? What is your obligation to protect privacy? Do you offer use of the chapel? Do you request that the ceremony occur outside?

A Competent Patient Should Have the Absolute Right to Limit the Sharing of His or Her Personal Clinical Data

There is emphasis on "competent," both to address the issues of minors and incompetent adults, whether temporarily incapacitated while unconscious or suffering from mental illness. There also is emphasis on "absolute," so that there is no wiggle room on the interpretation by organizational staff. If the patient says no to sharing her information, even if the staff member feels that a husband should know about a wife's medical condition, it is not the staff member's call to make. For the purpose of this principle, when not in conflict with other principles, this right is absolute. Staff should not share the information. Does there need to be a query tree that identifies who decides how privacy is managed when a patient is not competent? In the case of the brain-dead woman carrying the 22-week-old fetus, who should make the decision about how much information to share with the husband who caused the injury? In the UK, Google is routinely given individually identifiable health information without patient consent and under the guise of direct care, though it looks more like analytics (secondary data use).[5] Should patients opt in before their data is shared, or at least have the right to opt out once informed?

A Guardian's Principles Should Have Great Weight in the Management of a Patient Not Deemed Competent to Make His or Her Own Decisions

This would apply to incompetent patients who may be managed by a family member, a legal representative, or the state. In contrast to the prior principle, "absolute" is *not* used. Why would guardians not have the same absolute right patients would if they were making their own decisions? Is it possible that the guardian may consider some unstated secondary gain in their decision which is directly or indirectly harmful to the patient? What should happen when parents do not want their children to get life-saving treatment due to religious principles? What if the child wants the treatment? What about the reverse when neither the child nor the parents want the treatment? Does it matter if the child is 6 or 16? Conversely, what if the parents want the child fully informed, but the provider is concerned about how the child might interpret the information? What if a legal guardian is not a parent, and wants an unconscious celebrity's information released to the media? What if the legal guardian is the celebrity's agent? What if the guardian was a friend when named as attorney for health matters, but is now a professional competing for an acting role? How deeply should staff investigate whether a guardian might have an interest that is counter to the patient's?

Staff May Not Use Patient Data for Any Purpose Other than Direct Performance of Their Jobs

While this is also a legal requirement under the Health Insurance Portability and Accountability Act (HIPAA) and aligned with the HHS privacy principle of Collection, Use, and Disclosure Limitation,[4] it is also worth considering as an ethical principle of behavior. It will not hurt and might help to have the legal and privacy rationales, as well as the moral view in your organizational principles. As mentioned above, people have their own, often unstated principles. Your organization is unlikely to know which principles your staff will value as most important during a time of personal crisis (e.g., financial stress). Sometimes a staff member will respond to a legal threat and other times may just need a moral push. Your organization cannot predict which of an employee's personal principles will be battling each other, so it seems reasonable to expect that presenting this issue in two ways is better than presenting it in only one.

Healthcare Organizations Should Not Sell Patient Data without Patient Consent

Every healthcare organization is looking for ways to increase revenues and cut costs in these austere times and may consider the sale of patient data as a way to meet those goals. Though HIPAA requires explicit consent for sale of data, many healthcare facilities have very broad global consents into which such a global consent for sale of data could be inserted. Even if highlighted by a separate signature or initials, many patients feel obligated to sign these broad consents in order not to offend those from whom they desire high-quality care. Sometimes selling patient data does not result in a check, but a cost reduction. If an EHR vendor offers "free" services in return for access to your organization's patient data, is this ethical? What if the vendor's intention is to use the data to push pharmaceutical ads disguised as decision support recommendations which might raise organizational costs or even harm the patient?

How should data sharing be managed with business associates? Should the easiest process that meets the needs of the organizations be sufficient or should only the minimum data needed be shared? When sharing data beyond the minimum needed in order for the business associate to meet the terms of the agreement with the covered entity, should de-identified data be shared? If de-identified data sets are to be released to business associates, is the HIPAA standard for de-identification adequate to remove the possibility of identifying a patient, or should more effective techniques be used?

Healthcare Organizations Should Limit Secondary Use of Patient Data to Those Permitted by HIPAA

It is convenient to use HIPAA as a starting point rather than list all of the secondary uses it permits. To complete the exercise, an organization may wish to list each HIPAA-permitted use in a separate principle and evaluate whether to use that principle as written in HIPAA or modify it to better fit the organization. Your organization may determine that some of the secondary uses are ethical in many situations, but not all, and would benefit from some additional restrictions.

Finding Balance

There are few absolutes in our universe. Even in nature, the optimal approach is generally to find the best balance between competing options, actions, and forces. The organism that grows too quickly consumes all available resources and dies. The organism that grows too slowly loses competitively to organisms that grow more quickly. The organism that grows at the optimal pace grows faster than slower organisms, but not so quickly as to outpace the growth of the resources that it needs to survive.

Here is one approach to selecting and balancing your organizational principles in a manner that can be implemented:

1. Identify organizational goals

   When considering a balanced approach to ethical issues in your organization, it is important to first identify your organization's goals. The goals you have set should have been guided by your mission, which is aspirational, while your goals should be actionable. If you do not begin by identifying what you are trying to achieve, it is unlikely that you will reach those goals.

2. Define the principles that support those goals

   Most organizations have longstanding principles based on their mission, such as "We value our customers" or "We always do what is best for the patient." Some of these principles will tie directly to one or more goals, and in some cases you may need to define new principles that both reflect your organizational mission and support the goal to be achieved.

3. Prioritize goals and principles

   Goals and principles must be prioritized and weighted so that a hierarchy or blended approach is possible when goals or principles conflict, as they often do. The ethical approach requires that everyone is aware of the rules and that the rules be applied consistently. The greater flexibility there is for individual judgment to impact outcomes, the greater the variability of individual treatment and the higher the likelihood for unethical actions to occur. Individuality and innovation are valuable when developing products, but they permit our natural human variability to apply unequal treatment when commonly and broadly allowed in the determination of what is ethical. There is a place for flexibility in ethics, but it should be a narrow perspective for organizations to permit flexibility. The less flexibility permitted, the less variability in implementation, and the less opportunity for unethical actions or unequal treatment of different patients in similar circumstances.

Examples

We will provide just three examples for your organization to test its ability to apply principles to ethical dilemmas. To frame the key challenges, each example begins with a limited set of information. Subsequent information presented about each scenario is intended to repeatedly test the reader's perspective as the paradigm of the problem(s) changes. Your organization is encouraged to develop similar examples and discuss them in focus groups within your organization. Similar scenarios are common, so the reader should not have much difficulty crafting scenarios from personal experiences and those of your colleagues. By creating local examples, your organization's staff will build familiarity with and ownership of the process. The process will belong uniquely to your organization. The principles that your organization derives from the examples will best fit with your organizational mission and goals, as well as your organizational culture.

Privacy Among Partners

A woman insists to her physician that he not share any of her medical information with her husband. What ethical principles should your staff consider when deciding whether to honor this request? Does an individual have the right to limit who has access to her information? Would she or he (the husband) be harmed in some way if the request were granted? Would her relationship with her husband be harmed in some way? Should the provider take that into account, or simply accept the woman's request?

With additional discussion, the woman admits that she knows she is pregnant and she does not want her husband to know. Are there additional ethical principles at play? Does he have a right to know that his wife is pregnant? Doesn't the child have his DNA as well as hers?

The woman further admits that she was raped by her husband's brother and is concerned that the child may not be her husband's. How does knowledge of this alleged reprehensible and illegal action change your staff's duty to the woman's privacy? How would the information impact the family dynamic? Does your organization's perspective on the potential harm to the patient's relationship with her husband change?

The woman asks your staff to perform or refer her for an abortion. She is approximately 7 weeks pregnant and has no major health issues. Each staff member should consider the questions, "Do you personally agree with her request? Would you personally insist that her husband must know? Would you personally insist that her brother-in-law, the alleged rapist, also know? How should your organization respond?"

The woman says that she is scared of her husband. He sometimes drinks too much, flies into a rage, and beats her. Does her description of his behavior impact your organization's willingness to keep information from him? Why or why not?

The woman says that she was married to her husband when she was 14. She is now 18. Does your staff have legal reporting responsibilities which go beyond privacy? When does the law trump privacy principles?

Contemplated Activity

A middle-aged male patient who is new to a medical practice tells your staff that he frequently thinks about killing his wife. Whom should staff notify? How much additional information does your staff want beforehand? How quickly does your staff need to take an action?

He appears to weigh less than 100 pounds and he says that his wife is a former boxer with a temper. She has broken things in the home, but never hit him. Do his small size and her fighting skills affect your practice's initial answers? Would it matter if her husband had not claimed that she had a temper?

He is a gun enthusiast. He describes with great pride in his voice his cache of weapons ranging from 9 mm handguns to assault weapons. Does this make your staff more or less concerned about his initial statements? Would it be different if he were describing his insect collection with great pride? Would your staff ask if he handled poisonous insects? How much information is needed to determine the likelihood that he might take a regrettable action? Does that likelihood affect whether to inform his wife or the authorities?

His wife arrives after being delayed in traffic. She is muscular and fit. She says, with him in the room, that recently he has been acting strangely. She clearly does not fear him. Does your staff tell her what he has been saying? Is this a privacy issue or is there a larger safety issue? Would *his* safety be at risk if she knows what he has been saying? Who is more likely to be harmed by sharing or not sharing the information?

A Celebrity in Our Midst

An international pop music celebrity is admitted to your hospital through the emergency room after her bus was struck by a train. She is unconscious, in intensive care for observation, but in stable condition. How does your staff manage her identity in the hospital? Does your organization give her a pseudonym to maintain her privacy? If so, who is permitted to know it? What is the risk of maintaining her privacy compared to the risk of misidentifying a blood sample or giving her an incorrect medication? What information does your organization release to the media? With her unconscious, who can give permission?

Two days later she is awake and transferred to the floor. She was dating a motocross racer after a very hard break-up with an actor 3 months before. She does not recognize the racer and wants to have the actor with her at all times. The racer wants to know about her condition and whether her memory will return. What is your staff's duty to her not to talk to him versus the reasonableness of his request to get some idea as to whether she will ever remember their former relationship?

None of these incidents are real, but each of them is similar to a real event. The ethical issues raised are real. Some are easier to resolve than others. All can be resolved in a consistent way if your organization has defined, prioritized principles formalized into policies which are consistently enforced.

Developing Answers

How does your organization implement a consistent process? The four steps below are much simpler to describe than they are to implement, but the effort involved in the process will yield results that will help make complicated challenges easier to resolve in the moment.

Step 1: Ensure that your organizational goals are consistent with your organizational mission—most organizations have already completed such a step. If your organization has not, there are many resources to assist your organization in that exercise.

Step 2: Identify the principles that your organization supports. Your organization can start with the ones listed earlier in this chapter and modify them to meet your organizational needs or have a series of discussions to develop better ones. Given the importance of information privacy in the current environment, privacy frameworks—such as the HHS Privacy and Security Framework—can also inform this process. To ensure consistency, develop and use a formally documented process to add principles to this list over time.

Step 3: When an ethical question arises, determine whether the issue is already addressed by your organization's current policies in a way that is consistent with your identified principles. If so, keep your existing policy and move to the next issue. If not, consider beginning with a review by your ethics committee and develop policies to manage similar situations. When developing new policies, identify which of your organizational principles apply.

Step 4: Consider how the principles interact with each other. Are they complementary, in that they all support the same conclusion, or are there areas where they conflict? In the areas of conflict, prioritize the principles to develop a blended approach to the resolution of those conflicts. Finding balance and effectively using nuance is difficult, but will lead to more fair and equal treatment of patients, family, visitors, and staff.

Let us consider a few questions from the "Privacy among Partners" scenario. Now knowing the full scenario, we have an 18-year-old pregnant wife who says that she is periodically beaten by her husband and, unknown to her husband, was allegedly raped by her brother-in-law.

To demonstrate how the process might work in your organization, we will begin by assuming that your organization has already completed Steps 1 and 2. Your principles will be different, but *for this example,* the principles adopted in Step 2 are the sample principles previously defined in this chapter.

Before beginning Step 3, there is an important caveat to state again. Organizations should develop a set of core principles which are periodically reviewed and redefined, with new principles added as conditions warrant. For the purpose of this exercise, only the principles previously defined above will be considered, but organizations should consider all of the principles they have when considering their own examples. The principles defined in this chapter are, in themselves, *examples*. Your organization may or may not subscribe to them, so keep in mind that the process described below uses only the principles in this chapter. As a result, you personally, and your organization more generally, may come to very different answers than the author does when following this process using different principles. This is *not* a test to see if you get the same answers as the author; only an example of how to employ the process.

Per Step 3, which of the sample principles apply to the "Partners" scenario? You may personally feel the urge to completely skip this discussion because you have already come to your conclusion. Individuals have that option. However, it is important for organizations not to take shortcuts. Organizations should not "go with their gut," because there is no shared gut. Organizations often develop a better understanding of the issues by following a consistent process. Organizations are made up of many individuals, each of whom will interpret the examples described above in different ways. Absent clear direction from your organization, it is possible that individuals would manage the privacy issues consistent with their own ethical perspectives, but very differently from each other. While there is no guarantee, completing the full process in each circumstance will promote a consistent resolution among similar issues.

The author would suggest that the sample principles applying to the "Partners" scenario are: respecting the patient's wishes; valuing human life highly; ranking a patient's personal principles higher than those of your organization (or its staff); and giving substantial weight to a guardian's principles.

In Step 4, we consider how the principles interact and which ones take priority. The author would suggest that the principles do conflict and would rank them in this situation as follows: valuing human life highly; ranking a patient's personal principles higher than those of your organization (or its staff); respecting the patient's wishes with regard to the release of personal health information; and giving substantial weight to a guardian's principles. Your organization or you personally may come to a different conclusion. Based on this ranking, the author would suggest notifying local authorities about the abuse and not informing either male about the pregnancy.

The policy which supports this conclusion might look like this (and might have already been adopted at the time of the incident):

> *Staff will not share a patient's medical information with anyone else if specifically requested not to do so by a competent patient. Exceptions are made for legal guardians of the patient and other individuals who may have an independent right to the information, unless such a release would risk harm to or death of the patient. Examples of cases where another party may have a right to know may include the partner of an HIV-positive patient or the father of an unborn child.*

Your organization may come to a different conclusion and develop a different policy. The value of following a process based on your organization's principles is that the principles and how they are ranked support the decision made in this circumstance and all similar circumstances.

Managing the ethical issues in particularly complex situations is challenging, whether the issues are limited to privacy or not. With a consistent approach, your organization should be able to successfully and consistently navigate these challenges.

Special thanks to Bonnie Kaplan, PhD, FACMI*, for her thorough review and comments on the first version of this chapter.

Notes

1. Merriam-Webster. Ethic. Available at: http://www.merriam-webster.com/dictionary/ethic.
2. The Free Dictionary by Farlex. Principle. Available at: http://www.thefreedictionary.com/principle..
3. U.S. Department of Health & Human Services, Office of the National Coordinator for Health Information Technology. The nationwide privacy and security framework for electronic exchange of individually identifiable health information; December 15, 2008. Available at: https://www.healthit.gov/policy-researchers-implementers/nationwide-privacy-and-security-framework-electronic-exchange.
4. The Collection, Use, and Disclosure Limitation principle states that individually identifiable health information should be collected, used, and/or disclosed only to the extent necessary to accomplish a specified purpose.
5. "Revealed: Google AI has access to huge haul of NHS patient data" New Scientist, accessed 12/31/16 https://www.newscientist.com/article/2086454-revealed-google-ai-has-access-to-huge-haul-of-nhs-patient-data/.

---

* Yale Law School Information Society Project Faculty Fellow, Yale Interdisciplinary Bioethics Program Scholar, Yale Center for Medical Informatics, Yale University, New Haven, CT.

Chapter 3

The Role of Information Security in Protecting Privacy in the Healthcare Environment

By Julie S. McEwen, CISSP, PMP, FIP,
CIPP/G, CIPP/US, CIPT, CIPM

Contents

Protecting information within the healthcare environment can be challenging, especially because it is necessary to share very sensitive healthcare-related information among a number of authorized parties, while at the same time protecting that information from unauthorized access, disclosure, use, modification, and retention. Information security and privacy are two distinct disciplines, but they are linked. This chapter will provide an overview of security and suggest ways for security and privacy efforts to work together to protect information in the healthcare environment.

What Is Information Security?

Information security is defined as "protecting information and information systems from unauthorized access, use, disclosure, disruption, modification, or destruction."[1] The many functions of healthcare are dependent upon the use of information technology, and protecting the information collected, used, shared, and stored is critical to the healthcare mission. Information security should never be an afterthought; it should be built into all aspects of information system development, operations, maintenance, and management. Information security is accomplished through the implementation of a comprehensive security program across the enterprise. The security program should assess vulnerabilities and potential threats and implement security protections that address security threats and manage security risk. Ongoing monitoring of an organization's systems and networks, as well as employee behavior, is important in order to be able to readily adapt security approaches as the system environment changes and new threats emerge.

For the healthcare environment, the Health Insurance Portability and Accountability Act (HIPAA) Security Standards for the Protection of Electronic Protected Health Information (the Security Rule)[2] establishes a national set of security standards for protecting certain health information that is stored or transmitted in electronic form. Electronic protected health information (ePHI) is defined as all individually identifiable health information that a covered entity creates, receives, maintains, or transmits in electronic form.[3] The Security Rule contains definitions of the primary three objectives of information security: confidentiality, integrity, and availability. Confidentiality is defined as ensuring that access to and disclosure of information are provided only to authorized individuals or processes. Integrity is preventing the unauthorized modification or deletion of information, which ensures that information is genuine and valid. Availability is ensuring that information can be accessed and used by an authorized person upon demand.[4,5]

Information Security Safeguards in the Healthcare Environment

The HIPAA Security Rule requires covered entities to maintain appropriate security safeguards for protecting ePHI. The Security Rule describes security safeguards that covered entities must implement to protect ePHI.[6] The security safeguards listed in the Security Rule represent the three traditional types of safeguards: administrative, physical, and technical. *Administrative safeguards* are policies, procedures, and actions used to manage the selection, development, implementation, and maintenance of appropriate security measures to protect ePHI. For example, planning and risk assessment controls are administrative—they focus on actions taken to assess risk and select and manage information system security measures. Risk management actions include conducting continuous monitoring of security protection, as well as performing periodic reviews and evaluations. Administrative safeguards are also used to respond to security incidents and to manage the behavior of employees within a covered entity in order to protect ePHI, such as determining appropriate employee access to information. *Physical safeguards* are physical measures, policies, and procedures that protect information systems and related buildings and equipment from natural and environmental hazards and unauthorized access and/or intrusion. Physical safeguards include policies and procedures for media reuse and disposal of ePHI and/or the media or hardware on which the ePHI is stored.[7] *Technical safeguards* are technology and the policy and procedures for the technology's use in order to control access to and protect ePHI. The area of system and communications protection features a number of technical controls, such as encryption, which is "the use of an algorithmic process to transform data into a form in which there is a low probability of assigning meaning without use of a confidential process or key."[8] Encryption is used to protect data from access by unauthorized individuals when they are stored or transmitted. The HIPAA Security Rule also describes organizational measures that should be implemented, such as business associate contracts, as well as requirements to develop policies and procedures for complying with the Security Rule and maintain documentation of those policies and procedures.

Because covered entities vary in size and also have different business models and available resources, the Security Rule is designed to be flexible and scalable so that covered entities can select and implement security approaches that fit the characteristics of their specific environments. Covered entities must regularly examine and revise their security measures if needed so that ePHI is protected as changes occur within their environments.[9] When selecting security measures, covered entities should consider the following characteristics within their environments:[10]

- Size, complexity, and capabilities
- Technical, hardware, and software infrastructure
- Costs of security measures
- Likelihood and possible impact of potential risks to ePHI

As part of this flexibility, implementation specifications in the Security Rule are identified as being either required or addressable. Covered entities must implement required implementation specifications that are listed for each security standard. In addition, covered entities must assess whether addressable specifications that are listed for each security standard are reasonable and appropriate safeguards for protecting the ePHI in their specific environment. If an addressable specification is identified as reasonable and appropriate, then it must be implemented. If an addressable specification is identified as not reasonable and appropriate, the covered entity must document why the specification is not reasonable and appropriate to implement within the entity's environment and select and implement another safeguard that is equivalent.[11] A detailed list of the HIPAA Security Rule standards and implementation specifications is provided in Table 3.1. Required specifications are denoted by (R), while addressable specifications are denoted by (A).

Additional Security Incident Response Requirements

As reflected in Table 3.1, incident response and reporting activities are a required implementation specification in the HIPAA Security Rule. The Security Rule defines a security incident as "attempted or successful unauthorized access, use, disclosure, modification or destruction of information or interference with system operations in an information system."[12] Incident response is the development and implementation of policies and procedures to address security incidents, and incident response activities typically

Table 3.1 HIPAA Security Rule Standards and Implementation Specifications

Section of HIPAA Security Rule	HIPAA Security Rule Standards	Implementation Specifications
Administrative Safeguards		
164.308(a)(1)(i)	Security Management Process: Implement policies and procedures to prevent, detect, contain, and correct security violations.	
164.308(a)(1)(ii)(A)		Risk Analysis (R): Conduct an accurate and thorough assessment of the potential risks and vulnerabilities to the confidentiality, integrity, and availability of electronic protected health information held by the covered entity.
164.308(a)(1)(ii)(B)		Risk Management (R): Implement security measures sufficient to reduce risks and vulnerabilities to a reasonable and appropriate level to comply with Section 164.306(a).
164.308(a)(1)(ii)(C)		Sanction Policy (R): Apply appropriate sanctions against workforce members who fail to comply with the security policies and procedures of the covered entity.
164.308(a)(1)(ii)(D)		Information System Activity Review (R): Implement procedures to regularly review records of information system activity, such as audit logs, access reports, and security incident tracking reports.
164.308(a)(2)	Assigned Security Responsibility: Identify the security official who is responsible for the development and implementation of the policies and procedures required by this subpart for the entity.	

(Continued)

Table 3.1 (Continued)   HIPAA Security Rule Standards and Implementation Specifications

Section of HIPAA Security Rule	HIPAA Security Rule Standards	Implementation Specifications
164.308(a)(3)(i)	Workforce Security: Implement policies and procedures to ensure that all members of its workforce have appropriate access to ePHI, as provided under paragraph (a)(4) of this section, and to prevent those workforce members who do not have access under paragraph (a)(4) of this section from obtaining access to ePHI.	
164.308(a)(3)(ii)(A)		Authorization and/or Supervision (A): Implement procedures for the authorization and/or supervision of workforce members who work with ePHI or in locations where it might be accessed.
164.308(a)(3)(ii)(B)		Workforce Clearance Procedure (A): Implement procedures to determine that the access of a workforce member to ePHI is appropriate.
164.308(a)(3)(ii)(C)		Termination Procedure (A): Implement procedures for terminating access to ePHI when the employment of a workforce member ends or as required by determinations made as specified in paragraph (a)(3)(ii)(B) of this section.
164.308(a)(4)(i)	Information Access Management: Implement policies and procedures for authorizing access to ePHI that are consistent with the applicable requirements of subpart E of this part.	
164.308(a)(4)(ii)(A)		Isolating Healthcare Clearinghouse Functions (R): If a healthcare clearinghouse is part of a larger organization, the clearinghouse must implement policies and procedures that protect the ePHI of the clearinghouse from unauthorized access by the larger organization.

(Continued)

Table 3.1 (Continued)   HIPAA Security Rule Standards and Implementation Specifications

Section of HIPAA Security Rule	HIPAA Security Rule Standards	Implementation Specifications
164.308(a)(4)(ii)(B)		Access Authorization (A): Implement policies and procedures for granting access to ePHI, for example, through access to a workstation, transaction, program, process, or other mechanism.
164.308(a)(4)(ii)(C)		Access Establishment and Modification (A): Implement policies and procedures that, based upon the entity's access authorization policies, establish, document, review, and modify a user's right of access to a workstation, transaction, program, or process.
164.308(a)(5)(i)	Security Awareness and Training: Implement a security awareness and training program for all members of its workforce (including management).	
164.308(a)(5)(ii)(A)		Security Reminders (A): Periodic security updates.
164.308(a)(5)(ii)(B)		Protection from Malicious Software (A): Procedures for guarding against, detecting, and reporting malicious software.
164.308(a)(5)(ii)(C)		Log-in Monitoring (A): Procedures for monitoring log-in attempts and reporting discrepancies.
164.308(a)(5)(ii)(D)		Password Management (A): Procedures for creating, changing, and safeguarding passwords.
164.308(a)(6)(i)	Security Incident Procedures: Implement policies and procedures to address security incidents.	
164.308(a)(6)(ii)		Response and Reporting (R): Identify and respond to suspected or known security incidents; mitigate, to the extent practicable, harmful effects of security incidents that are known to the covered entity; and document security incidents and their outcomes.

(Continued)

Table 3.1 (Continued)   HIPAA Security Rule Standards and Implementation Specifications

Section of HIPAA Security Rule	HIPAA Security Rule Standards	Implementation Specifications
164.308(a)(7)(i)	Contingency Plan: Establish (and implement as needed) policies and procedures for responding to an emergency or other occurrence (for example, fire, vandalism, system failure, and natural disaster) that damages systems that contain ePHI.	
164.308(a)(7)(ii)(A)		Data Backup Plan (R): Establish and implement procedures to create and maintain retrievable exact copies of ePHI.
164.308(a)(7)(ii)(B)		Disaster Recovery Plan (R): Establish (and implement as needed) procedures to restore any loss of data.
164.308(a)(7)(ii)(C)		Emergency Mode Operation Plan (R): Establish (and implement as needed) procedures to enable continuation of critical business processes for protection of the security of ePHI while operating in emergency mode.
164.308(a)(7)(ii)(D)		Testing and Revision Procedure (A): Implement procedures for periodic testing and revision of contingency plans.
164.308(a)(7)(ii)(E)		Applications and Data Criticality Analysis (A): Assess the relative criticality of specific applications and data in support of other contingency plan components.
164.308(a)(8)	Evaluation: Perform a periodic technical and nontechnical evaluation, based initially upon the standards implemented under this rule and subsequently, in response to environmental or operational changes affecting the security of ePHI that establishes the extent to which an entity's security policies and procedures meet the requirements of this subpart.	

(Continued)

Table 3.1 (Continued) HIPAA Security Rule Standards and Implementation Specifications

Section of HIPAA Security Rule	HIPAA Security Rule Standards	Implementation Specifications
164.308(b)(1)	Business Associate Contracts and Other Arrangements: A covered entity, in accordance with § 164.306, may permit a business associate to create, receive, maintain, or transmit ePHI on the covered entity's behalf only if the covered entity obtains satisfactory assurances, in accordance with § 164.314(a), that the business associate will appropriately safeguard the information.	
164.308(b)(4)		Written Contract or Other Arrangement (R): Document the satisfactory assurances required by paragraph (b)(1) of this section through a written contract or other arrangement with the business associate that meets the applicable requirements of §164.314(a).
Physical Safeguards		
164.310(a)(1)	Facility Access Controls: Implement policies and procedures to limit physical access to its electronic information systems and the facility or facilities in which they are housed, while ensuring that properly authorized access is allowed.	
164.310(a)(2)(i)		Contingency Operations (A): Establish (and implement as needed) procedures that allow facility access in support of restoration of lost data under the disaster recovery plan and emergency mode operations plan in the event of an emergency.
164.310(a)(2)(ii)		Facility Security Plan (A): Implement policies and procedures to safeguard the facility and the equipment therein from unauthorized physical access, tampering, and theft.

(Continued)

Table 3.1 (Continued)   HIPAA Security Rule Standards and Implementation Specifications

Section of HIPAA Security Rule	HIPAA Security Rule Standards	Implementation Specifications
164.310(a)(2)(iii)		Access Control and Validation Procedures (A): Implement procedures to control and validate a person's access to facilities based on their role or function, including visitor control and control of access to software programs for testing and revision.
164.310(a)(2)(iv)		Maintenance Records (A): Implement policies and procedures to document repairs and modifications to the physical components of a facility which are related to security (for example, hardware, walls, doors, and locks).
164.310(b)	Workstation Use: Implement policies and procedures that specify the proper functions to be performed, the manner in which those functions are to be performed, and the physical attributes of the surroundings of a specific workstation or class of workstation that can access ePHI.	
164.310(c)	Workstation Security: Implement physical safeguards for all workstations that access ePHI to restrict access to authorized users.	
164.310(d)(1)	Device and Media Controls: Implement policies and procedures that govern the receipt and removal of hardware and electronic media that contain ePHI into and out of a facility, and the movement of these items within the facility.	
164.310(d)(2)(i)		Disposal (R): Implement policies and procedures to address the final disposition of ePHI and/or the hardware or electronic media on which it is stored.
164.310(d)(2)(ii)		Media Reuse (R): Implement procedures for removal of ePHI from electronic media before the media are made available for reuse.

(Continued)

Table 3.1 (Continued)   HIPAA Security Rule Standards and Implementation Specifications

Section of HIPAA Security Rule	HIPAA Security Rule Standards	Implementation Specifications
164.310(d)(2)(iii)		Accountability (A): Maintain a record of the movements of hardware and electronic media and any person responsible therefore.
164.310(d)(2)(iv)		Data Backup and Storage (A): Create a retrievable exact copy of ePHI, when needed, before movement of equipment.
Technical Safeguards		
164.312(a)(1)	Access Control: Implement technical policies and procedures for electronic information systems that maintain ePHI to allow access only to those persons or software programs that have been granted access rights as specified in § 164.308(a)(4).	
164.312(a)(2)(i)		Unique User Identification (R): Assign a unique name and/or number for identifying and tracking user identity.
164.312(a)(2)(ii)		Emergency Access Procedure (R): Establish (and implement as needed) procedures for obtaining necessary ePHI during an emergency.
164.312(a)(2)(iii)		Automatic Logoff (A): Implement electronic procedures that terminate an electronic session after a predetermined time of inactivity.
164.312(a)(2)(iv)		Encryption and Decryption (A): Implement a mechanism to encrypt and decrypt ePHI.
164.312(b)	Audit Controls: Implement hardware, software, and/or procedural mechanisms that record and examine activity in information systems that contain or use ePHI.	
164.312(c)(1)	Integrity: Implement policies and procedures to protect ePHI from improper alteration or destruction.	

(Continued)

Table 3.1 (Continued)   HIPAA Security Rule Standards and Implementation Specifications

Section of HIPAA Security Rule	HIPAA Security Rule Standards	Implementation Specifications
164.312(c)(2)		Mechanism to Authenticate ePHI (A): Implement electronic mechanisms to corroborate that ePHI has not been altered or destroyed in an unauthorized manner.
164.312(d)	Person or Entity Authentication: Implement procedures to verify that a person or entity seeking access to ePHI is the one claimed.	
164.312(e)(1)	Transmission Security: Implement technical security measures to guard against unauthorized access to ePHI that is being transmitted over an electronic communications network.	
164.312(e)(2)(i)		Integrity Controls (A): Implement security measures to ensure that electronically transmitted ePHI is not improperly modified without detection until disposed of.
164.312(e)(2)(ii)		Encryption (A): Implement a mechanism to encrypt ePHI whenever deemed appropriate.
Organizational		
164.314(a)(1)	Business Associate Contracts or Other Arrangements: (i) The contract or other arrangement between the covered entity and its business associate required by § 164.308(b) must meet the requirements of paragraph (a) (2)(i) or (a)(2)(ii) of this section, as applicable. (ii) A covered entity is not in compliance with the standards in § 164.502(e) and paragraph (a) of this section if the covered entity knew of a pattern of an activity or practice of the business associate that constituted a material breach or violation of the business associate's obligation under the contract or other arrangement, unless the covered entity took reasonable steps to cure the breach or end the violation, as applicable, and, if such steps were unsuccessful— (A) Terminated the contract or arrangement, if feasible; or (B) If termination is not feasible, reported the problem to the Secretary.	

(Continued)

Table 3.1 (Continued) **HIPAA Security Rule Standards and Implementation Specifications**

Section of HIPAA Security Rule	HIPAA Security Rule Standards	Implementation Specifications
164.314(a)(2)(i)		Business Associate Contracts (R): The contract between a covered entity and a business associate must provide that the business associate will—(A) Implement administrative, physical, and technical safeguards that reasonably and appropriately protect the confidentiality, integrity, and availability of the ePHI that it creates, receives, maintains, or transmits on behalf of the covered entity as required by this subpart; (B) Ensure that any agent, including a subcontractor, to whom it provides such information agrees to implement reasonable and appropriate safeguards to protect it; (C) Report to the covered entity any security incident of which it becomes aware; (D) Authorize termination of the contract by the covered entity if the covered entity determines that the business associate has violated a material term of the contract.
164.314(a)(2)(ii)		Other Arrangements: When a covered entity and its business associate are both governmental entities, the covered entity is in compliance with paragraph (a)(1) of this section, if—(1) It enters into a memorandum of understanding with the business associate that contains terms that accomplish the objectives of paragraph (a)(2)(i) of this section; or (2) Other law (including regulations adopted by the covered entity or its business associate) contains requirements applicable to the business associate that accomplish the objectives of paragraph (a) (2)(i) of this section.

(Continued)

Table 3.1 (Continued)   HIPAA Security Rule Standards and Implementation Specifications

Section of HIPAA Security Rule	HIPAA Security Rule Standards	Implementation Specifications
164.314(b)(1)	Requirements for Group Health Plans: Except when the only ePHI disclosed to a plan sponsor is disclosed pursuant to § 164.504(f) (1)(ii) or (iii), or as authorized under § 164.508, a group health plan must ensure that its plan documents provide that the plan sponsor will reasonably and appropriately safeguard ePHI created, received, maintained, or transmitted to or by the plan sponsor on behalf of the group health plan.	
164.314(b)(2)(i)		Group Health Plan Implementation Specification (R): The plan documents of the group health plan must be amended to incorporate provisions to require the plan sponsor to—(i) Implement administrative, physical, and technical safeguards that reasonably and appropriately protect the confidentiality, integrity, and availability of the ePHI that it creates, receives, maintains, or transmits on behalf of the group health plan.
164.314(b)(2)(ii)		Group Health Plan Implementation Specification (R): The plan documents of the group health plan must be amended to incorporate provisions to require the plan sponsor to—(ii) Ensure that the adequate separation required by § 164.504(f)(2)(iii) is supported by reasonable and appropriate security measures.
164.314(b)(2)(iii)		Group Health Plan Implementation Specification (R): The plan documents of the group health plan must be amended to incorporate provisions to require the plan sponsor to—(iii) Ensure that any agent, including a subcontractor, to whom it provides this information agrees to implement reasonable and appropriate security measures to protect the information.

(Continued)

Table 3.1 (Continued)   HIPAA Security Rule Standards and Implementation Specifications

Section of HIPAA Security Rule	*HIPAA Security Rule Standards*	*Implementation Specifications*
164.314(b)(2)(iv)		Group Health Plan Implementation Specification (R): The plan documents of the group health plan must be amended to incorporate provisions to require the plan sponsor to—(iv) Report to the group health plan any security incident of which it becomes aware.
Policies and Procedure and Documentation Requirements		
164.316(a)	Policies and Procedures: Implement reasonable and appropriate policies and procedures to comply with the standards, implementation specifications, or other requirements of this subpart, taking into account those factors specified in § 164.306(b)(2)(i), (ii), (iii), and (iv). This standard is not to be construed to permit or excuse an action that violates any other standard, implementation specification, or other requirements of this subpart. A covered entity may change its policies and procedures at any time, provided that the changes are documented and are implemented in accordance with this subpart.	
164.316(b)(1)	Documentation: (i) Maintain the policies and procedures implemented to comply with this subpart in written (which may be electronic) form; and (ii) If an action, activity or assessment is required by this subpart to be documented, maintain a written (which may be electronic) record of the action, activity, or assessment.	
164.316(b)(2)(i)		Time Limit (R): Retain the documentation required by paragraph (b)(1) of this section for 6 years from the date of its creation or the date when it last was in effect, whichever is later.

(Continued)

Table 3.1 (Continued) HIPAA Security Rule Standards and Implementation Specifications

Section of HIPAA Security Rule	HIPAA Security Rule Standards	Implementation Specifications
164.316(b)(2)(ii)		Availability (R): Make documentation available to those persons responsible for implementing the procedures to which the documentation pertains.
164.316(b)(2)(iii)		Updates (R): Review documentation periodically, and update as needed, in response to environmental or operational changes affecting the security of the ePHI.

Source: Adapted from National Institute of Standards and Technology. SP 800-66, *An Introductory Resource Guide for Implementing the Health Insurance Portability and Accountability Act, (HIPAA) Security Rule,* October 2008.

include detection, analysis, containment, eradication, and recovery from security incidents. Incident response activities should be coordinated with contingency planning activities, which are activities to address maintaining essential business functions despite an information system disruption, compromise, or failure. Contingency planning includes using backup systems, as well as having procedures for recovering a failed or compromised system or recovering data. Lessons learned from handling previous incidents should be incorporated into incident response procedures and training.

The HITECH Act, which is Title XIII of the American Recovery and Reinvestment Act of 2009 (ARRA),[13] requires data breach notification for unauthorized uses and disclosures of "unsecured PHI," which refers to unencrypted PHI. HHS has issued regulations that implement provisions of the HITECH Act requiring covered entities under HIPAA to notify individuals when their health information is breached.[14] A breach is defined as the compromise of the security or privacy of information via unauthorized acquisition, access, use, or disclosure of the information. The regulations require covered entities to promptly notify affected individuals of a breach. The HHS Secretary and the media must also be notified of breaches when more than 500 individuals are affected. Breaches that affect fewer than 500 individuals must be reported to the HHS Secretary on an annual basis. In addition, business associates of covered entities are required to notify the covered entity of any breaches that the business associates experience. In turn, the covered entity is responsible for the required notifications to the affected individuals and/or HHS. The regulations specify that covered entities that secure health information through the use of encryption or destruction as described in the regulations do not have to perform breach notification for the secured information if a breach occurs.[15]

Tools for Selecting and Assessing Security and Privacy Measures in the Healthcare Environment

The National Institute of Standards and Technology (NIST) has published guidance and tools on information security that healthcare practitioners can use to address security protection in the healthcare environment. NIST SP 800-66, *An Introductory Resource Guide for Implementing the Health Insurance Portability and Accountability Act (HIPAA) Security Rule*,[16] lists security measures from NIST publications that are relevant to each section of the Security Rule. SP 800-66 provides a table that lists the information and activities a covered entity may wish to consider when implementing the Security Rule. NIST has also developed a HIPAA Security Rule Toolkit, which can be used by organizations to perform a risk assessment of security controls to protect ePHI and identify where new security controls need to be implemented or where existing security controls need to be improved.[17] The toolkit addresses the 45 implementation specifications identified in the HIPAA Security Rule. The toolkit is also based on the HITECH Act and several NIST guidance documents.[18]

In addition, within the U.S. federal government, the Committee on National Security Systems (CNSS) has developed an Instruction entitled CNSSI 1253F, Attachment 6, which is the Privacy Overlay document.[19] NIST Special Publication (SP) 800-53, Revision 4,[20] and CNSS Instruction 1253[21] provide guidance on the underlying controls that are needed in order to protect national security systems. However, PII is distinct from other types of data since, in addition to protecting PII, the collection, use, and sharing of PII needs to meet Federal requirements. The Privacy Overlays are based on the Fair Information Practice Principles (FIPPs) and federal privacy requirements. They provide a way to select privacy and security controls for protecting PII that leverages the structure of NIST and CNSS guidance while also addressing the unique requirements for PII. The Privacy Overlays document consists of four Privacy Overlays that identify control specifications required to protect PII, including PHI, in national security systems. The document is to be used for security and privacy control selection to reduce privacy risks for national security systems, but can be used by any organizations in any environment, including those with systems that are not national security systems, such as federal government agencies in the executive branch or organizations in private industry. The document provides guidance for determining the risk level of PII using NIST risk management guidance to categorize the PII risk level for a system as low, moderate, or high. It contains three overlays that specify controls at each of the three risk levels identified by NIST. A fourth overlay in the document provides the minimum set of control specifications for PHI based on the HIPAA Privacy and Security Rules. Systems with PHI need to apply both the applicable low, moderate, or high overlay based on the risk level of the PHI and also apply the separate PHI overlay in order to select privacy and security controls that are appropriate for their environment.

Information Security and Privacy as Distinct Disciplines

Although the terms "privacy" and "security" are often used interchangeably, these are two distinct disciplines. As discussed in Chapter 1, privacy focuses on the ability of an individual to control the collection, use, dissemination, and retention of his or her personally identifiable information (PII). PII is defined as information that uniquely identifies an individual when used alone or when used in combination with other information and includes PHI. Privacy is based on a set of foundational principles known as the Fair Information Practice Principles (FIPPs). One version of FIPPs is provided by HHS in the *Nationwide Privacy and Security Framework for Electronic Exchange of Individually Identifiable Health Information*[22]:

- Individual access
- Correction
- Openness and transparency
- Individual choice
- Collection, use, and disclosure limitation
- Data quality and integrity
- Safeguards
- Accountability

The standards and implementation specifications in the HIPAA Privacy Rule pertain to actions that organizations need to take in order to protect privacy, and the specifications are based on FIPPs. The specifications prescribe what uses and disclosures of PHI are allowed and also what the rights of individuals are to request privacy protection of PHI, obtain access to and amend their PHI, and obtain an accounting of the disclosure of their PHI.[23]

In contrast, information security focuses on protecting information and information systems. The HIPAA Security Rule implementation specifications (see Table 3.1) include protecting systems from threats to their security, providing physical protection to systems, and also providing disaster recovery and incident response capabilities. These activities all relate to the security objectives of confidentiality, integrity, and availability discussed earlier in this chapter.

In the end, information security and privacy are two distinct disciplines, but they are linked. Just because a system has good security protection, it does not automatically mean that the system also has good privacy protection. A system can be very secure while, at the same time, it can have inadequate privacy protection if policies, procedures, and technology are not in place to protect the privacy of the individuals about whom data are collected in accordance with foundational privacy principles.

How Security and Privacy Efforts Work Together

As mentioned above, security measures are needed to protect the privacy of individuals. For example, the HIPAA Security Rule operationalizes the protections contained in the HIPAA Privacy Rule by specifying the safeguards that covered entities must implement in order to secure ePHI. In fact, security is one of the privacy principles in several widely used versions of FIPPs, including those established by OECD.[24] Techniques and tools that by design or configuration support privacy are known as privacy-enhancing technologies, and privacy-enhancing technologies are often security technologies whose use protects individuals' privacy. Privacy-enhancing technologies can be used to perform functions such as enabling appropriate access and use of data internally and preventing inappropriate disclosure of data externally. However, just as security mechanisms are used to help with privacy efforts, some privacy measures also help with security efforts. Examples of how technical security mechanisms and privacy measures work together in the healthcare environment are provided below.

Access Control

Access control mechanisms are technical security mechanisms that are used to protect the security objective of confidentiality, since access control limits the user's access to information about individuals based on the user's role. Access controls also help to protect the security objective of integrity, since they limit the user's ability to modify or delete ePHI. Examples of access control security mechanisms include assigning a unique name or number for identifying and tracking a user's identity, implementing procedures that terminate an electronic session after a predetermined time of inactivity, and encrypting ePHI. Because access controls limit the user's access to ePHI based on the user's role and the purposes for which the user is entitled to access the ePHI, the use of access controls also helps to meet the privacy objective of limiting the use of ePHI to only those uses that are authorized for the purposes of the system and for the purposes for which the ePHI was collected in the first place. Thus, privacy measures include identifying who needs access to specific ePHI, and the resulting access determinations are used as input when configuring security mechanisms for access control.

Accountability

Accountability is the process of ensuring that individuals use data in accordance with established security and privacy rules and guidance. In the areas of both privacy and security, accountability is typically addressed through the use of governance, monitoring, risk management, and assessment efforts. On the privacy side, monitoring includes following the trail of disclosure of information about individuals to ensure that the information is shared appropriately based on predetermined privacy guidance. Security measures that help with accountability include implementing actual technical mechanisms such as audit trails to track individuals' access to information.

Aggregation

Aggregation occurs when data from different sources are combined into one data set. Aggregation of data has the potential to impact privacy, since individual pieces of data about a person may not be sensitive when standing alone, but may become sensitive when combined together. For example, name, date of birth, place of birth, and mother's maiden name are each not sensitive by themselves, but, when combined, could be readily used to identify an individual, and could then be used to commit identity theft. In the healthcare environment, a list of names and a list of medical diagnoses are not sensitive when they are separate, but they become sensitive information when they are linked together. A sound privacy practice is to allow aggregation or derivation of new information about individuals only if the new information is authorized by law or necessary to fulfill a stated purpose. Privacy measures with respect to aggregation include determining the sensitivity level and the privacy impact of aggregated data. The identified sensitivity level is then used as input to determine what security mechanisms, such as encryption, should be implemented to protect aggregated data.

Data Minimization

As mentioned above, one of the foundational privacy principles is to collect only the information about individuals that is needed for the purpose of an organization's function or mission, and privacy policies and procedures to minimize the amount of ePHI collected should be used to ensure that organizations in the healthcare environment meet this privacy principle. Limiting the amount of data that is collected makes it easier to protect the data since there is less data to protect in the first place, so the privacy measure of data minimization helps security efforts.

Disclosure

Disclosure is when one entity shares data about individuals with other entities. The HIPAA Privacy Rule requires covered entities to limit the use or disclosure of PHI to the minimum necessary to accomplish the intended purpose.[25] Individuals within organizations who have responsibility for making disclosure determinations typically decide who should have access to information about individuals based upon the functions that the recipients perform, the categories or types of ePHI needed, and whether the recipients need access to the ePHI in order to perform their job functions. By working up front to determine potential privacy risks related to ePHI disclosure and develop disclosure guidance, privacy measures help with security efforts, since the disclosure guidance can be used to determine appropriate security mechanisms to protect the ePHI from inappropriate disclosure.

Integrity

Integrity is the process of maintaining correct data and guarding against the improper modification or deletion of data. With respect to integrity, the main privacy goal is to ensure that incorrect information about an individual is not used to make an inappropriate decision about that person, so data accuracy is very important for privacy. Technical security mechanisms are used to confirm that ePHI has not been subject to unauthorized alteration or deletion.

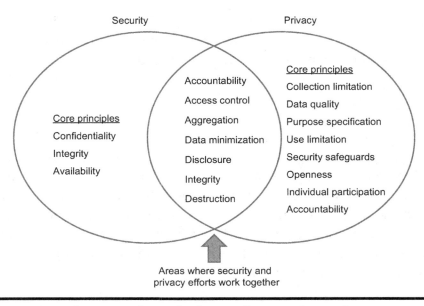

Figure 3.1   Areas where security and privacy efforts work together.

Destruction

Destruction is the process of rendering data unusable. Privacy practices regarding destruction address the need for the complete elimination of information about individuals that has been collected once the information has served its purpose, and it is important to identify and follow retention periods for the information. Technical security mechanisms are used to ensure that information cannot be recovered once it has been deleted.

Figure 3.1 illustrates the core concepts behind security and privacy and also shows the areas where security and privacy efforts typically work together.

Privacy and Security and Risk Management

In order for ePHI to be appropriately protected, it is important to select security and privacy controls that are commensurate with the level of security and privacy risk to the data on the system. A basic risk management process has several steps that should be integrated into the system development life cycle[26]:

■ Identify potential system threats and vulnerabilities and determine the level of privacy and security risk for the system based on the threats and vulnerabilities. Determine the level of impact if the system has a security or privacy incident. Both the impact of an incident upon the individuals whose information is stored on the system or used via the system and the impact of the incident upon the organization that owns and manages the system should be considered.

■ Select security and privacy safeguards based upon the level of security and privacy risk identified. For the HIPAA Security Rule, determine how the required specifications will be implemented for the system. Also, determine whether addressable specifications are reasonable and appropriate. If they are not, then select equivalent safeguards to implement.

■ Implement the selected security and privacy safeguards within the information system and its environment of operation.

■ Assess the implemented security and privacy safeguards to determine the extent to which they are implemented correctly, operating as intended, and producing the desired outcome regarding the system's security and privacy requirements.

■ Monitor the security and privacy safeguards in the information system on an ongoing basis and report on the security and privacy state of the system to appropriate managers.

To determine the level of risk to ePHI, organizations within the healthcare environment should perform the following actions[27]:

■ Identify what ePHI resides in an organization's environment and its physical and logical location. It is difficult, if not impossible, to protect ePHI when an organization does not know what ePHI exists and where it is located. Documenting the location and type of ePHI is critical in order for an organization to appropriately protect the ePHI.

■ Categorize the ePHI according to the level of security and privacy impact that would result if a privacy or security incident occurred, such as if the ePHI is inappropriately used or disclosed, if more ePHI is collected than is needed, or if appropriate notice or consent is not provided to individuals. Levels of impact are often categorized as being low, medium, or high, with high being the level with the most negative impact. The level of impact varies depending upon the characteristics of the ePHI being used. Characteristics of the ePHI to consider when determining potential impact include:

– *Identifiability.* Determine how easy it is to identify an individual based upon the ePHI available (e.g., a Social Security Number [SSN] directly identifies an individual while a medical diagnosis code standing alone can be linked to a group of people).

– *Quantity of ePHI.* Consider how many individuals can be identified from the available ePHI. Organizations may want to vary their incident response approaches based on the number of individuals who are affected.

– *Data field sensitivity.* Evaluate the sensitivity of individual data fields when standing alone (e.g., an SSN standing alone is extremely sensitive since it directly identifies an individual, while a phone number is significantly less sensitive in most cases), or when combined with other data fields (e.g., name and medical diagnosis code, when combined, is a more sensitive set of data).

– *Context of use.* Evaluate the purpose for which ePHI is used; this can affect the impact level. For example, two sets of identical ePHI data would have different impact levels if one set is used to determine who is on a public mailing list, while the second set identifies individuals who have a major illness.

– *Obligation to protect the security and privacy of ePHI.* Consider if there are specific laws, regulations, or guidance that apply to an organization and require ePHI to be protected in a certain way. HIPAA and the HITECH Act are the primary laws that apply to ePHI. State laws that are contrary to the Privacy Rule are preempted by the federal requirements, unless a specific exception applies. Examples of exceptions include laws that:

  • Relate to the privacy of PHI and provide greater protection of privacy.
  • Provide for the reporting of disease or injury, child abuse, birth, or death, or for public health surveillance, investigation, or intervention.
  • Require certain health plan reporting, such as for management or financial audits.

So, there may be other laws that should be considered by organizations in the healthcare environment regarding security and privacy measures to protect ePHI.

– *Access to and location of ePHI*. Consider the location of ePHI and how frequently it is accessed. There is higher potential security and privacy risk for ePHI that is accessed often, accessed by a large number of users, or accessed remotely.

It is already an accepted practice in systems engineering to design security into systems at the start of the system development life cycle when the systems are still conceptual. In addition, the idea of *Privacy by Design*,[28] has gained widespread acceptance. Privacy by Design supports the idea that organizations should ensure that they protect privacy by default. This is accomplished not just through compliance with regulatory frameworks, but also by building privacy protection into business practices and the physical design of systems as well as policies. Privacy should be integrated into each layer of the organization; this comprehensive approach ensures that privacy risk is fully and proactively addressed.

Leveraging existing systems engineering processes and integrating privacy into them instead of creating separate processes to address privacy risk is a sound approach to use to implement Privacy by Design. The process of *privacy engineering* does this by integrating activities and associated methods that support privacy's unique features (e.g., notice, consent, PII collection limitation, individual access) throughout the systems engineering life cycle from the very beginning. The figure below shows the stages of the classic systems engineering life cycle and maps the core privacy engineering activities to the different life cycle phases. The privacy engineering activities can be mapped to any systems engineering life cycle regardless of type (e.g., agile, waterfall) since the core activities exist in every life cycle (Figure 3.2).

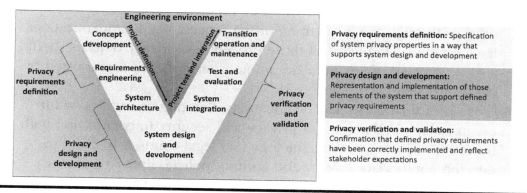

Figure 3.2   Privacy engineering framework.

Key elements of privacy engineering include addressing privacy in design documentation, explicitly identifying technical privacy requirements for a system, constructing privacy tests based on those requirements, executing the privacy tests, identifying residual privacy risks, and determining how to address them. Privacy requirements must take into account architectural, technical, and policy controls, and address privacy risks beyond compliance. Many organizations currently complete these life cycle activities with respect to security, but may not fully complete them regarding privacy, resulting in privacy risks not being adequately addressed. System documentation that should discuss privacy considerations includes design and requirements documents, test case specifications, test plan results, post-test results documents/risk register, and remediation plans. In addition, if a Privacy Impact Assessment (PIA) or other similar type of privacy risk analysis is completed, it should be updated at each milestone in the systems engineering process.

Implementing Privacy by Design by including privacy within the risk management process and as part of the system development process will lead to better privacy and security protection and lower costs for both privacy and security measures, since privacy issues and associated security mechanisms that are needed will be identified and addressed early in the system development process, when it is typically easier and less costly to make system changes.

Protecting Information Security and Privacy in Operations

In the day-to-day operations within the healthcare environment, there are two key ways that privacy and security organizations should work together:

- In many cases, data breaches are first reported to information security officials through the incident reporting procedures that organizations have established. As part of those procedures, privacy officials should also be notified of any breaches immediately when it is suspected or confirmed that ePHI is involved.
- Close coordination should be encouraged among executives within organizations in the areas of privacy and security in conjunction with the areas of information technology and legal counsel. In order to develop appropriate privacy and security policies and procedures, address operational issues related to privacy and security protection for ePHI, and appropriately respond to incidents involving ePHI,

knowledge is needed in all of these areas of expertise. Organizations should strive to have good working relationships among these groups, especially among senior leadership.

In addition, once operational, as the system's security state is continuously monitored, its privacy state should also be continuously monitored and updated when needed in order to improve privacy protection.

Conclusion

Information security and privacy are two distinct disciplines that are linked together; in order to have appropriate privacy protection, sound security mechanisms are needed. Given the sensitivity of information about individuals that is collected, used, and shared within the healthcare environment, it is important to select and implement appropriate security mechanisms that will protect ePHI and the privacy of individuals. Implementing Privacy by Design through privacy engineering by defining security and privacy requirements and selecting and implementing security and privacy controls during the beginning phases and throughout the remainder of the system development life cycle, and updating security and privacy protection as needed once the system is operational based on ongoing security and privacy risk management, are all key to ensuring that security and privacy are both adequately addressed in systems. It is also critical to have individuals in the information security and privacy organizations work together to manage security and privacy protection. Doing so will help to better detect possible security and privacy issues and develop and implement approaches to address them, and will also aid quick response to security and privacy incidents when they occur.

Notes

1. National Institute of Standards and Technology. Federal Information Security Management Act of 2002. Available at: http://csrc.nist.gov/drivers/documents/FISMA-final.pdf.
2. U.S. Department of Health & Human Services. The Security Rule. Available at: www.hhs.gov/ocr/privacy/hipaa/administrative/securityrule/index.html.
3. U.S. Department of Health & Human Services. Summary of the HIPAA Security Rule. Available at: www.hhs.gov/ocr/privacy/hipaa/understanding/srsummary.html.

4. U.S. Department of Health & Human Services, Office for Civil Rights. HIPAA Administrative Simplification: Regulation Text. Available at: www.hhs.gov/sites/default/files/hipaa-simplification-201303.pdf.
5. U.S. Department of Health & Human Services. Summary of the HIPAA Security Rule. Available at: www.hhs.gov/ocr/privacy/hipaa/understanding/srsummary.html.
6. U.S. Department of Health & Human Services. Summary of the HIPAA Security Rule. Available at: www.hhs.gov/ocr/privacy/hipaa/understanding/srsummary.html.
7. U.S. Department of Health & Human Services, Summary of the HIPAA Security Rule. www.hhs.gov/ocr/privacy/hipaa/understanding/srsummary.html.
8. U.S. Department of Health & Human Services. The Security Rule. Available at: www.hhs.gov/ocr/privacy/hipaa/administrative/securityrule/index.html.
9. U.S. Department of Health & Human Services. Summary of the HIPAA Security Rule. Available at: www.hhs.gov/ocr/privacy/hipaa/understanding/srsummary.html.
10. U.S. Department of Health & Human Services. Summary of the HIPAA Security Rule. Available at: www.hhs.gov/ocr/privacy/hipaa/understanding/srsummary.html.
11. U.S. Department of Health & Human Services. The Security Rule. Available at: www.hhs.gov/ocr/privacy/hipaa/administrative/securityrule/index.html.
12. U.S. Department of Health & Human Services, Office for Civil Rights. HIPAA Administrative Simplification: Regulation Text. Available at: www.hhs.gov/ocr/privacy/hipaa/administrative/privacyrule/adminsimpregtext.pdf.
13. American Recovery and Reinvestment Act of 2009. Available at: www.gpo.gov/fdsys/pkg/BILLS111hr1enr/pdf/BILLS-111hr1enr.pdf.
14. U.S. Department of Health & Human Services. HIPAA Administrative Simplification: Enforcement. 74 Federal Register, 209; October 30, 2009. Available at: www.hhs.gov/ocr/privacy/hipaa/administrative/enforcementrule/enfifr.pdf.
15. U.S. Department of Health & Human Services. HITECH Breach Notification Interim Final Rule. Available at: www.hhs.gov/ocr/privacy/hipaa/understanding/coveredentities/breachnotificationifr.html.
16. Adapted from National Institute of Standards and Technology. SP 800-66, *An Introductory Resource Guide for Implementing the Health Insurance Portability and Accountability Act, (HIPAA) Security Rule*, October 2008. Available at: http://csrc.nist.gov/publications/nistpubs/800-66-Rev1/SP-800-66-Revision1.pdf.
17. National Institute of Standards and Technology. *HIPAA Security Rule Toolkit*. Available at: http://scap.nist.gov/hipaa/.
18. National Institute of Standards and Technology. *HIPAA Security Rule Toolkit*. Available at: http://scap.nist.gov/hipaa/.
19. CNSSI 1253F, Attachment 6, *Privacy Overlay*; April 23, 2015. Available at: https://www.cnss.gov/cnss/.
20. NIST SP 800-53, Recommended Security Controls for Federal Information Systems, Revision 4, April 30, 2013. Available at: http://nvlpubs.nist.gov/nistpubs/SpecialPublications/NIST.SP.800-53r4.pdf.

21. Committee on National Security Systems (CNSS) Instruction 1253, Security Categorization and Security Control Selection for National Security Systems; March 2014.

22. Office of the National Coordinator for Health Information Technology, U.S. Department of Health & Human Services. Nationwide Privacy and Security Framework for Electronic Exchange of Individually Identifiable Health Information; December 15, 2008. Available at: http://healthit.hhs.gov/portal/server.pt?open=512&objID=1173&parentname=CommunityPage&parentid=34&mode=2& in_hi_userid=10732&cached=true.

23. U.S. Department of Health & Human Services, Office for Civil Rights. HIPAA Administrative Simplification: Regulation Text. Available at: www.hhs.gov/ocr/privacy/hipaa/administrative/privacyrule/adminsimpregtext.pdf.

24. Organization for Economic Co-operation and Development. *OECD Privacy Principles*. Available at: http://oecdprivacy.org/.

25. U.S. Department of Health & Human Services. Health Information Privacy, Minimum Necessary Requirement. Available at: www.hhs.gov/ocr/privacy/hipaa/understanding/coveredentities/minimumnecessary.html.

26. Adapted from National Institute of Standards and Technology, SP 800-122. *Guide to Protecting the Confidentiality of Personally Identifiable Information;* April 2010. Available at: http://csrc.nist.gov/publications/nistpubs/800-122/sp800-122.pdf.

27. Adapted from National Institute of Standards and Technology, SP 800-122. *Guide to Protecting the Confidentiality of Personally Identifiable Information,* April 2010. Available at: http://csrc.nist.gov/publications/nistpubs/800-122/sp800-122.pdf.

28. Information and Privacy Commissioner/Ontario, *About Privacy by Design*, https://www.privacybydesign.ca/index.php/about-pbd/.

Chapter 4

The Legal Framework for Health Information Privacy

By Robert D. Belfort, JD, and Susan R. Ingargiola, MA
Updated by Linda D. Koontz for current edition

Contents

An array of federal and state laws restricts the use and disclosure of individually identifiable health information by healthcare providers and other health industry stakeholders. The most comprehensive of these laws is The Health Insurance Portability and Accountability Act (HIPAA),[1] which establishes a national legal foundation for health information privacy. But a patchwork of other state and federal laws are layered on top of HIPAA, imposing more stringent requirements on particular types of entities or certain types of information. As a result, an organization's privacy obligations may vary from one context to another. This chapter provides a summary of HIPAA's privacy requirements, as amended by the Health Information Technology for Economic and Clinical Health (HITECH) Act, and an overview of the other state and federal laws that are likely to affect the use and disclosure of health information.

Health Insurance Portability and Accountability Act

Statutory and Regulatory History

HIPAA was enacted on August 21, 1996. The statute set forth broad principles and required the Department of Health and Human Services (HHS) to issue more detailed privacy and security standards if Congress did not do so itself within a specified time period. Congress did not act within the mandated time frame and HHS undertook the task of developing privacy and security standards. HIPAA's Privacy Rule, which is the subject of this chapter, regulates when individually identifiable health information may be used and disclosed. The Privacy Rule became effective on April 14, 2003.

In February 2009, Congress enacted the American Recovery and Reinvestment Act of 2009 (ARRA).[2] Title XIII of ARRA is known as the HITECH Act. The HITECH Act, which authorized investments in health information technology infrastructure, also includes a number of provisions that significantly modify and expand the scope of the HIPAA Privacy Rule. HHS released two Notices of Proposed Rulemaking (in July 2010 and May 2011, respectively), implementing certain provisions, but not yet finalizing them. Thus, this chapter discusses only the statute.

Applicability of HIPAA: Definition of Covered Entities

The Privacy Rule does not apply to every entity that maintains health information. Initially, the Privacy Rule applied only to "covered entities." Under HITECH, as discussed further below, the Privacy Rule was made applicable to vendors of covered entities, referred to as "business associates." A business associate is any person or organization that receives, maintains, accesses, uses, or discloses protected health information (PHI) in connection with assisting a covered entity in carrying out its operations.

There are three types of covered entities:

- *Health plans*: Health plans include a wide range of public and private entities providing health insurance benefits. These entities include, among others, health maintenance organizations (HMOs), state-licensed health insurance companies, self-funded employee health benefit plans, and Medicare and Medicaid.
- *Healthcare providers conducting HIPAA transactions*: A healthcare provider is a person or entity that furnishes or bills for healthcare in the normal course of business, such as a hospital, physician, nursing home,

home health agency, pharmacy, or clinical laboratory. However, not all healthcare providers are covered entities. A healthcare provider is a covered entity only if it conducts one or more of the transactions governed by the HIPAA Transactions and Code Sets Rule electronically. These transactions include the common transactions conducted between providers and health plans, such as the submission of claims and verification of eligibility. Virtually all sizable healthcare providers conduct one or more of these transactions electronically and, therefore, are covered entities. But some smaller providers, such as physicians who accept payment only from patients and do not bill insurers, are not subject to HIPAA.

■ *Healthcare clearinghouses*: A healthcare clearinghouse assists healthcare providers and/or health plans in converting transactions that are not in a format that complies with the Transactions and Code Sets Rule into a compliant format, or vice versa.[3] A healthcare clearinghouse could be operated by a billing service or repricing company, for example.

Scope of Data Covered

Definition of Protected Health Information

The Privacy Rule protects all "individually identifiable health information" held or transmitted by a covered entity or its business associate, in any form or media, whether electronic, paper, or oral. This type of information is referred to as protected health information or PHI. There are narrow exceptions to the definition of PHI covering employment and educational records, which are not subject to HIPAA. "Individually identifiable health information" is information, including demographic data, that (i) relates to the individual's past, present, or future physical or mental health or condition; the provision of healthcare to the individual; or the past, present, or future payment for the provision of healthcare to the individual; and (ii) identifies the individual or for which there is a reasonable basis to believe it can be used to identify the individual.[4]

Standards for De-Identification of Health Information

The Privacy Rule places no restrictions on the use or disclosure of de-identified health information. De-identified health information is health information that does not identify an individual or provide a reasonable basis for identification.

There are two ways to de-identify protected health information. First, a person who is experienced with generally accepted statistical and scientific principles and methods for rendering information de-identified may provide an opinion that there is little risk that the information could be used, alone or in combination with other reasonably available information, by an anticipated recipient of the information to identify the subject of the information.

Second, 18 identifiers may be removed from the record. These identifiers are listed in Table 4.1. Covered entities cannot have actual knowledge

Table 4.1   Identifiers That Must Be Removed to De-Identify Health Information

1	Names
2	All geographic subdivisions smaller than a state, including street address, city, county, precinct, ZIP code, and equivalent geographical codes, except for the initial three ZIP code numbers, if according to the current publicly available data from the Bureau of the Census the geographic unit formed from those ZIP codes contains more than 20,000 people or, if less than 20,000 people, the digits are changed to 000
3	All elements of dates (except year) that are directly related to an individual, including birth date, admission date, discharge date, date of death, and all ages over 89, and all elements of dates (including year) indicative of such age, except that such ages and elements may be aggregated into a single category of age 90 or older
4	Telephone numbers
5	Fax numbers
6	Email addresses
7	Social Security numbers
8	Medical record numbers
9	Health plan beneficiary numbers
10	Account numbers
11	Certificate/license numbers
12	Vehicle identifiers and serial numbers, including license plate numbers
13	Device identifiers and serial numbers
14	Web universal resource locators (URLs)
15	Internet protocol (IP) address numbers
16	Biometric identifiers, including finger and voice prints
17	Full-face photographic images and any other comparable images
18	Any other unique identifying number, characteristic or code, unless otherwise permitted by the Privacy Rule for re-identification

Source: 45 CFR § 164.154.

that any information used alone, or in combination with other information, would identify an individual who is a subject of the information.[5]

Restrictions on Use and Disclosure of PHI

PHI may be used or disclosed without an individual's authorization only for specified purposes. The term "use" refers to the sharing, employment, application, utilization, examination, or analysis of PHI within the entity that maintains it. The term "disclosure" refers to any release, transfer, provision of access to, or divulging of PHI outside that entity.[6]

Treatment, Payment, and Healthcare Operations

A covered entity may use and disclose PHI for its own treatment, payment, and healthcare operations activities. A covered entity also may disclose PHI for (i) the treatment activities of any healthcare provider; (ii) the payment activities of another covered entity or any other healthcare provider; or (iii) the healthcare operations of another covered entity involving either quality or competency assurance activities or fraud and abuse detection and compliance activities, if both covered entities have or had a relationship with the individual and the PHI pertains to the relationship. Treatment, payment, and healthcare operations are defined as follows:

- *Treatment* is the provision, coordination, or management of healthcare and related services for an individual by one or more healthcare providers, including consultation between providers regarding a patient and referral of a patient by one provider to another.
- *Payment* encompasses (i) activities of a health plan to collect premiums, determine or fulfill responsibilities for coverage and provision of benefits, and furnish or obtain reimbursement for healthcare delivered to an individual; and (ii) activities of a healthcare provider to obtain payment or be reimbursed for the provision of healthcare to an individual.
- *Healthcare operations* include but are not limited to the following activities: (a) quality assessment and improvement activities, including case management and care coordination; (b) competency assurance activities, including provider or health plan performance evaluation, credentialing, and accreditation; (c) conducting or arranging for medical reviews, audits, or legal services, including fraud and abuse detection and compliance programs; (d) specified insurance functions, such

as underwriting, risk rating, and reinsuring risk; (e) business planning, development, management, and administration; and (f) business management and general administrative activities of the entity, including but not limited to de-identifying PHI.[7]

Uses and Disclosures for Public Interest Purposes

The Privacy Rule also permits use and disclosure of PHI for a range of "public interest" purposes. One key public interest purpose is medical research. Research is defined as any systematic investigation designed to develop or contribute to generalizable knowledge. The Privacy Rule permits a covered entity to use and disclose PHI for research purposes without an individual's authorization, provided the covered entity obtains: (i) a waiver of the authorization requirement from an institutional review board or privacy board; (ii) representations from the researcher that the use or disclosure of PHI is solely to prepare a research protocol or for similar purpose preparatory to research, that the researcher will not remove any PHI from the covered entity, and that PHI for which access is sought is necessary for the research; or (iii) representations from the researcher that the use or disclosure sought is solely for research on the PHI of decedents, that the PHI sought is necessary for the research, and, at the request of the covered entity, documentation of the death of the individuals about whom information is sought. A covered entity also may use or disclose a limited data set of PHI for research purposes if the researcher enters into a "data use agreement."[8]

The remaining public interest purposes are listed in Table 4.2.

The Minimum Necessary Requirement

Under the Privacy Rule, a covered entity must make reasonable efforts to use, disclose, and request only the minimum amount of PHI needed to accomplish the intended purpose of the use, disclosure, or request. Among other things, covered entities must establish and implement policies and procedures for routine, recurring disclosures that limit the PHI disclosed to that which is the minimum amount reasonably necessary to achieve the purpose of the disclosure. Individual review of each disclosure is not required. For nonroutine, nonrecurring disclosures, a covered entity must develop criteria designed to limit disclosures to the information reasonably necessary to accomplish the purpose of the disclosure, and review each of these requests individually in accordance with the established criteria.

Table 4.2 Public Interest Uses and Disclosures for Which Patient Authorization Is Not Required under the HIPAA Privacy Rule

Required by Law	Covered entities may use and disclose PHI without individual authorization as required by law (including by statute, regulation, or court orders).
Public health activities	Covered entities may disclose PHI to (1) public health authorities authorized by law to collect or receive such information for preventing or controlling disease, injury, or disability and to public health or other government authorities authorized to receive reports of child abuse and neglect; (2) entities subject to FDA regulation regarding FDA-regulated products or activities for purposes such as adverse event reporting, tracking of products, product recalls, and postmarketing surveillance; (3) individuals who may have contracted or been exposed to a communicable disease when notification is authorized by law; and (4) employers, regarding employees, when requested by employers, for information concerning a work-related illness or injury or workplace-related medical surveillance, because such information is needed by the employer to comply with the Occupational Safety and Health Administration (OHSA), the Mine Safety and Health Administration (MHSA), or similar state law.
Victims of abuse, neglect, or domestic violence	In certain circumstances, covered entities may disclose PHI to appropriate government authorities regarding victims of abuse, neglect, or domestic violence.
Health oversight activities	Covered entities may disclose PHI to health oversight agencies (as defined in the Rule) for purposes of legally authorized health oversight activities, such as audits and investigations necessary for oversight of the healthcare system and government benefit programs.
Judicial and administrative proceedings	Covered entities may disclose PHI in a judicial or administrative proceeding if the request for the information is through an order from a court or administrative tribunal. Such information may also be disclosed in response to a subpoena or other lawful process if certain assurances regarding notice to the individual or a protective order are provided.

(Continued)

Table 4.2 (Continued)   Public Interest Uses and Disclosures for Which Patient Authorization Is Not Required under the HIPAA Privacy Rule

Law enforcement purposes	Covered entities may disclose PHI to law enforcement officials for law enforcement purposes under the following six circumstances, and subject to specified conditions: (1) as required by law (including court orders, court-ordered warrants, subpoenas) and administrative requests; (2) to identify or locate a suspect, fugitive, material witness, or missing person; (3) in response to a law enforcement official's request for information about a victim or suspected victim of a crime; (4) to alert law enforcement of a person's death, if the covered entity suspects that criminal activity caused the death; (5) when a covered entity believes that PHI is evidence of a crime that occurred on its premises; and (6) by a covered healthcare provider in a medical emergency not occurring on its premises, when necessary to inform law enforcement about the commission and nature of a crime, the location of the crime or crime victims, and the perpetrator of the crime.
Decedents	Covered entities may disclose PHI to funeral directors as needed, and to coroners or medical examiners to identify a deceased person, determine the cause of death, and perform other functions authorized by law.
Cadaveric organ, eye, or tissue donation	Covered entities may use or disclose PHI to facilitate the donation and transplantation of cadaveric organs, eyes, and tissue.
Serious threat to health or safety	Covered entities may disclose PHI that they believe is necessary to prevent or lessen a serious and imminent threat to a person or the public, when such disclosure is made to someone they believe can prevent or lessen the threat (including the target of the threat). Covered entities may also disclose to law enforcement if the information is needed to identify or apprehend an escapee or violent criminal.
Essential government functions	An authorization is not required to use or disclose PHI for certain essential government functions. Such functions include assuring proper execution of a military mission, conducting intelligence and national security activities that are authorized by law, providing protective services to the President, making medical suitability determinations for U.S. State Department employees, protecting the health and safety of inmates or employees in a correctional institution, and determining eligibility for or conducting enrollment in certain government benefit programs.
Workers compensation	Covered entities may disclose PHI as authorized by, and to comply with, workers' compensation laws and other similar programs providing benefits for work-related injuries or illnesses.

Source: 45 CFR § 164.152.

If another covered entity makes a request for PHI, a covered entity may rely, if reasonable under the circumstances, on the request as complying with this minimum necessary standard. Similarly, a covered entity may rely upon requests as being the minimum necessary PHI from (a) a public official; (b) a professional (such as an attorney or accountant) who is the covered entity's business associate, seeking the information to provide services to or for the covered entity; or (c) a researcher who provides the documentation or representation required by the Privacy Rule for research.

The minimum necessary requirement does not apply to the use or disclosure of PHI for treatment purposes. It is also inapplicable to (a) disclosure to an individual who is the subject of the information, or to the individual's personal representative; (b) use or disclosure made pursuant to an authorization; (c) disclosure to HHS for complaint investigation, compliance review, or enforcement; (d) use or disclosure that is required by law; or (e) use or disclosure required for compliance with the HIPAA Transactions Rule or other HIPAA Administrative Simplification Rules.[9]

In the past, the determination of the minimum necessary data set was left to the judgment of the covered entity. However, the HITECH Act requires covered entities to use or disclose only a "limited data set" if sufficient to carry out the intended purpose. A limited data set excludes names, street addresses, social security numbers, and other identifiers, but is not fully "de-identified" in accordance with HIPAA standards. HITECH directed the HHS to issue regulations within 18 months of HITECH's enactment, providing additional guidance on what constitutes the minimum necessary information. The limited data set requirement sunsets when such regulations are issued.[10]

Elements of Valid Patient Authorization

Covered entities must obtain an individual's written authorization for any use or disclosure of PHI that is not for treatment, payment, or healthcare operations or otherwise permitted by the Privacy Rule. All authorizations must be in plain language and contain specific information regarding the information to be used or disclosed, the person(s) disclosing and receiving the information, an expiration date, and the right to revoke the authorization.[11]

Business Associates

To conduct business, covered entities must share PHI with service providers that are not covered entities. Any person or organization that receives, maintains, accesses, uses, or discloses PHI in connection with assisting a covered entity in carrying out its operations is referred to under HIPAA as a business associate.

Prior to sharing PHI with a business associate, a covered entity must enter into a written business associate agreement with the business associate. The agreement must state, among other things, that the business associate (i) will generally use or disclose PHI only for specified purposes that are related to the provision of services to the covered entity and are consistent with the Privacy Rule; (ii) will employ appropriate safeguards to prevent improper use or disclosure of the PHI; (iii) will ensure that any subcontractors abide by the same restrictions applicable to the business associate; (iv) will report any improper use or disclosure to the covered entity; (v) will assist the covered entity in responding to certain requests by patients relating to their information; (vi) will make records available to HHS upon request; and (vii) will return or destroy the PHI upon termination of the services arrangement unless infeasible.[12]

Prior to the enactment of the HITECH Act, HIPAA regulations could not be enforced directly against business associates (i.e., business associates were not subject to the civil or (arguably) criminal penalties that may be imposed by the federal government against covered entities). The sole remedy against a business associate for a privacy or security violation was a breach of contract claim by a covered entity. The HITECH Act significantly changed the way in which business associates are regulated under HIPAA. Under the HITECH Act, effective February 17, 2010, business associates are subject to direct regulation and punishment under HIPAA.

Two key obligations are imposed on business associates under the HITECH Act. First, business associates must adhere to the privacy requirements of their business associate agreements and the HITECH Act's privacy requirements. Second, business associates must comply with the HIPAA Security Rule.[13] This latter obligation is a significant one for business associates, which were previously required under their business associate agreements only to implement reasonable, but unspecified, administrative, physical, and technical safeguards.

Privacy Safeguards

Under the Privacy Rule, a covered entity must have in place appropriate administrative, physical, and technical safeguards to protect the privacy of PHI and reasonably safeguard it from any intentional or unintentional use or disclosure that is in violation of the Privacy Rule. This requirement applies to all PHI (i.e., PHI in any form, including paper or electronic). For electronic PHI (or ePHI), covered entities must implement detailed safeguards set forth in the HIPAA Security Rule.[14]

Patient Rights

The Privacy Rule requires covered entities to afford patients certain rights with respect to any PHI maintained about them in medical records, billing records, or other records used to deliver healthcare services or provide health benefits. These rights include the following:

- The right to adequate notice of how a covered entity may use and disclose PHI about the individual, as well as his or her rights and the covered entity's obligations with respect to that information. To afford patients this right, most covered entities must develop and provide individuals with a "notice of privacy practices."
- The right to obtain access to or copies of their information. The HITECH Act added an additional patient right beyond what was included in the HIPAA Privacy Rule. That is, if the information is maintained in an "electronic health record," the information must be provided in electronic form at the patient's request.
- The right to request amendments to the entity's records if deemed inaccurate or incomplete by the patient. The covered entity is not obligated to make all requested amendments, but it must note the request and the entity's response in its records.
- The right to restrict the manner in which the patient's information is used or disclosed, even if otherwise permitted by HIPAA.
- The right to an accounting of certain disclosures of the patient's information made by the covered entity. Prior to the enactment of the HITECH Act, the accounting did not have to include disclosures made for treatment, payment, or healthcare operations. However, under the HITECH Act, these disclosures must be accounted for if made "through an electronic health record." The HITECH Act requires HHS to issue a regulation specifying what must be included in such an "accounting of disclosures;" that regulation is forthcoming.
- The right to request an alternative means or location for receiving communications of PHI by means other than those that the covered entity typically employs.[15]

Breach Notification

The HITECH Act imposes a new security breach notification requirement on covered entities and business associates.[16] In the event of a security breach of "unsecured PHI," a covered entity must notify the affected individuals and HHS without unreasonable delay, but in no event more than 60 days after discovery of the breach. To enable a covered entity to comply with this requirement, a business associate must notify the covered entity of a security breach involving any of the covered entity's information within the same time frame. The covered entity is responsible for applicable notifications related to the breach at the business associate site, still within the statutory time frame.

PHI is considered "unsecured" unless it is maintained or transmitted in accordance with encryption standards adopted by HHS. These standards are as follows:

- For data at rest, encryption must be in accordance with NIST Special Publication 800-111, *Guide to Storage Encryption Technologies for End User Devices*.
- For data in motion, encryption must be in accordance with Federal Information Processing Standards (FIPS) 140-2. These include, as appropriate, standards described in NIST Special Publications 800-52, *Guidelines for the Selection and Use of Transport Layer Security (TLS) Implementations*; 800-77, *Guide to IPsec VPNs*; or 800-113, *Guide to SSL VPNs*, and may include others which are FIPS 140-2-validated.

HHS has defined a breach as an unauthorized disclosure of PHI that poses "a significant risk of financial, reputational, or other harm" to the individual whose PHI was breached.[17] The "risk of harm" standard has been controversial because privacy advocates believe that it gives covered entities too much flexibility to determine when there is a breach. At the same time, covered entities have expressed concern that the standard is vague and ill defined, thereby opening them up to liability for making an incorrect determination about whether there has been a significant risk of harm. HHS has announced that it is reconsidering the significant risk of harm standard.

Relationship to State Privacy Laws

State laws that are contrary to the Privacy Rule are generally preempted (i.e., they are superseded by federal laws). "Contrary" means that it would be impossible for a covered entity to comply with both the state and federal requirements, or that the provision of state law stands as an obstacle to the objectives of HIPAA.

There are several exceptions to the federal preemption rule. Most importantly, a state law is not preempted if it provides greater privacy protections or privacy rights with respect to such information. As a result, more stringent state privacy laws continue to apply to covered entities.[18]

Penalties

Both civil monetary penalties and criminal sanctions may be imposed for violations of HIPAA. As amended by the HITECH Act, civil monetary penalties under HIPAA range from $100 to $50,000 per violation and up to $1.5 million for identical violations in a calendar year.[19]

Criminal penalties may be imposed on any person who knowingly misuses PHI. The base penalty is a fine of up to $50,000 and/or imprisonment of up to 1 year. If a person commits an offense under false pretenses, the maximum penalty increases to a $100,000 fine and/or imprisonment of not more than 5 years. If a person commits an offense with intent to sell, transfer, or use individually identifiable health information for commercial advantage, personal gain, or malicious harm, a court may fine the person up to $250,000 and/or imprison the person for not more than 10 years.[20]

Federal Protection of Substance Abuse Treatment Records

The confidentiality of certain alcohol and drug abuse treatment records is subject to more stringent federal protection than is afforded other health information under HIPAA. The stricter regulatory scheme reflects the particularly sensitive nature of records relating to substance abuse treatment. These records are protected under 42 CFR Part 2, which are frequently referred to as the Part 2 Rules.[21] This means that, with respect to this type of data, the Part 2 Rules apply.

Types of Organizations Covered by Part 2 Rules

The Part 2 Rules are applicable to "alcohol and drug abuse patient records which are maintained in connection with the performance of any federally assisted alcohol and drug abuse program." A "program" is any person or entity that holds itself out as providing, and actually provides, alcohol or drug abuse diagnosis, treatment, or referral for treatment. A general medical facility is *not* a "program," except for an identified alcohol or drug abuse unit therein. A program is federally assisted if:

- It is conducted by a federal agency or department.
- It is carried out under a federal license or certification, including but not limited to (a) Medicare provider status; (b) methadone maintenance authorization; or (c) registration to dispense controlled substances.
- It is supported by funds from a federal department or agency. Support includes general federal funding not linked to the program or federal revenue-sharing funds provided to state governments.
- It has been granted a tax exemption by the IRS.

The regulations do not apply to the following: (i) records of the Veterans Administration; (ii) certain records of the armed forces; (iii) the exchange of information by personnel within a program or between a program and its controlling entity; (iv) disclosures to law enforcement officials in connection with the commission of a crime by the patient on the program's premises; and (v) reports of suspected child abuse or neglect pursuant to state law.[22]

Elements of a Valid Consent

If no exception is available, records governed by the Part 2 Rules may be disclosed only with written patient consent. The consent form must contain many of the same elements as a valid HIPAA authorization, but must specifically reference the specially protected nature of the substance abuse treatment records. The consent form must include:

- The name of the program.
- The name of the recipient of the records.
- The name of the patient.
- The purpose of the disclosure.
- A description of the information being disclosed.
- The signature of the patient or a minor patient's parent or guardian.
- The date of the signature.
- A statement that the consent is subject to revocation.

■ The date or event upon which the consent expires. The consent may remain in effect no longer than is reasonably necessary to achieve its purpose.[23]

Exceptions to Consent Requirement

Records subject to the Part 2 Rules may be disclosed without the patient's consent in the following circumstances: (a) subject to certain limitations, to a central registry or another detoxification or maintenance program within 200 miles of the facility to prevent multiple enrollments by the patient; (b) in medical emergencies for treatment purposes; (c) to the FDA for certain purposes; (d) to a researcher if certain safeguards are employed; and (e) to governmental or third-party payer audit personnel for on-site program audits if certain conditions are satisfied.[24] The information disclosed must be limited to the amount necessary for the particular purpose.

Mandatory Warning Notice Accompanying Disclosures

Third-party payers and entities controlling programs that receive protected records from a program may not redisclose the records except as permitted by the Part 2 Rules. Redisclosure is also prohibited by any person who receives notice from a program that the protected records are subject to the Part 2 Rules.

Each disclosure made pursuant to a patient's consent must include the following warning notice: "This information has been disclosed to you from records protected by Federal confidentiality rules (42 CFR part 2). The federal rules prohibit you from making any further disclosure of this information unless further disclosure is expressly permitted by the written consent of the person to whom it pertains or as otherwise permitted by 42 CFR Part 2. A general authorization for the release of medical or other information is *not* sufficient for this purpose. The federal rules restrict any use of the information to criminally investigate or prosecute any alcohol or drug abuse patient."[25]

Relationship between Programs and Qualified Service Organizations

Programs may disclose information to a qualified service organization (QSO) without the patient's consent. The QSO concept is similar to the business associate framework under HIPAA. A QSO is a person or agency that provides services—such as data processing, dosage preparation, laboratory analyses, vocational counseling, or legal, medical, accounting, or other professional services—to a program that the program does not provide for itself. The QSO must enter a written agreement with the program in which it acknowledges that it is bound by the Part 2 Rules, promises not to redisclose patient-identifying information to which it gains access, and promises to resist unauthorized efforts to gain access to any patient-identifying information that may come into its possession.[26]

Penalties

Any person who violates the Part 2 Rules may be subject to a criminal fine of up to $500 for the first offense and up to $5,000 for each subsequent offense.[27] Criminal penalties may be imposed only if there is criminal intent. There is no private civil right of action.

Other Federal Health Privacy Statutes and Regulations

A substantial number of other federal statutes and regulations impose confidentiality obligations on the use and disclosure of certain types of health information. A couple of prominent examples of such statutes and regulations are summarized below.

Title X Family Planning Program

The Title X Family Planning program is a federal grant program dedicated to providing individuals with comprehensive family planning and related preventive health services. The Title X program provides access to contraceptive services, supplies, and information. Title X grantees provide family planning services through a network of community-based clinics that include state and local health departments, tribal organizations, hospitals, university health centers, independent clinics, community health centers, faith-based organizations, and other public and private nonprofit agencies.[28]

Title X family planning services must be provided on a confidential basis. The regulations governing the Title X program provide that "[a]ll information as to personal facts and circumstances obtained by the project staff about individuals receiving services must be held confidential and must not be disclosed without the individual's documented consent, except as may be necessary to provide services to the patient or as required by law, with appropriate safeguards for confidentiality. Otherwise, information may be disclosed only in summary, statistical, or other form which does not identify particular individuals."[29]

Medicare and Medicaid

Healthcare providers participating in the Medicare or Medicaid programs must satisfy certain "conditions of participation," referred to as COPs. The COPs include requirements relating to the confidentiality of medical records. For example, the Medicare COPs applicable to hospitals provide that only authorized persons may have access to patient records, and that a participating hospital must ensure that unauthorized individuals cannot gain access to or alter patient records. Failure to satisfy a Medicare COP jeopardizes reimbursement under the Medicare and Medicaid programs.[30]

State Privacy Laws

Both before and after the enactment of HIPAA, states have adopted a patchwork of health information privacy laws that are applicable to covered entities if they are more stringent than the HIPAA Privacy Rule. Some states have passed comprehensive laws similar in scope to HIPAA, while other states have enacted laws that are focused on certain types of providers or sensitive health information such as mental health, substance abuse, HIV/AIDS, genetic testing, and family planning records. In addition, many states protect the confidentiality of health information through healthcare provider licensing laws, laws that grant patients the right to access their own health information, breach notification laws, and new state laws that govern the electronic exchange of health information among healthcare providers and other health industry stakeholders. These disparate approaches to protecting health information privacy are discussed briefly below.

Comprehensive Medical Privacy Laws

One example of a comprehensive state privacy law is the California Confidentiality of Medical Information Act (CMIA). The CMIA provides that "no provider of health care shall disclose medical information regarding a patient of the provider without first obtaining an authorization." Exceptions include, but are not limited to, disclosures (i) pursuant to a court order;

(ii) for purposes of diagnosis and treatment of the patient; and (iii) to an insurer, employer, healthcare service plan, governmental authority, or other entity responsible for determination of payment.

Under the CMIA, healthcare providers must follow certain procedures to document a patient's authorization to disclose confidential medical information. The authorization form must satisfy specific requirements, including minimum font size. A recipient of medical information pursuant to such an authorization may not further disclose that information except in accordance with a new authorization.[31] This is more stringent than HIPAA, which expressly states that once PHI has been disclosed to a party that is not a covered entity, it is no longer protected by the statute.

Laws Governing Sensitive Health Information

HIV/AIDS Information

According to the "Report on State Law Requirements for Patient Permission to Disclose Health Information," prepared for the Health Information Security and Privacy Collaboration (HISPC), the majority of states have statutes or regulations that specifically regulate the disclosure of HIV test results and/or information related to HIV, or to information related to communicable diseases, including HIV.[32] Strong confidentiality requirements are included in most state statutes governing HIV/AIDS information, as are penalties for disclosure of confidential HIV/AIDS information. At the same time, such statutes generally permit (and sometimes require) disclosure of results to health practitioners, emergency workers, sexual partners, and state and federal health officials.[33] States that require patient consent to disclose HIV-related information generally mandate that such consent be in writing.[34]

Mental Health Information

Many states have enacted laws specifically restricting the disclosure of the records of patients who have received mental health treatment. In some cases, these laws apply to any mental health information; in other cases, obligations are imposed only on specialized mental health providers, such as licensed mental health facilities, psychiatrists, or other mental health practitioners.

For example, many states have laws that govern the disclosure of information maintained by facilities that provide inpatient mental health treatment. Such laws often protect a broad range of information and records. Laws in New Jersey, as well as in several other states, protect "certificates, applications, records and reports" identifying individuals presently or formerly receiving mental health services, a practice which serves to keep private even the fact that the person has sought or obtained mental health services. As is the case under the Part 2 Rules, laws in several states prohibit the recipients of health information originating from these mental health facilities from further disclosing the information except as authorized under the terms of the law.[35]

Genetic Testing Information

State laws often provide heightened protection for information related to individuals' genetic makeup. Some of these state laws afford protection solely to genetic testing and testing-related information, while others are broader and also protect other information tied to genetic makeup, such as family health history or information about inherited characteristics. According to the HISPC report referenced above, genetic information laws in 14 states generally require the permission of the test subject for disclosure of such information, even for treatment. Laws in three states expressly permit the disclosure of genetic information without patient permission to another provider for treatment.[36]

Family Planning Information

States may also have laws that protect the confidentiality of family planning information. In New York, for example, General Business Law § 394-e forbids healthcare providers from disclosing "a report of a referral for abortion services or a report of an inquiry or request therefore, to any person," absent the written authorization of the subject of the report or in other limited circumstances. The authorization must identify the name and address of the requestor. Violators may be subject to both civil and criminal penalties.

Information about Minors

Most states allow minors to consent to the provision of certain medical services on their own, without the consent of a parent or guardian. These "minor consent" services commonly include family planning, mental health, and substance abuse treatment services. In many states, information relating to a service for which a minor has provided informed consent is controlled by the minor. This means that such information cannot be shared with the minor's parent or guardian without the minor's consent. In addition, only the minor, and not the minor's parent or guardian, may consent to the disclosure of the information to another person or entity when consent for the disclosure is required by law.

Laws Relating to Licensure of Facilities and Professionals

As a condition of licensure, various states require healthcare professionals to maintain the confidentiality of medical information. State licensing laws applicable to healthcare facilities frequently impose similar requirements. The Florida hospital licensure law, for example, provides that "patient records are confidential and must not be disclosed without the consent of the person to whom they pertain," though this requirement is subject to exceptions.[37]

Privilege Statutes

Almost all states have statutes making patient–physician communications privileged. This means that medical records may not be obtained through discovery in litigation or entered into evidence in a court proceeding without the subject's authorization.

The extent of the physician–patient privilege depends upon the specific provisions of the statute. Privilege statutes often establish requirements relating to the identity of the healthcare provider, the existence of a physician–patient relationship, and the type of information that will be privileged. New York was the first state to enact a physician–patient privilege. Under New York law, "[u]nless the patient waives the privilege, a person authorized to practice medicine . . . shall not be allowed to disclose any information which he acquired in attending a patient in a professional capacity."[38]

Patient Access Laws

The HIPAA Privacy Rule does not preempt state laws that grant individuals more extensive rights to access and amend health information than the rights provided under HIPAA. According to a 2009 HISPC report, entitled "Report on State Medical Record Access Laws," nearly every state has some statutory or regulatory provisions that grant individuals the right to access their medical records maintained by healthcare providers. While most state medical record access laws are less detailed than HIPAA, they generally include provisions that address individuals' right of access to their health information; the maximum time doctors and/or hospitals have to respond to such a request; and the maximum copying fees doctors and/or hospitals may charge for furnishing the record.[39]

Breach Notification Laws

As of January 2012, 46 states, the District of Columbia, Puerto Rico, and the Virgin Islands had enacted laws requiring notification of affected individuals in the event of a data security breach involving personal information. These laws are generally designed to prevent identity theft and other types of financial fraud. As a result, personal information is commonly defined to include an individual's first name or initial and last name combined with social security number, driver's license or state ID number, account number, credit or debit card number, or similar types of financial information. Thus, only those breaches of medical records that contain such identifiers are subject to these state laws. A few states include all medical information and/or health insurance information in their breach notification statutes.

While there are variations among state security breach notification laws, they generally contain the following key elements: (i) delineating who must comply with the law; (ii) defining the terms "personal information" and "breach of security"; (iii) establishing the elements of harm that must occur, if any, for notice to be triggered; (iv) adopting requirements for notice; (v) creating exemptions and safe harbors; (vi) clarifying preemption and relationships to other federal laws; and (vii) establishing penalties, enforcement authorities, and remedies.[40]

Recent Regulation of Regional and Other Health Information Exchanges

State and regional electronic health information exchanges (HIEs) are the building blocks of a national electronic health information network. But before a national health data network can become a reality, privacy issues will have to be resolved to the satisfaction of a divergent group of stakeholders. A handful of states have recently attempted to resolve some of the privacy issues raised by widespread electronic HIE through new legislation.

For example, North Carolina recently adopted the North Carolina Health Information Exchange Act (the Act), which authorizes the creation and operation of a voluntary, statewide health information exchange network (HIE network). The Act supersedes other state laws and permits the widespread exchange of medical information through the HIE network for purposes allowed under HIPAA. The Act grants patients the right to opt out of the exchange of their information through the HIE network, except in a medical emergency. It also provides immunity for any healthcare provider who, in treating a patient, in good faith relies upon information provided through the HIE network.[41]

Conclusion

The various federal and state laws described above create a patchwork quilt of requirements governing the use and disclosure of individually identifiable health information. One of the implications of this legal framework for health information privacy is that an organization's privacy obligations may vary from one context to another. But, perhaps even more importantly, the variations in existing health information privacy laws may stand as a barrier to nationwide electronic health information exchange.

Notes

1. Pub. L. No. 104-191.
2. Pub. L. No. 111-005.
3. 45 CFR §§ 160.102 & 103.
4. 45 CFR § 160.103.
5. 45 CFR § 164.514(a)-(c).
6. 45 CFR § 160.103.
7. 45 CFR §§ 164.501 & 506(c).
8. 45 CFR §§ 164.501 & 512(i).
9. 54 CFR §§ 164.502(b)(2) & 514(d). Section 13405(b) of the HITECH Act requires HHS to release minimum necessary guidance though it is unclear when the guidance will be released.
10. See Section 13405(b) of the HITECH Act.
11. 45 CFR § 164.508(a) & (c).
12. 45 CFR §§ 160.103 & 164.504(e)(2).
13. See section 13401(a) of the HITECH Act.
14. 45 CFR § 164.530(c).

15. See 45 CFR §§ 164.520, 522, 524, 526, & 528. Note that a covered entity does not have to agree to all restriction requests. However, under Section 13405(a) of the HITECH Act, effective February 17, 2010, covered entities must agree to a request not to disclose information relating to a particular medical service to the patient's insurer if the patient agrees to pay for the service out-of-pocket in full.

16. The Privacy Rule obligated covered entities to mitigate the potentially harmful effects of an improper disclosure of protected health information, but it did not necessarily mandate notification of affected individuals or government agencies. 45 CFR § 164.530(f). See section § 13402(b) of the HITECH Act.

17. 74 Fed. Reg. 42740. HHS published an interim final rule explaining how covered entities must comply with the HITECH Act's breach notification requirement in the August 25, 2009 *Federal Register*.

18. 45 CFR §§ 160.202 & 203.

19. 45 CFR §§ 160.402(a) & 404.

20. 42 U.S.C.§ 1320d-6(b).

21. The description of 42 CFR Part 2 requirements reflects those in place as of September 2016. In February 2016, the U.S. Department of Health and Human Services Secretary announced proposed changes to this regulation, intended to facilitate information exchange while protecting individuals' privacy.

22. See 42 CFR §§ 2.3(a), 2.11 & 2.12.

23. 42 CFR § 2.31.

24. 42 CFR §§ 2.34, 2.51, 2.52 & 2.53.

25. 42 CFR § 2.32.

26. 42 CFR §§ 2.11 & 2.12.

27. 42 U.S.C. § 290dd-2(f).

28. Office of Population Affairs, U.S. Department of Health & Human Services. History of Title X. Available at: http://www.hhs.gov/opa/title-x-family-planning/.

29. 42 CFR § 59.11.

30. See 42 CFR §§ 440.10(a)(3)(iii), 440.20(a)(3)(ii) & 440.140 indicating that hospitals are required to meet the Medicare COPs in order to participate in Medicaid.

31. See Cal. Civ. Code §§ 56.10, 11 & 13.

32. Health Information Security and Privacy Collaboration. Report on State Law Requirements for Patient Permission to Disclose Health Information. August 2009. Available at: https://www.healthit.gov/sites/default/files/disclosure-report-1.pdf.

33. DeWitt R, Ellis Harton A, Hoffmann WE Jr., Keenan R III, Russell M. 3-16 Treatise on Health Care Law § 16.05 (2011).

34. See, e.g. N.Y. Pub. Health Law Article 27-F and 10 N.Y.C.R.R. Part 63.

35. Health Information Security and Privacy Collaboration. Report on State Law Requirements for Patient Permission to Disclose Health Information. August 2009. Available at: https://www.healthit.gov/sites/default/files/disclosure-report-1.pdf. See also N. J. Admin. Code § 10:37-6.79(a)(1) (2008).

36. Health Information Security and Privacy Collaboration. Report on State Law Requirements for Patient Permission to Disclose Health Information. August 2009. Available at: https://www.healthit.gov/sites/default/files/disclosure-report-1.pdf.
37. DeWitt R, Ellis Harton A, Hoffmann WE Jr., Keenan R III, Russell M. 3-16 Treatise on Health Care Law § 16.02 (2011). See also Fla. Stat. Ann. § 395.3025.
38. DeWitt R, Ellis Harton A, Hoffmann WE Jr., Keenan R III, Russell M. 3-16 Treatise on Health Care Law § 16.02 (2011). See also N.Y. C.P.L.R. 4504[a].
39. Health Information Security and Privacy Collaboration. Privacy and Security Solutions for Interoperable Health Information Exchange: Report on State Medical Record Access Laws. August 2009. Available at: https://www.healthit.gov/sites/default/files/290-05-0015-state-law-access-report-1.pdf.
40. Stevens G. Congressional Research Service. Data Security Breach Notification Laws. April 10, 2012.
41. For more information see http://hiea.nc.gov/.

Chapter 5

Privacy Challenges in Health Information Exchange

By Linda Dimitropoulos, PhD

Contents

The capability to share health information that will come from the adoption and use of electronic health records (EHR) and health information exchange has the potential to produce significant benefits to healthcare providers, patients, and the healthcare delivery system. Interoperable health information systems will also support critical public health functions, including real-time case reporting, disease surveillance, and disaster response and can support data aggregation for research, which will lead to improved clinical guidelines and practices. In addition, interoperability will also support the integration of administrative and clinical data to enable value-based payment. However, networked electronic records also create privacy risks, such as the loss of patients' control over their health information and misuse of information, as well as the potential for security breaches. Many fear that such risks, if realized, might lead to a loss of patients' trust in their doctors and the healthcare delivery system. This chapter will explore the privacy risks associated with health information exchange and approaches to mitigating these risks.

The Need for Nationwide Electronic Health Information Exchange

The term "health information exchange" is used as a verb when describing the sharing of information among organizations and between patients and providers; and as a noun to describe a health information exchange (HIE), which is an organization that provides services that enable widespread sharing of health information (sometimes referred to as an HIO). In this chapter, we will use HIE as the noun to refer to the organization. Electronic health information exchange is the key to unlocking the wealth of information that is currently held in paper records. The capability to share information electronically in a usable format is necessary to transform the way we deliver care to improve quality, safety, and efficiency, resulting in a healthy, engaged population.[1,2] Ready access to clinical information by healthcare providers will streamline the care coordination necessary to support the healthcare transformation called for in the Patient Protection and Affordable Care Act (ACA). The ability to share clinical information among members of care teams is necessary to support innovative care models, such as person-centered health homes, and payment reform approaches, such as the Medicare Shared Savings Program for Accountable Care Organizations.

Health information exchange is also necessary to support the goals of the Medicare and Medicaid EHR Incentive programs, created by the American Recovery and Reinvestment Act (ARRA) in February 2009 to provide a financial incentive for the "meaningful use" (MU) of certified EHRs to achieve a number of health and efficiency objectives. These include using certified EHRs in meaningful ways, such as (1) for electronic prescribing; (2) to share clinical information electronically to improve care coordination and quality;

and (3) to submit clinical quality and other measures. In the future, interoperable information sharing will allow us to integrate clinical information with other sources of health data such as genomic data to enable precision medicine[3,4] and self-generated health data collected by monitoring devices and smartphone applications.[5]

Making Electronic Health Information Exchange a Reality

To advance nationwide sharing of electronic health information requires the widespread adoption and use of interoperable EHRs, a common set of data and interoperability standards, and a policy infrastructure to govern the exchange and use of health information.

EHR Adoption

Significant investments have been made to promote EHR adoption through the Health Information Technology for Economic and Clinical Health (HITECH) Act, which is part of ARRA. The Department of Health and Human Services (HHS) established programs to advance the MU of certified EHR technology and secure health information exchange by establishing the Medicare and Medicaid EHR Incentive programs. The Medicare and Medicaid EHR Incentive programs pay incentives to eligible healthcare professionals and hospitals when they adopt certified EHR technology and use it to achieve specified objectives for improving care as outlined in the MU regulations. The regulations outline the requirements that eligible professionals and hospitals must meet to be eligible for the incentive payments, which include gradually more robust requirements for exchanging health information to improve care coordination. Altogether, more than $27 billion in incentive payments are available to eligible providers and hospitals that meet the MU objectives.[6]

Since the implementation of the EHR incentive programs there has been dramatic growth in the adoption of EHRs, but interoperability is still lagging. As of July 2015, 41 percent of hospitals routinely access electronic clinical information from outside providers for treatment. In 2014, 78 percent of hospitals electronically sent a summary of care document and 56 percent received a summary of care document. However, fewer than 50 percent of those hospitals integrate the data received into the patient's current record.[7]

Although the Medicare and Medicaid EHR Incentive Programs have increased the adoption and use of certified EHR technology among eligible hospitals and providers, they have not catalyzed the widespread information sharing necessary to achieve the vision of a person-centered, data-driven healthcare system. The current business environment does not incentivize information sharing. The Medicare Access and CHIP Reauthorization Act (MACRA) legislation paves the way for widespread sharing of health information by shifting payment models from volume- to value-based payment and quality reporting programs.[8] Many healthcare payment models pay for volume of services rather than quality of care and improved patient outcomes. Shifting to payment models that reward value versus volume creates a compelling business case for providers to invest in the technology that will enable them to use interoperable health information in care delivery. MACRA will consolidate current physician reporting programs, including the Medicare and Medicaid EHR Incentive Program, into a unified Merit-Based Incentive Payment System (MIPS). The move to payment for quality versus quantity is key to creating the business case for interoperability.[9]

The HITECH Act also directed HHS to establish programs that support private and secure electronic health information exchange. ONC has also been instrumental in providing support to the development of state-level HIEs by establishing the State Health Information Exchange Cooperative Agreements Program, which was designed to develop the technical and legal infrastructure for health information exchange in each state and territory. The goal of the program is to promote health information exchange by advancing mechanisms for information sharing among healthcare organizations at the state level. The state HIEs are focused on developing the statewide policy, governance, technical infrastructure, and business practices needed to support the delivery of health information exchange services.

Data Standards and Interoperability

ONC, as the lead federal agency with respect to advancing health information exchange, has launched a number of programs aimed at developing a standards and interoperability framework for nationwide sharing of electronic health information. Interoperability is defined as "the ability of two or more systems or components to exchange information and to use the information that has been exchanged."[10] There are numerous standards and many standards development organizations (SDOs), so it is important to adopt those standards that will facilitate interoperable information exchange and minimize the need to develop new standards. The Health Information Technology Standards Panel (HITSP) served as a public–private collaborative to guide harmonization of data and interoperability standards developed by standards-setting organizations such as Health Level 7 (HL7) and the American National Standards Institute (ANSI) from 2005 to 2010. The Standards and Interoperability (S&I) Framework project is currently focused on developing a set of integrated functions, tools, and processes to guide HIE activities among various stakeholders.[11]

The Nationwide Health Information Network (NwHIN), which is a set of standards, services, and policies that enable the secure exchange of health information over the Internet, has been a key facilitator for nationwide health information exchange. NwHIN standards are being used in three major federal initiatives: NwHIN Exchange, Direct Project, and the CONNECT software solution. The NwHIN exchange is comprised of a group of federal agencies and private organizations working together to develop and test the NwHIN standards, services, and policies through live health information exchange. The focus of the NwHIN Exchange has been the exchange of information for patient care, disability claims processing, and public health information tracking.

The Direct Project (Direct) was launched in March 2010, as a simple, secure, scalable, standards-based method for sending authenticated, encrypted health information directly from an authorized entity to authorized users over the Internet.[12,13] Direct supports point-to-point information transfers that address basic needs for information exchange. Direct exchanges include pushing laboratory results to physicians; physician-to-physician exchange of patient records; physician-to-hospital exchange for patient admission; the push of hospital discharge data back to physicians; and the submission of clinical information to public health agencies. The Direct point-to-point exchange provides a relatively easy way to meet the MU requirements for health information exchange by allowing any two participants or organizations to exchange information without going through an HIE or similar organization. A recent survey conducted by the Healthcare Information and Management Systems Society (HIMSS) demonstrates how widespread use of Direct messaging is among provider organizations.[14] Although Direct is seen as a key facilitator of health information exchange, and nearly half of the HIE initiatives participating in the eHealth Initiative's 2011 survey reported plans to incorporate Direct into their offerings,[15] it is not expected to be a long-term solution to the interoperability issue because it supports only pushed communications. True interoperability requires meaningful communication between systems, including the ability to query and pull information from other systems.

CONNECT is an open source software solution that was developed out of the need for federal agencies with a healthcare line of business to be able to exchange health information. The CONNECT software solution uses the NwHIN standards to support information exchange at both the national and local level and helps to ensure that HIE initiatives are using compatible standards and policies.[16] The CONNECT solution provides a means for supporting both NwHIN exchange and DIRECT exchange. These federal initiatives are driving toward the shared set of standards necessary to achieve nationwide health information exchange.

Privacy Considerations for Health Information Exchange

The privacy of health information continues to be a concern both among individuals and organizations that manage health information. However, research shows that people do see the value of sharing their health information and they are willing to share their information under the right conditions.[17] Recent studies have begun to shed some light on individuals' preferences with respect to sharing their health information. A recent survey of individuals' attitudes toward health information exchange reported that their main concern is the potential for an unauthorized person to access their health information and commit fraud, deny credit, or deny employment. Despite these concerns, most individuals who participated in the survey recognize the benefits of health information exchange, with a clear majority citing better care coordination, a reduction in the number of tests needed, and improvements in care quality as benefits of health information exchange. In addition, many believe that the benefits of sharing their health information outweigh the risks to privacy and security, at least in some situations, and they are willing to permit health information exchange among some of their healthcare providers. About half of those surveyed wanted to choose which providers could have access to and share their information. However, when asked if they would permit the sharing of their health information among providers that were not directly involved in their care, most said that they wanted to limit access to only those providers that were directly involved in their care and treatment. (See Figure 5.1.)

> If you could choose the health care providers that could electronically access and share your health information, would you grant permission to all of your health care providers, specific health care providers, or none of your health care providers?
>
> - 38% would permit sharing among any healthcare provider
> - 52% would limit sharing to specific treating providers
>
> If you could choose the amount of information that health care providers could access and share electronically, would you choose to share all of your information, some of your information, or none of your information?
>
> - 50% would share all of their health information
> - 32% would share some of their health information
> - 12% would not share any of their health information

Figure 5.1   Individual preferences for limiting access to health information. (From Dimitropoulos, L.L. et al., *Am J Managed Care*. 17 (Special Issue): SP95– SP100, 2011.)

Another study similarly reported that although most patients understand the value of data sharing among treating providers, they want some control over which providers can see what information, especially with respect to mental and behavioral health information.[18]

More recently a study of individuals' willingness to exchange health information electronically using mobile devices found that participants were willing to exchange appointment reminders, general health tips, medication reminders, laboratory/test results, and symptoms. Older participants were somewhat less willing to share any type of information.[19]

Finally, an analysis of trends in individuals' perceptions of privacy and security of medical records and health information exchange conducted between 2012 and 2014 indicates that individuals' concerns regarding information sharing and the privacy of their medical records has declined.[20] For example, in 2012, 72 percent of respondents said they were somewhat or very concerned about the privacy of their medical records and in 2014 only 52 percent of respondents expressed that concern. Although this trend coincides with expanded adoption of EHRs and information sharing, there is no evidence to indicate a causal relationship. It may be that with the proliferation of social media, individuals are more willing to share personal information and are less concerned with privacy overall. The authors note that these findings reflect individuals' perceptions prior to the announcement in 2015 of several large healthcare information breaches, which may have negatively impacted individuals' perceptions related to the privacy of their medical records and the exchange of their health information.[21]

Challenges in Addressing Privacy of Health Information Exchange

The specific privacy concerns reported in the literature suggest a clear need to improve individuals' participation in decisions about who may access an individual's health information and how the information will be used. Providing individuals with meaningful choice in decisions about how their health information is shared is expected to increase consumer confidence in electronic health information exchange. The Privacy and Security TIGER team of the Health IT Policy Committee (federal advisory committee to the Office of the National Coordinator for Health Information Technology [ONC]) recommended that toward this goal patients should be given the opportunity to provide "meaningful consent," as depicted in Figure 5.2.

The concept of "meaningful consent" is described as "the ability of patients to thoughtfully and clearly express preferences to limit access to some parts of their record, and to change their minds at any time."[22] Further, the TIGER team recommended that both "opt-in" and "opt-out" consent models are acceptable if the choice provided is "meaningful." Opt-in consent models typically require an explicit, written consent by the individual to participate in HIE and, as implemented today, tend to be "all or nothing"

Meaningful Consent

- Allows the individual time to make a decision. (e.g., outside of the urgent need for care.)
- Is not compelled or used for discriminatory purposes. (e.g., consent to participate in an HIO is not a condition of receiving necessary medical services.
- Provides full transparency and education. (i.e., the individual gets a clear explanation of the choice and its consequences, in consumer-friendly language.)
- Is commensurate with the circumstances. (i.e., the more sensitive, personally exposing, or inscrutable the activity, the more specific the consent mechanism. Activities that depart significantly from reasonable patient expectations require a greater degree of education, time to make decision, opportunity to discuss with provider, etc.)
- Must be consistent with reasonable patient expectations for privacy, health, and safety; and
- Must be revocable. (i.e., patients should have the ability to change their consent preferences at any time. It should be clearly explained whether such changes can apply retroactively to data copies already exchanged or whether they apply only "going forward.")

Figure 5.2 Meaningful consent elements. (Adapted from Health IT Policy Committee Meeting Notes. Sept. 1, 2010.)

with no option for restricting the types of information shared, although opt-in models that allow some restrictions are being used by some organizations. Opt-out models default to allow sharing of a person's data unless the person specifically opts out. As with opt-in models, there are opt-out models that permit some restrictions by type of data, provider, or purposes for sharing the data.[23]

HIEs are making progress toward offering more individual choice regarding what information is shared and with whom when it comes to obtaining consent to participate in HIE. According to the 2011 eHealth Initiative Report on Health Information Exchange, HIEs are implementing both opt-in and opt-out approaches to obtaining consent, and they are offering more opportunities for individuals to have some limited choice in what information is shared and with whom. For example, more than half of the 255 initiatives reporting allowed individuals to make decisions by provider, data type (lab or radiology), encounter, disclosing organization, data field (demographics only), and certain types of sensitive data such as mental health, HIV status, and genetic data. The report noted that HIEs were using a Health Insurance Portability and Accountability Act notice of privacy practices (HIPAA NPP) at the point of care to inform individuals of these choices. However, the details describing what options individuals were offered regarding updating their preferences or revoking consent were not reported.

There are a number of key challenges to adequately providing meaningful choice in the consent models offered by HIEs. First, the technology needs to have the capability to capture individual preferences for data sharing, including (1) the type of data; (2) who will have access; (3) under what circumstances; and (4) the time frame for access. There also needs to be a mechanism for maintaining and updating those preferences and their specific context, and the capability to apply these rules to data coming from multiple sources.

Data segmentation refers to the process of "sequestering from capture, access, or view certain data elements that are perceived by a legal entity, institution, organization, or individual as being undesirable to share."[24] However, current clinical systems are not very sophisticated with respect to having the capability to parse or segment specific data elements in a way that will allow a policy-driven consent management system to apply the appropriate algorithms. One key challenge is getting the data into structured data fields that can be tagged and coded. Structured data fields within EHRs can be an excellent, efficient way to capture and display certain types of data such as blood pressure, lab results, and other basic information.

However, structured data fields have been met with sharp criticism by providers when they are overly restrictive and do not fit the provider's work flow. For example, providers have reported being frustrated by drop-down lists that do not have the appropriate choice available or that have hundreds of choices to scroll through to find the right one. In some cases, doctors have reported entering data into other open data fields or in the notes to create a "work around" for poorly designed structured data fields in their EHRs.[25]

In addition to the technical complexity of segmenting data to allow for individual preferences, both individuals and their healthcare providers need to be engaged and motivated to implement a decidedly new and different consent process. Individuals will need to be willing to take responsibility for making decisions about their preferences, which may be confusing for many. Patients must be educated regarding the implications, positive and negative, of the consent decisions they make. A recent telephone survey found that only 18 percent of individuals want to have the sole responsibility for determining their privacy settings when offered the choice to restrict access to dates and locations of treatment, diagnoses/treatments, prescribed medications, laboratory and genetic tests, HIV tests, sexually transmitted disease (STD) tests, or mental health treatment information. Most people want to have their physicians involved in these decisions. Twenty-six percent said that they would like to have their physician help them determine their settings and nearly 40 percent preferred that they, their physicians, and their family determine their privacy settings. Only 4 percent of the respondents wanted their provider to make these decisions for them. Nearly 80 percent of those responding indicated they would want a physician to override their privacy settings in a medical emergency in order to treat them. Providers also have preferences that must be considered, particularly the need to be certain that they have complete and accurate information to make diagnosis and treatment decisions. The needs of both sides of the patient–provider relationship must be considered, and the desire of individuals to have their providers engaged in their decisions about restricting access opens the door for a conversation in which both sides can share concerns and the individual can make informed decisions. Understanding what individuals want in terms of privacy protections is an important first step, but there are multiple social and technical challenges to be resolved before we can manage personal preferences in a truly meaningful way.

The privacy concerns that individuals raise also suggest a need to continue to improve people's trust in technology and the healthcare system overall. The Nationwide Privacy and Security Framework developed by HHS outlined eight key principles for the protection of individually identifiable health information (IIHI). These principles were distilled from a number of national and international sources, including the Code of Fair Information Practice and the Fair Information Practice Principles.[26,27] The eight key principles include individuals' right to access their information and have corrections made if errors are found; and the need for transparency about policies, procedures, and technologies that affect patients or their health information. Education about data security, individual rights, and recourse in cases of unauthorized disclosures and misuse of information may help build trust in the use of electronic information. The ability to readily obtain a list of disclosures may also help build a stronger trust relationship. In the survey cited earlier, 71 percent of respondents indicated that they would request an accounting of disclosures that their provider had made related to treatment and payment and 95 percent of those who would request the list of disclosures wanted to know what information was disclosed, when, by whom, and for what purpose.

State and Federal Health Information Privacy Policy and Regulation

Perhaps the biggest challenge we face in protecting the privacy of health information is how we develop a policy infrastructure that takes into account individual preferences and concerns about privacy, the technical complexity of data segmentation, and the interplay between state and federal laws and regulations governing HIE. The current environment leaves many of these challenges to the states, which creates a network of "learning laboratories," as each state works to identify the appropriate combination of policy and regulation that works for their stakeholders. This means, however, that it is also important to have a guiding set of principles such as those found in the Privacy and Security Framework for states to follow to promote a consistent approach across the country.

The variation in state privacy laws remains a key challenge for interstate health information exchange.[28,29] Although meeting MU requirements and payment reform are putting pressure on states to focus on information exchange issues among stakeholders within their borders, many states, especially those with populations that cross state lines for healthcare, are also focused on the challenges of interstate HIE.

The Health Information Security and Privacy Collaboration (HISPC) was the first coordinated, nationwide effort aimed at assessing the impact of the variation in organization-level business practices, policies, and state laws governing the privacy and security of electronic health information on the nation's ability to ensure adequate privacy protections and advance health information exchange.[30] The HISPC project found that health information privacy practices, policies, and state laws had been developed over time, state by state and organization by organization, without a comprehensive plan or approach.[31] The privacy laws are found in many chapters of code and sometimes conflict with one another within a given state. Most of the laws were written for paper-based systems and did not anticipate the potential for electronic collection, storage, and sharing of health information. The study also found gaps in the regulations that needed to be addressed to accommodate the shift to electronic systems. There were also some regulations that would need to be revisited because they posed direct barriers to the electronic sharing of information, for example, by requiring handwritten signatures on paper forms.

In addition to the challenges posed by the variation in state laws, the study found key challenges in how organizations interpret federal and state laws specifically related to consent and authorization for disclosures, authentication and authorization, and data linkage. Organizations struggled to understand the HIPAA Privacy and Security Rules and how and when state laws apply. Some states defer to the HIPAA Privacy Rule, which serves as a floor or baseline of protections upon which states may, but often do not choose, to enact stricter state laws. Many organizations also lacked a solid understanding of the need for an actual process of capturing patient consent or authorization to disclose health information. The confusion stems from a basic misunderstanding of whether and when the HIPAA Privacy Rule requires patients' permission for certain disclosures and a misconception that such permission is required to disclose information for treatment. Some states do require consent to disclose health information in some, if not all, circumstances, and in some cases it is an organizational policy decision to require patients' consent as an added protection to reduce the risk of liability for wrongful disclosure. There also are substantial differences in state privacy and consent rules.

Confusion also exists about the terms used for obtaining patients' permission. This is partly a result of the HIPAA Privacy Rule's use of different terms and requirements for permissions that are related to different purposes: the term *consent* applies to a patient's written permission to use and disclose health information for treatment, payment, and healthcare operations, while the term *authorization* is used to describe a patient's permission to use and disclose health information for purposes not otherwise permitted or required by the rule. Adding to the confusion, terms such as *consent*, *authorization*, and *release*, to describe a patient's written permission to disclose health information, also may vary by state.

Trust between organizations also was found to be impacted by the methods used for authentication and authorization and record matching. Organizations pointed to the need to develop a set of standards for authentication and authorization to ensure that the protocols were acceptable to all partners in the exchange. The lack of a standard, reliable way to accurately match records to patients introduces the potential for inappropriate use or disclosure of personal health information from the wrong patient, which presents both a clinical and a privacy risk. This risk is particularly acute when information is shared across institutions that use different methods of patient and record identification. Recent developments in patient-generated data and personal health records (PHRs) have added to the need to establish a consistent and reliable method for linking data from multiple sources. Correctly identifying patients and providers is critical in the delivery of high-quality care and for electronic HIE, but also is a fundamental issue in authentication and authorization.

Currently, the State Health Policy Consortium (SHPC) supports states' efforts to develop solutions to some of the many challenges to interstate HIE.[32] To date, 28 states have participated in demonstration projects to identify and test potential solutions to policy questions related to interstate HIE. Some of the consortiums are tackling longstanding issues such as the differences in requirements for obtaining patient consent and how to better integrate behavioral health and primary care data. Other consortiums are focused on the need to share information when natural disasters (e.g., Hurricane Katrina) or acute situations (e.g., 9/11) make it necessary to share information across borders, and the development of policies to establish trust through strong governance over the access and use of health information. Each of these multistate groups is working on key issues that are complicated by the variation in state regulations and their lessons will be instructive as we move toward true nationwide HIE.

Management of State Consent Requirements

Policies and laws governing patient consent to disclose health information vary from state to state. In an interstate transaction, the releasing state must comply with local law regardless of policies and laws in the receiving state. For example, Minnesota law requires written patient consent for each information disclosure in a nonemergency setting. Conversely, in emergencies, no written consent is required for any type of data. To comply, Minnesota providers must obtain proof of a signed consent form before they disclose data for treatment in response to requests from neighboring states. Although the surrounding states do not have the same restrictions for authorizing disclosure for treatment, they do have restrictions that apply to various types of specially protected data. Figure 5.3 provides a summary of the variation in requirements for patient consent in both emergency and nonemergency situations.[33]

Challenged with the variations in their state laws and looking for a way to get their providers to meet Stage 1 of MU, Minnesota, Illinois, North Dakota,

Disclosure in Nonemergencies:

	Disclosure of general health information	Disclosure from hospitals	Consent is required for disclosure of health information on sensitive conditions								
			Alcohol and substance abuse treatment	Mental health *	HIV/AIDS	STDs	Developmental disability	Genetic testing	Sexual assault and abuse	Child abuse and neglect	Abuse of adult with disability
IL	☐		☐	☐	☐	☐	☐	☐	☐		☐
MN	☐	☐	☐	☐	☐	☐	☐	☐	☐	☐	☐
ND		☐	☐								
SD			☐			☐					
WI			☐	☐			☐				

* Does not include "Psychotherapy note" as defined by HIPAA at 45 CRF 164.501, which are subject to additional authorization

For Disclosure in an Emergency (Definition Varies by State Statute)

	Disclosure of general health information	Disclosure from hospitals	Consent is required for disclosure of health information on sensitive conditions								
			Alcohol and substance abuse treatment	Mental health *	HIV/AIDS	STDs	Developmental disability	Genetic testing	Sexual assault and abuse	Child abuse and neglect	Abuse of adult with disability
IL	☐		☐	☐	☐	☐	☐	☐	☐		☐
MN	☐	☐	☐								
ND		☐									
SD			☐			☐					
WI											

* Does not include "Psychotherapy note" as defined by HIPAA at 45 CRF 164.501 which are subject to additional authorization

Figure 5.3   Example of variation in requirements for written consent by state. Matrix is adapted from the model developed by the Upper Midwest HIE Consortium.

South Dakota, and Wisconsin have worked to develop a common consent solution to manage the differences in state consent requirements. Working together the group developed (1) a standard, common consent form that meets the requirements of all participating states; (2) policies and procedures for using the form; and (3) a consent matrix that serves as a framework for developing an electronic interstate consent management solution in the future. The goal is to take a phased approach to facilitating information exchange, starting with the simplest path forward. The common consent form covers direct exchanges of information for treatment, payment, and operations as defined by the HIPAA Privacy Rule, as well as by data covered under the federal Confidentiality of Alcohol and Drug Abuse Patient Records law (42 CFR Part 2). The common consent form is an all-or-nothing solution that does not allow for individuals to restrict access to specific elements of their health information.

The challenges to interstate information exchange become even more complex when discussions turn to segregation of the various categories of sensitive information. Not only are there the challenges discussed earlier related to managing personal preferences, but state laws governing sensitive data vary widely.

Behavioral Health Data Exchange

Many HIEs have focused their resources on exchanging general clinical information for treatment, payment, and operations because the regulations regarding consent tend to be less complicated to navigate, making it more technically feasible for them to begin exchanging information as organizations build trust among stakeholders. Most plan to incorporate sensitive data types such as mental health, alcohol and substance abuse, genetic test results, and HIV/AIDS information at a later date, after they have worked out the technical and policy issues governing general clinical data. Critical care coordination issues necessitate the sharing of sensitive data, which creates some urgency around understanding the issues and developing solutions to ensure that patients get appropriate care.

One example is information related to behavioral and mental health and substance abuse. Many local and state HIEs have chosen not to exchange patient data from behavioral health facilities due to the sensitive nature of the data, the additional complexities and ambiguities of federal and state laws, and the penalties associated with failure to comply. Patients with behavioral health issues are particularly vulnerable to harm from data breaches because of the stigma associated with such conditions, yet they may not receive appropriate care if their physicians are not aware of ongoing behavioral health issues. Many individuals who suffer from chronic illnesses such as diabetes and cardiovascular disease also suffer from a mental illness. For example, diabetes patients are twice as likely to suffer from depression than the general population.[34] Mental illness is also associated with a higher prevalence of substance abuse.[35] In addition, a large volume of mental and behavioral healthcare is delivered in the primary care setting.[36] It is clear that better integration of behavioral health and primary care data is needed. Behavioral health stakeholders are largely supportive of information sharing to improve patient care, although the debate over whether to integrate behavioral and mental health data with general medical data is far from over.[37] It is clear that the regulatory landscape becomes quite complex and HIEs are struggling with how to manage patient consent requirements for behavioral health data disclosure.

Compliance with the federal Confidentiality of Alcohol and Drug Abuse Patient Records law (42 CFR Part 2), which specifies the conditions and requirements for disclosure of patient information regarding substance abuse treatment programs, is a significant concern in the behavioral health community. The Part 2 regulation requires patient authorization before an individual's substance abuse treatment information can be disclosed to external entities. In addition, the regulations prohibit the redisclosure of this information without patient consent. HHS's release of Frequently Asked Questions in July 2010 helped resolve some ambiguity regarding 42 CFR Part 2, which applies to certain federally funded substance abuse treatment programs by explaining the circumstances under which an individual's information can be exchanged electronically while also meeting the requirements of Part 2 for patient consent.[38]

With respect to inpatient mental health information, many state laws impose additional requirements for sharing behavioral and mental health information, prohibiting disclosure, and/or redisclosure of sensitive data by providers in the absence of patient consent. In addition, the HIPAA Privacy Rule includes restrictions on sharing psychotherapy notes. Patients do not have the right to access providers' psychotherapy notes if they are kept separately from the patient's record unless state law supersedes this regulation.[39] Providers are also prohibited from disclosing psychotherapy notes to health plans without patient consent. This is another area where the capability to segment electronic data will be needed to comply with the regulations governing behavioral and mental health information. In addition, electronic systems and workflows will also need to be changed to manage the multiple types of patient consents needed to disclose sensitive data between states. The regulations provide important privacy protections, but they also present significant technical implementation challenges to the electronic exchange of data between behavioral health and primary care providers.

Alabama, Florida, Kentucky, New Mexico, Nebraska, and Michigan believe that there is a path forward for electronically enabling the engagement of behavioral health facilities in HIE, and they are working to develop a set of implementation policies and procedures that addresses the special laws that apply to behavioral health data. These states have formed the Behavioral Health Data Exchange Consortium to pilot the interstate exchange of behavioral health treatment records among treating healthcare providers using the Direct messaging protocols.[40] This is particularly timely as the number of behavioral and mental health providers now participating in HIEs has grown rapidly.

This multistate team is currently developing policies and procedures for the electronic release of behavioral health patient data using Direct messaging from a provider in one state to a healthcare provider directly involved in treating a patient in another state. The states are drawing upon the concepts outlined in the July 2010 Frequently Asked Questions on applying the substance abuse confidentiality regulations published by the Substance Abuse and Mental Health Services Administration (SAMHSA). The goal is to enable electronic exchange of patient data that falls under the regulation of 42 CFR Part 2 and some state-specific laws governing the disclosure of mental health records for participating states. This is especially important because many of the substance abuse treatment facilities also provide mental health services to patients. This approach will ensure that the policies and procedures developed by this group of states comply with both state and federal regulations. Once the policies and procedures governing this interstate exchange are developed and agreed upon, a subset of these states will conduct a Direct-enabled pilot to provide a proof-of-concept demonstration that the policies and procedures align with the technical capacity to execute the exchange.

Interstate Information Exchange in the Event of a Disaster

In the aftermath of Hurricane Katrina in 2005, we were left with a very real example of how important it is to have access to health information "whenever and wherever" it is needed. Having a specific plan for HIE in the event of a disaster is a key element for disaster preparedness. Although the disclosure of health information during a disaster is often permitted across state lines under emergency provisions, the processes and procedures for doing so have been lacking. Ensuring the appropriate access to data needed to treat patients displaced by a disaster has technical, legal, and policy issues that must be resolved to incorporate HIE into regional disaster planning processes.

The states in the Southeast Regional HIT-HIE Collaboration (SERCH)—Florida, Louisiana, Texas, Georgia, Alabama, and Arkansas—examined the challenges of coordinating multiple state-level HIEs after a disaster.[41] Based on the lessons learned from KatrinaHealth, an online service designed to help individuals affected by Hurricane Katrina to work with their healthcare providers to access their electronic prescription medication records, this consortium developed an approach that would leverage the existing exchange infrastructure (such as provider-to-provider exchange using Direct), and lay the foundation for more advanced state-level HIE coordination in the future. Their goal was to examine the legal and technical issues of HIE during disaster situations and to develop a framework for states to review and assess their legal and technical infrastructure. Based on this work, the group developed an action plan to improve HIE capabilities to provide better access to patient information both during and following a disaster.

Their recommendations include

1. Understand the state's disaster response policies and align with the state agency designated for the emergency support function related to public health and medical services.
2. Develop standard procedures and gain the approval of relevant public and private stakeholders to share electronic health information across state lines.
3. Consider enacting the Mutual Aid Memorandum of Understanding to establish a waiver of liability for the release of records when an emergency is declared and to default state privacy and security laws to HIPAA in a disaster. States should also consider using the Data Use and Reciprocal Support Agreement (DURSA) in order to address and/or expedite patient privacy, security, and health data-sharing concerns.
4. Assess the state's availability of public and private health information sources and the ability to electronically share the data using HIE(s) and other health data-sharing entities.

5. Develop a phased approach to establishing interstate electronic health information-sharing capabilities.

The issues of coordinating between state-level HIEs in a disaster go beyond discussions between state-designated entities. The policies and procedures also need to be incorporated into emergency management and disaster preparedness planning, including working closely with the Federal Emergency Management Agency's (FEMA) Emergency Support Functions, which coordinate multihazard preparedness across federal, regional, and state authorities. This interaction with the federal government provides a natural conduit for spreading these procedures to other states as a core part of disaster preparedness going forward.

New Day, New Challenges: Establishing Trusted Entities

The Western States Consortium, comprised of Oregon, California, Arizona, Hawaii, Utah, Nevada, Alaska, and New Mexico, has been working to tackle technical and policy barriers to electronically exchanging health information across their borders.[42] Its goal is to develop a common set of policies and technology solutions to ensure trust and security within the exchange community. The states will develop the policies and procedures to be followed when issuing the digital certificates used for secure web-based health information exchange among HIEs within their states. The group also will develop an approach to linking and sharing their provider directories across states and communities to promote easier access to the Direct addresses of providers in the region. The objective is to ensure that all HIE participants can find, know, and trust the identity, credentials, and technical security of those with whom they are exchanging their patients' health information.

As part of their work, they have taken up the challenge of variation in exchange policies governing exchange services provided by Health Information Service Providers (HISPs) and are trying to identify ways to manage trusted relationships using digital certificates. This is a fairly new set of issues for states to grapple with, but their lessons will be valuable beyond their borders. A HISP is an organization that provides the basic framework for the secure exchange of clinical messages over the Internet. HISP enables users to easily send information using Direct protocols by structuring a secure interface. The HISP interface allows providers to access a database of verified organizational and individual Direct addresses, and authenticates the identity of both the sender and the recipient of the messages. However, while each HISP has the technical capacity to transmit information to and receive information from another HISP system, they are sometimes reluctant to trust the procedures and practices of competing HISPs. For this reason, a Direct message sent from a provider through a gateway provided by one HISP may not be delivered to the receiving provider if the recipient provider is using a different HISP. To solve this problem, the Western States Consortium is developing documentation regarding the use of standard policies to encourage exchange among HISPs, give providers and other stakeholders' confidence that Direct is being implemented in a manner that supports widespread information exchange, and enable the development of trust communities at the regional and state level.

Some states have developed "trust anchors" by promoting documentation (such as a Memorandum of Understanding), allowing regional HISPs to establish that they are following basic mandatory procedures that all entities agree are sufficient. This agreement allows free market development between HISPs and also encourages their cooperation. This solution does not address connectivity between states, however, and does not leverage the directory mechanisms available across HISPs. Establishing regional trust anchors and trust services will allow interstate exchange using Direct, and could lead to establishing regional provider directory services.

Discussion

Reaping the benefits of widespread sharing of health information requires a policy framework that ensures transparency and allows individuals to have a say in decisions about the use of their health information. The National Privacy and Security Framework and the Health IT Privacy and Security Toolkit developed by ONC offer a solid basis for the development of not only a national framework, but also for states to ensure the development of state-level policies that are consistent across the country. The benefits of widespread and meaningful health information exchange to healthcare providers, patients, and the healthcare delivery system are great, but the risks to privacy, perceived or otherwise, need to be addressed. This chapter has explored some of the privacy risks associated with health information exchange and some approaches to mitigating these risks that hold promise going forward.

As the policy framework for protecting privacy continues to evolve and develop, it will be important to balance the need for interoperable sharing of health information to improve health and healthcare with an individual's need for privacy protections, including the right to transparency regarding the use of health information and to be able to grant and revoke consent to access the data. Individuals are willing to share their information for treatment with providers involved with their care, but they become more concerned about sharing the information as the circle widens. This means that there needs to be very clear and transparent approaches taken to sharing information for secondary uses such as clinical research, data analytics, and public health reporting. The focus on secondary uses of data should be a priority, especially as HIEs are looking at new ways to become sustainable and as tools such as new data analytics methods, big data, data mining, and cloud computing become more prevalent.

The lessons we are learning from states as they work to share data across borders can and should inform the further development of federal plans for ensuring protected health information exchange. The states have concerns about the complexity of the regulatory environment which is, in many cases, driving a very deliberative approach to information sharing. For example, some states such as New Hampshire are sharing patient data only in provider-to-provider exchanges and related only to an individual's care.[43] This measured approach to developing trust between patients and the organizations looking to share their information, and working through these complex policy decisions is necessary, particularly given the privacy concerns of individuals and organizations and the potential for inadvertent disclosures that could jeopardize progress toward the goals of improving health and healthcare and reducing costs. However, continued sharing of lessons learned from state-level initiatives with those responsible for developing the federal "rules of the road" will ensure that the needs of the states are taken into account as federal leaders move forward, and it will ensure that the states develop policies that are aligned with federal plans.

Notes

1. *National Strategy for Quality Improvement in Health Care.* Washington, DC: National Quality Forum; March 2011.
2. West DM. Enabling personalized medicine through health information technology: advancing the integration of information; December 2010. Available at: www.brookings.edu/research/papers/2011/01/28-personalized-medicine-west.

3. Collins, FS and Varmus, H. A New Initiative on Precision Medicine. *N Engl J Med* 2015; 372:793–5; February 26. DOI: 10.1056/NEJMp1500523.

4. Shapiro M, Johnston D, Wald J, Mon D. Patient-Generated Health Data. White paper produced for the Office of the National Coordinator for Health IT; April 2012.

5. CMS EHR Incentive program. Available at: www.cms.gov/Regulations-and-Guidance/Legislation/EHRIncentivePrograms/index.html?redirect=/EHRIncentivePrograms.

6. Charles D, Swain M, Patel V. (July 2015) Interoperability among U.S. Non-federal Acute Care Hospitals. ONC Data Brief, no. 28. Washington, DC: Office of the National Coordinator for Health Information Technology.

7. Medicare Access and CHIP Reauthorization Act of 2015 (MACRA). Available at: https://www.federalregister.gov/articles/2016/05/09/2016-10032/medicare-program-merit-based-incentive-payment-system-mips-and-alternative-payment-model-apm.

8. Connecting Health and Care for the Nation, A Shared Nationwide Interoperability Roadmap, version 1.0; December 2015. Available at: https://www.healthit.gov/sites/default/files/nationwide-interoperability-roadmap-draft-version-1.0.pdf.

9. President's Council of Advisors on Science and Technology. Report to the President: Realizing the full potential of health information technology to improve healthcare for Americans: The path forward; December 2010. Available at: www.whitehouse.gov/sites/default/files/microsites/ostp/pcast-health-it-report.pdf.

10. See *IEEE Standard Computer Dictionary: A Compilation of IEEE Standard Computer Glossaries*; 1990. New York, NY: IEEE.

11. See the Standards & Interoperability Framework. Available at: http://www.siframework.org/.

12. See the DIRECT and NwHIN CONNECT under the HIMSS Ambulatory HIE Toolkit. Available at: http://www.himss.org/ehealth-exchange-direct-project-and-connect-ambulatory-hie-faq.

13. See also the Direct project. Available at: http://directproject.org.

14. HIMSS Interoperability and HIE Committee, HIE and Direct Messaging Survey; June 22, 2015. Available at: http://www.himss.org/hie-and-direct-messaging-survey.

15. eHealth Initiative (2011). Report on Health Information Exchange: The changing landscape. Based on Results from eHealth Initiative's Eighth Annual Survey of Health Information Exchange. Washington, DC: eHealth Initiative.

16. See also CONNECT. Available at: www.connectopensource.org.

17. Dimitropoulos LL, Patel V, Scheffler SA, Posnack S. Public attitudes towards health information exchange: Perceived benefits and concerns. *Am J Managed Care*. 2011; 17 (Special Issue): SP95–SP100.

18. Report of the Secretary's Advisory Committee on Automated Personal Data Systems (1973). Available at: http://aspe.hhs.gov/DATACNCL/1973privacy/tocprefacemembers.htm.

19. Serrano KJ, Yu M, Riley W, Patel V et al. Willingness to exchange health information via mobile devices: findings from a population-based survey. *Ann Fam Med.* 2016;14 (1):34–40.

20. Patel V, Hughes P, Barker W, Moon L. Trends in Individuals' Perceptions regarding Privacy and Security of Medical Records and Exchange of Health Information: 2012–2014. ONC Data Brief, no. 33; February 2016. Washington, DC: Office of the National Coordinator for Health Information Technology.

21. Office of the National Coordinator for Health Information Technology. Breaches of unsecured protected health information, Health IT Quick - Stat #53; February 2016. Available at: http://dashboard.healthit.gov/quickstats/pages/breaches-protected-health-information.php.

22. Federal Trade Commission (1998). Privacy Online: A Report to Congress: Fair Information Practice Principles. Available at: https://www.ftc.gov/reports/privacy-online-report-congress.

23. Markle Foundation. Markle Survey: The Public and Doctors Agree on Importance of Specific Privacy Protections for Health IT, Markle Survey on Health in a Networked Life; January 2011. Available at: http://www.markle.org/sites/default/files/7_PrivacyPolicies.pdf.

24. Office of the National Coordinator for Health IT. Privacy and Security Framework Requirements and Guidance for the State Health Information Exchange Cooperative Agreement Program, Program Information Notice; March 2012. Available at: https://www.healthit.gov/sites/default/files/hie-interoperability/onc-hie-pin-003-final.pdf.

25. Goldstein MM, Rein AL. Consumer consent options for electronic health information exchange: Policy considerations and analysis; March 23, 2010. Available at: https://www.healthit.gov/sites/default/files/privacy-security/cover-page-and-executive-summary-032610.pdf.

26. Goldstein MM, Rein AL. Data segmentation in electronic health information exchange: Policy consideration and analysis; September 29, 2010. Available at: https://www.healthit.gov/sites/default/files/privacy-security/gwu-data-segmentation-final-cover-letter.pdf.

27. Dimitropoulos LL. Barriers to meeting meaningful use among Medicaid providers. Presented at fourth annual CMS Multi-State Medicaid HITECH Conference, Baltimore, MD; April 2012.

28. Pritts J, Lewis S, Jacobson R, Lucia K, Kayne K. Privacy and security solutions for interoperable health information exchange: Report on state law requirements for patient permissions to disclose health information. Office of the National Coordinator for Health IT; 2009.

29. eHealth Initiative. The State of health information exchange: Connecting the nation to achieve meaningful use; 2010.

30. Dimitropoulos LL. Health Information Security and Privacy Collaboration (HISPC). Reports on State Law, Business Practices, and Policy Variations. Office of the National Coordinator for Health

Information Technology; January 2010. Updated April 9, 2010. Available at: https://www.healthit.gov/policy-researchers-implementers/health-information-security-privacy-collaboration-hispc.

31. Dimitropoulos LL, Risk S. A state-based approach to privacy and security for interoperable health information exchange. *Health Affairs*. 2009; Available at: http://content.healthaffairs.org/content/28/2/428.abstract.

32. State Health Policy Consortium. Available at: http://www.rti.org/publication/state-health-policy-consortium-summary-projects-and-outcomes-final-report.

33. The Upper Midwest State Health Policy Consortium on Health Information Exchange. Final Report; October 2011. Available at: http://www.healthit.nd.gov/wp-content/uploads/sites/2/sites/2/2010/07/UMHIE_Final_Report_Oct-2011.pdf. Note: State laws change frequently and although these data were current as of the writing of this chapter, some changes may have occurred since publication.

34. Egede LE, Zheng D, Simpson K. Comorbid depression is associated with increased health care use and expenditures in individuals with diabetes. *Diabetes Care*. 2002;25(3):464–470.

35. Martins S, Gorelick D. Conditional substance abuse and dependence by diagnosis of mood or anxiety disorder or schizophrenia in the U.S. population. *Drug and Alcohol Dependence*. 2011;119(1–2):28–36.

36. Centers for Disease Control and Prevention. National Ambulatory Medical Care Survey; 2008.

37. Conaboy C. Clipboard: Who should have access to mental health records? Available at: http://www.boston.com/whitecoatnotes/2012/06/21/clipboard-who-should-have-access-mental-health-records/fHb9nH5e4TcW7DdQLdTCtM/story.html.

38. Wattenburg S. Frequently Asked Questions: Applying the Substance Abuse Confidentiality Regulations to Health Information Exchange (HIE); SAMHSA; July 2010. Available at: http://www.samhsa.gov/sites/default/files/faqs-applying-confidentiality-regulations-to-hie.pdf.

39. Holloway J. More protections for patients and psychologists under HIPAA. *Monitor on Psychology* 2003;34(2):22.

40. See the Direct Implementation Protocols. Available at: https://www.healthit.gov/policy-researchers-implementers/direct-project.

41. Southeast Regional HIT-HIE Collaboration (SERCH): Final Report. Available at: http://www.healthit.gov/sites/default/files/pdf/SERCH-White-Paper.pdf.

42. State Health Policy Consortium - Behavioral Health Data Exchange. Available at: https://www.healthit.gov/sites/default/files/bhdeconsortiumfinalreport_06182014_508_compliant.pdf.

43. State Health Policy Consortium - Behavioral Health Data Exchange. Available at: https://www.healthit.gov/sites/default/files/bhdeconsortiumfinalreport_06182014_508_compliant.pdf.

Chapter 6

Maintaining a Holistic Approach to Privacy

By Kris Miller, JD, LLM, MPA, CIPP/US/G/E, SMP

Contents

Experts anticipate that advances in health IT will improve healthcare delivery and enable patients to assume greater responsibility for managing their health. But while provider effectiveness and consumer empowerment are important goals, health IT adoption is raising new privacy issues and concerns. The fact remains that the unintended or inappropriate collection, use, or disclosure of sensitive protected health information (PHI) can lead to a variety of harms ranging from inconvenience, to embarrassment, to discrimination.

The healthcare industry in the United States is on a steady path toward modernization. With financial encouragement from the federal government, doctors and hospitals are investing in health IT solutions. Examples include electronic health records (EHRs), which are electronic versions of traditional paper medical records that can be updated and shared in near real time with other healthcare providers, and patient portals, which enable patients to view their health records, schedule appointments, and communicate with their providers. Moreover, private technology companies are innovating rapidly in the health space, as seen by the explosive growth of wearable fitness technologies and health-related applications. These companies are not regulated by the Health Insurance Portability and Accountability Act (HIPAA), and they rely heavily on user consent when collecting and processing health-related data. For EHRs, portals, and other health-related technologies to succeed, patients must not only maintain trust in their providers (and technology companies), but they must also trust the systems that collect, use, and disseminate their personal information. Without trust, patients are likely to withhold sensitive personal information, healthcare delivery may be degraded, and health IT investments may not achieve their anticipated benefits.

One way to establish trust and advance privacy is to obtain patient consent prior to sharing PHI. However, there is a healthy debate among experts regarding how and to what extent consent should be implemented in the context of electronic health information exchange. For example, issues regarding the specific transactions that should require consent and the form of that consent are regularly discussed topics among privacy professionals.

Regardless of the outcome of the consent debate, one should not lose sight of the long-established tenet that a holistic, multifaceted approach to privacy, based on FIPPs, is a valuable approach for protecting the privacy of PHI. FIPPs are an internationally recognized set of principles that aim to protect individual privacy. They were originally promulgated by the Department of Health, Education & Welfare in the early 1970s, and today, FIPPs are the foundation for the data privacy frameworks of many organizations, both public and private. In an increasingly complex world in which digital records are collected, used, and disseminated among a growing legion of third-party intermediaries, this approach offers crucial flexibility and trust.

The Benefits and Risks of Health IT

Health IT offers potential benefits to both healthcare providers and consumers. Perceiving this value, the federal government has funded initiatives to improve healthcare delivery in recent years. The Health Information Technology for Economic and Clinical Health (HITECH) Act, passed as part of the American Recovery and Reinvestment Act of 2009 (ARRA), may be the federal government's most significant investment in health IT to date.

Subsidies for establishing EHR systems are a vital part of HITECH.[1] Billions of dollars have been reserved for Medicare and Medicaid incentive payments to healthcare providers to promote the meaningful use of certified EHR technologies.[2] For example, the EHR Incentive Program pays medical professionals and hospitals when they adopt, implement, upgrade, and demonstrate meaningful use of EHR technologies certified by the Centers for Medicare & Medicaid Services (CMS), an agency of the Department of Health and Human Services (HHS). Eligible professionals may receive up to $44,000 through the Medicare program, or $63,750 through the Medicaid program. CMS's incentive payments to eligible hospitals with certified EHRs vary, but they begin with a $2 million base payment.[3]

Health IT Benefits

HHS believes that widespread use of EHR systems will improve the quality and delivery of patient care. These benefits are discussed in Chapters 1 and 5, but a few are briefly mentioned here. The benefits listed in Table 6.1 can be found on the HHS website.[4]

Additionally, EHR systems provide functionality that paper records cannot. Unlike a hard copy chart that can be misplaced or is not available at a crucial moment, an EHR can be available for access at any time. EHRs can facilitate superior follow-up care by automating patient appointment reminders and treatment instructions, and EHRs can improve convenience by instantly ordering prescription drugs and filing insurance claims.[5]

Finally, some potential benefits are disputed, which is to be expected when major sectors like healthcare experience significant transformation. For example, the Secretary of HHS[6] has stated that migrating to health IT systems like EHRs will lower healthcare costs. But a study published in *Health Affairs* states that the use of health IT as a cost control strategy is

Table 6.1 Benefits of EHRs

Complete and accurate information	With electronic health records, providers have the information they need to provide the best possible care. Providers will know more about their patients and their health history before they walk into the examination room.
Better access to information	Electronic health records facilitate greater access to the information providers need to diagnose health problems earlier and improve the health outcomes of their patients. Electronic health records also allow information to be shared more easily among doctors' offices, hospitals, and across health systems, leading to better coordination of care.
Patient empowerment	Electronic health records will help empower patients to take a more active role in their health and in the health of their families. Patients can receive electronic copies of their medical records and share their health information securely over the Internet with their families.

Source: Office of the National Coordinator for Health Information Technology, Department of Health and Human Services.

unproven. Dr. Danny McCormick of Harvard Medical School, along with three colleagues, found that doctors with access to electronic records in an office setting ordered more tests rather than fewer tests, which drove up costs.[7] Additionally, in 2012, the *New York Times* reported that, according to its own analysis, hospitals that adopted EHRs experienced a 47 percent rise in Medicare payments from 2006 to 2010, whereas hospitals that did not receive EHR incentives showed only a 32 percent rise.[8] One explanation is that doctors were previously under-billing, and EHRs have corrected past errors (e.g., doctors are now using the right treatment codes).[9] But another possibility is that EHR systems are vulnerable to fraud and abuse in coding for services, a weakness documented by the Office of the Inspector General for HHS.[10] Additionally, as EHR implementations have grown in size and complexity, so have the costs, as experienced by several major health systems that are hoping such investments improve efficiency and their bottom line in the future.[11,12] Finally, as more patient data are digitally captured, EHR systems become more susceptible to internal breaches, as well as more attractive targets for hackers, and the average costs for data breaches and the number of breaches per year are growing annually. In the end, regardless of the outcome of the cost debate, the march toward digitizing patient data continues forward as vendors and the federal government seek to improve the efficacy of EHR systems.

Privacy Risks and Harms

As healthcare providers and hospitals modernize the way health information is collected, used, and disseminated, existing privacy and security risks are likely to persist or become amplified. Health records contain a wealth of sensitive personal information, and a lack of transparency, over-collection, or aggregation of PHI may cause significant harm to patients.

First, if fundamental privacy principles are not respected, PHI might be shared in ways that lack transparency and are inconsistent with patient expectations. This unforeseen sharing may lead to mere inconveniences, like spam or unsolicited marketing e-mails, or to publication in secondary or tertiary records that may become accessible to government agencies, law enforcement, or courts. Further, it may lead to personal embarrassment, especially if the data relate to innately private matters, like mental illness, STD, or abortion.

Second, inappropriate collection, use, or disclosure of PHI may lead to discrimination or harassment. For example, a 1999 survey found that more than one-third of *Fortune 500* companies viewed applicants' or employees' medical records before making hiring and promotion decisions.[13]

Third, patients may hide information or avoid treatment if they suspect PHI will not be adequately safeguarded. HHS has estimated that millions of Americans avoid treatment for early signs of cancer, mental illness, and STDs due to privacy concerns.[14]

Finally, one should not ignore certain security risks, which often exist in parallel with privacy risks. Specifically, EHRs and other health IT systems become attractive targets to hackers, fraudsters, or even curious employees when PHI is collected electronically. A single penetration of a centralized server could result in the compromise of thousands, if not millions of records. In 2015, the Identity Theft Resource Center (ITRC) reported 781 data breaches, the highest annual number since 2005, when the ITRC began tracking breaches.[15] The health/medical sector tallied the second highest number of breaches (35.5% of all breaches). Under HITECH, HHS maintains statistics regarding breaches reported by covered entities and their business associates,[16] and in 2015, breaches of PHI affected up to 113 million people.[17]

The Success of Health IT Depends on Public Trust

Public concern regarding the privacy of PHI is well documented.[18] To ensure the success of EHR systems, and health IT more broadly, the public must trust that new technologies will effectively protect patient confidentiality and safeguard the PHI that is collected, used, and disclosed. Simply stated, privacy and trust are interdependent.

Trust was an issue well documented by the Health IT Policy Committee (HIT Policy Committee), which was established by Congress under HITECH to address key policy issues regarding technological advances in the healthcare domain. The Office of the National Coordinator for Health Information Technology (ONC) managed the HIT Policy Committee, which was comprised of subsidiary committees. One of these subcommittees, the Privacy & Security Work Group (the PSWG, previously the Privacy & Security Tiger Team), was charged with making recommendations on privacy and security policies that will help build public trust. In one of its early reports, the PSWG listed the following core values:

- "The relationship between the patient and his/her healthcare provider is the foundation for trust in the health information exchange; thus, providers are responsible for maintaining the privacy and security of their patients' records."
- "Patients should not be surprised about or harmed by collections, uses or disclosures of their information."[19]
- "Ultimately, to be successful in the use of health information exchange to improve health and healthcare, we need to earn the trust of both consumers and physicians."[20]

Moreover, the HHS Final Rule regarding Standards for Privacy of Individually Identifiable Health Information provides the following:

> The need for privacy of health information, in particular, has long been recognized as critical to the delivery of needed medical care. More than anything else, the relationship between a patient and a clinician is based on trust. The clinician must trust the patient to give full and truthful information about their health, symptoms, and medical history. The patient must trust the clinician to use that information to improve his or her health and to respect the need to keep such information private. In order to receive accurate and reliable diagnosis and treatment, patients must provide healthcare professionals with accurate, detailed information about their personal health, behavior, and other aspects of their lives.[21]

Finally, this view is supported by the Healthcare Information and Management Systems Society (HIMSS). HIMSS publishes biannual Public Policy Principles, and its 2014–2016 report provides that "a well-functioning healthcare system requires the development and maintenance of a trust framework through recognition, management, and enforcement of privacy principles and risk-based security practices which, consistent with data stewardship, also allows for appropriate access and use, appropriate information flow in care delivery, and appropriate secondary uses to promote a learning health care system."[22]

If patients do not trust that doctors can keep their personal data confidential, patients may under-report information, which may have a negative impact of the quality of their care. If doctors do not trust the computer systems that manage patient information, they may not leverage health technology and their investments will go unrealized. Thus, without trust and privacy, it may be very difficult to achieve nationwide adoption of health IT solutions.

There Is a Healthy, Ongoing Debate regarding the Effectiveness of Patient Consent to Protect Patient Privacy

Trust may be enhanced if patients have a measure of control over their PHI. Current federal law and regulations (HIPAA and the HIPAA Privacy Rule) delineate the specific uses and disclosures of PHI that can be made by HIPAA-covered entities without patient authorization (consent); all other uses and disclosures require authorization. Privacy advocates arrive at different conclusions as to whether current consent policies and practices are adequate to protect patient privacy. This section briefly explores those views.

Current Practice under the Privacy Rule

The Privacy Rule provides for permitted uses and disclosures of PHI that may be executed without patient authorization. Covered entities,[23] which include most healthcare providers, health plans, and healthcare clearinghouses, can collect, use, and disclose patient PHI without a patient's consent for the following: (1) treatment,[24] (2) payment,[25] or (3) healthcare operations (TPO).[26] In addition to the consent exception for TPO purposes, the Privacy Rule permits covered entities to disclose patient PHI for public health purposes, as required by law, to report abuse or domestic violence, for health oversight, judicial or administrative proceedings, and for certain law enforcement purposes, provided that individuals retain the opportunity to intervene.[27] Additionally, covered entities may share patient data with family members, provided the patient does not object.[28]

For any uses or disclosures not specified in the Privacy Rule, covered entities must obtain patient "authorization" (the Privacy Rule uses the term "authorization" rather than "consent"). Authorization is required when patient data are used for marketing purposes, certain research, and especially for sensitive data like psychotherapy information (which can be shared without authorization only in emergency situations).[29]

Finally, it is important to note that HIPAA and the Privacy Rule are only a baseline; they do not preempt more stringent state laws that protect patient privacy. This means that states are at liberty to pass and maintain statutes and rules that create equivalent or more stringent legal obligations than the requirements set forth under federal laws and regulations.

An Argument for More Patient Control via Consent

Fostering individual control over PHI is one aspect of building trust and safeguarding patient privacy.[30] Indeed, "data protection law has historically been built based on the concept of individual control."[31] Essentially, privacy and trust are enhanced if patients are able to control with whom, how frequently, and in what manner their data are shared.

On its website, the Patient Privacy Rights Foundation, a nonprofit advocacy group, lists the following core privacy principles related to empowering patients.

- Recognize that patients own their health data
- Give patients control over who can access their electronic health records
- Give patients the right to opt-in and opt-out of electronic systems
- Give patients the right to segment sensitive information
- Require audit trails of every disclosure of patient information
- Require that patients be notified of suspected or actual privacy breaches
- Provide meaningful penalties and enforcement for privacy violations
- Require that health information disclosed for one purpose may not be used for another purpose without informed consent

- Ensure that consumers cannot be compelled to share electronic health records to obtain employment, insurance, credit, or admission to schools
- Deny employers access to employees' medical records
- Preserve stronger privacy protections in state laws[32]

Additionally, in 2010 the Coalition for Patient Privacy (the Coalition), a nonprofit patients' rights organization, outlined a vision for greater patient control in a letter to the Secretary of HHS. In its recommendations, the Coalition urged that HHS should eliminate not only what it termed "loopholes" in HIPAA and the Privacy Rule that permit PHI to be collected, used, and disclosed without patient consent, but HHS also should advance new laws and regulations that would enable patients to control PHI at the data element level.[33] Specifically, the Coalition recommended that as part of implementing Meaningful Use, HHS should require the use of sophisticated electronic consent and data segmentation technologies so that patients can control exactly what PHI is used or disclosed (even when covered entities process patient data for TPO purposes).[34] Under this approach, a patient would be contacted automatically by computer or by telephone if a data steward tries to use PHI in a manner inconsistent with a patient's stated rules or directives, or when third parties want to use PHI for any new purpose.[35] The Coalition proffered a stern warning if such advances in patient consent are not achieved: "If HHS does not require strong privacy policies and the enforcement of patients' rights to control PHI now, the United States will be destined to [sic] waste the billions in [health IT] and HIE investments," and the American public will reject health IT solutions, just as the British public rejected similar advances in the UK.[36]

Thus, there is a passionate argument that patients should be able to exercise a greater degree of control when PHI is collected, used, or disclosed. Some have even argued for a return to the earlier version of the Privacy Rule, which required patient consent for almost every transaction involving PHI (including transactions for TPO purposes).[37]

An Argument for Limited Sharing of PHI without Prior Patient Consent

Conversely, other experts and organizations support the current Privacy Rule paradigm, which permits covered entities to process PHI without patient consent for TPO and other limited purposes. HHS changed this require-ment in 2002, largely because of public comment that the previous rule could impede the provision of healthcare in many critical circumstances.[38] Additionally, some caution that relying too heavily on patient consent may be detrimental to privacy.

The Markle Foundation sponsors Connecting for Health, which is a public–private collaboration that unites thought leaders from more than 100 organizations to shape innovation and provide recommendations that advance health IT. The Markle Common Framework is the embodiment of the technology and policy best practices endorsed by Connecting for Health.

The Common Framework supports limited sharing of patient data without prior consent. For example, the Common Framework supports the use of record locator services (RLS) to route patient PHI between authorized users of an EHR or other health IT systems. An RLS contains an index of lim-ited patient data, which include the patient's name and some demographic information, but no clinical records. In order to exchange clinical records between providers, two steps are required. First, the provider or institu-tion holding the clinical records must decide which of those records are uploaded into the system for transmission. Second, based on the patient's predetermined consent and disclosure policies, clinical records are sent according to the patient's desires and expectations.[39]

Patients are automatically registered to participate in RLS systems; although patients may opt out, the default position is to be opted in. The Markle Connecting for Health Policy Subcommittee recognizes that an exception to prior patient consent is merited. Specifically, a "policy requiring individual consent prior to including a patient's information in the RLS might threaten robustness and viability of the system at an early stage, in addi-tion to placing large burdens on the institutions and providers involved."[40] Additionally, the Subcommittee determined the following:

- Requiring consent from patients before their data are listed in the RLS index would erect a significant barrier to establishing a functional sys-tem due to inevitable delays and excessive start-up costs.
- Requiring prior consent might create an incentive to obtain broader consent than necessary due to costs and time to establish the process.
- Managing individual consent is administratively and operationally chal-lenging for participants.
- Future expansion of the RLS system may not be possible without addi-tional consent, which increases time and costs.

■ If incremental consent were required for each individual transaction (such as for specific treatment purposes), then it may become very challenging to guarantee that participating institutions access only the information for these permitted purposes.[41]

In 2012, the Markle Foundation augmented the Common Framework by issuing Policies in Practice recommendations. One of these Policies in Practice discusses consent.[42] The recommendations caution that "focusing on consent policy without addressing the other FIPPs often provides only very weak privacy protection in practice."[43] Moreover, "relying on consent as the sole or most significant privacy policy shifts the burden of protecting health information to the individual," who must make a determination without the full benefit of protective policies and practices.[44]

Similarly, other organizations concerned with patient privacy suggest that consent alone is insufficient to protect patient privacy. A 2009 paper from the Center for Democracy and Technology (CDT) states that requiring patient consent for every exchange of health-related data would "provide fewer privacy safeguards and impose greater burdens on individuals, while undermining quality of care and access to services."[45] Furthermore, the paper highlights the following issues regarding prior consent:

■ Prior consent for every routine use of PHI may deny providers the ability to review patient records before a visit.
■ Prior consent may disrupt coordination among multiple providers.
■ Prior consent may delay the payment of health claims.
■ Prior consent for every transaction would inevitably lead to "consent fatigue," and such information overload would ultimately weaken consumer privacy.
■ Information sharing may be unnecessarily chilled because providers would be held liable for any inadvertent sharing not covered by a consent form.
■ A requirement for prior consent may inevitably lead to the creation of broad, all-inclusive, blanket consent forms that cover every possible transaction, thereby eviscerating the value of consent.[46]

Finally, the CDT paper suggests that relying too heavily on consent places a disproportionate burden on patients, and this reduction in bargaining power weakens the protection of PHI. In essence, "equating privacy with consumer consent relieves the holders of patient data of the responsibility for adopting comprehensive privacy protections."[47] Instead, the CDT paper advocates for more meaningful and granular consent, while still permitting the free flow of PHI among authorized healthcare entities for treatment, payment, and limited administrative purposes without requiring prior patient consent.

For now, and likely for the near future, the debate will persist among experts who support a range of positions from requiring consent for every transaction to permitting limited sharing of PHI without patient consent. One thing is certain: regardless of one's perspective, more work remains to be done as health IT solutions continue to evolve.

A Broad, Holistic Approach to Data Privacy Remains a Valuable Method for Protecting Patient Privacy

To design and maintain health IT systems that respect patient choice, protect privacy, and still enable providers to deliver quality care, one derives significant value by adopting a holistic privacy framework grounded in the FIPPs. This is not a novel concept; indeed, almost every organization that has recommended a privacy framework in the past 40 years has leveraged FIPPs. This section briefly discusses some of the advantages of such an approach and highlights three examples of privacy frameworks from the White House, the Markle Foundation, and HHS.

Benefits of a Holistic Approach

A holistic approach to privacy that leverages FIPPs is valuable because it is enduring, it fosters trust, and it is flexible. First, a holistic approach is historically well regarded. Today, privacy and security experts around the world are familiar with concepts like openness and transparency, collection limitation, individual participation and control, data integrity and quality, security safeguards and controls, and accountability. These concepts have stood the test of time, even when confronted with rapid advances in technology. Most organizations interested in privacy have embraced FIPPs as the starting point for their own frameworks, and by 2012 these principles have become part of a global privacy lexicon.

Second, the enduring nature of a FIPPs-based approach fosters public trust in health IT. Simply stated, FIPPs enable system designers to balance patients' rights and expectations with the provider's ability to use PHI. In its biannual Public Policy Principles, HIMSS expresses its support for the use of "Fair Information Practices as a basis for establishing sound information laws, policies, and practices to support and promote good data stewardship and foster public trust in the collection, access, use, and disclosure of individually identifiable health information."[48]

Third, a holistic approach is also valuable because it is flexible. Each fair information practice principle can be adapted as technologies and the user environment evolve. For example, FIPPs can be applied to any HIE, regardless of whether the HIE operates a federated model (in which PHI is stored locally on multiple end-user systems and queries are routed by an RLS), or a centralized model (in which PHI is stored in a central location and then delivered to authorized end-user systems).

Examples of Privacy Frameworks That Embrace FIPPs

During the past four decades, many organizations have embraced the value of a privacy approach based on FIPPs. The following brief examples demonstrate that regardless of the environment, FIPPs are an important point of departure when designing a framework that honors individual privacy.

1. *The White House Consumer Bill of Rights*: In February 2012, the White House published a framework for protecting consumer data privacy. The document, *Consumer Data Privacy in a Networked World: A Framework for Protecting Privacy and Promotion Innovation in the Global Digital Economy*, applies generally to all sectors of the American economy, not just healthcare. More specifically, this framework does not address entities already covered by HIPAA, but it does address entities not covered by HIPAA that collect, use, or disclose patient data. Within the framework, the White House proposes a Consumer Bill of Rights,[49] which is an example of a holistic, FIPPs-based approach to data privacy. The Consumer Privacy Bill of Rights includes the following principles:
   - Individual control
   - Transparency
   - Respect for context
   - Security
   - Access and accuracy
   - Focused collection

   The White House justified this approach by stating that it desired a framework that is "comprehensive, actionable, and flexible."[50] Moreover, the White House noted that FIPPs are the foundation for numerous international data privacy frameworks, and they continue to be relevant, despite significant changes in the way data stewards collect, store, and process personal information.[51] To support this view, each principle in the Consumer Bill of Rights is cross-referenced to similar principles in other frameworks, including those from the Organisation for Economic Co-operation and Development (OECD), the Department of Homeland Security, and the Asia Pacific Economic Cooperation (a forum of 21 Pacific Rim countries).

In November 2015, the White House re-emphasized similar principles as part of the Precision Medicine Initiative (PMI).[52] Specifically, the PMI privacy and trust principles include the following:
– Governance
– Transparency
– Respecting Participant Preferences
– Participant Empowerment through Access to Information
– Data Sharing, Access, and Use
– Data Quality and Integrity[53]

2. *The Markle Common Framework* establishes nine privacy principles based on the original FIPPs and the OEDC principles. These principles are depicted in Table 6.2.

As with other organizations, the Markle Foundation chose to adopt a holistic, FIPPs-based approach because of its flexibility and its track record of building trust. With regard to flexibility, the Markle website provides the following:

Considered and applied together, these principles enable the development of an integrated and comprehensive approach to privacy that can be built into any information-sharing system or network at the outset in order to ensure confidentiality and privacy of patient data. It is critical that the nine principles be balanced together and considered as part of one package, as elevating certain principles over others will weaken the overall architectural solution, and no one principle can assure confidentiality and privacy of patient data on its own.[54]

Additionally, the Markle Foundation asserts that a holistic approach fosters trust:

Table 6.2 **Markle Common Framework**[57]

Principle	Description
Openness and Transparency	There should be a general policy of openness about development, practices, and policies with respect to personal data. Individuals should be able to know what information exists about them, the purpose of its use, who can access and use it, and where it resides.
Purpose Specification and Minimization	The purposes for which personal data is collected should be specified at the time of collection, and the subsequent use should be limited to those purposes or others that are specified on each occasion of change of purpose.
Collection limitation	Personal health information should only be collected for specified purposes, should be obtained by lawful and fair means and, where possible, with the knowledge or consent of the data subject.
Use Limitation	Personal data should not be disclosed, made available, or otherwise used for purposes other than those specified.
Individual Participation and Control	Individuals should have access to their personal health information: • Individuals should be able to obtain from each entity that controls personal health data, information about whether or not the entity has data relating to them. Individuals should have the right to • Have personal data relating to them communicated within a reasonable time (at an affordable charge, if any), and in a form that is readily understandable. • Be given reasons if a request . . . is denied, and to be able to challenge such a denial. • Challenge data relating to them and have it rectified, completed, or amended.
Data Integrity and Quality	All personal data collected should be relevant to the purpose for which it is to be used and should be accurate, complete, and current.
Security Safeguards and Controls	Personal data should be protected by reasonable security safeguards against such risks as loss, unauthorized access, destruction, use, modification, or disclosure.
Accountability and Oversight	Entities in control of personal health data must be held accountable for implementing these information practices.
Remedies	Legal and financial remedies must exist to address any security breaches or privacy violations.

Source: Connecting for Health Common Framework, © 2006, Markle Foundation.

Ultimately, the goal of enacting a comprehensive set of privacy and security policies [based on FIPPs] is to build and maintain public trust in electronic health information sharing. Health information sharing efforts must implement policies necessary to achieve the goals of exchange, thereby maintaining an environment of trust in their communities.[55]

3. *The Nationwide Privacy and Security Framework for Electronic Exchange of Individually Identifiable Information.* As discussed in Chapter 1, HHS unveiled its own privacy framework in 2008. The methodology for developing the ONC Framework[56] included a review of several FIPPs-based frameworks, including the Markle Common Framework, the OECD principles, and models from the Federal Trade Commission and the International Security Trust and Privacy Alliance. ONC carefully evaluated these frameworks to determine which principles would best apply to the electronic exchange of health information data. The principles in the ONC Framework are provided in Table 6.3.

Viewed together, these three examples illustrate that regardless of the environment, organizations that are committed to establishing meaningful data privacy protections will embrace a broad, holistic approach and will look to FIPPs as their starting point.

Conclusion

Healthcare practitioners are embracing health IT solutions like EHRs to improve the quality of patient care. Health IT advances are expected to improve provider effectiveness and empower patients to take greater control for their data. However, for health IT solutions to gain traction and succeed, patients must trust both their providers and the health IT solutions they use to collect, use, and disclose patient PHI. Privacy professionals may disagree about the role that consent should play in fostering trust and improving privacy, but in the end, a robust, holistic approach to privacy that embraces all of the FIPPs remains a valuable and resilient methodology for protecting health information. By embracing a holistic approach to privacy, Federal agencies and the entities that are creating and using exciting new health-related technologies will be able to improve the health of the American public while maintaining people's trust and expectations for individual privacy.

Table 6.3 HHS ONC Framework Principles

Principle	Description
Individual Access	Individuals should be provided with a simple and timely means to access and obtain their individually identifiable health information in a readable form and format.
Openness and Transparency	There should be openness and transparency about policies, procedures, and technologies that directly affect individuals and/or their individually identifiable health information.
Individual Choice	Individuals should be provided a reasonable opportunity and capability to make informed decisions about the collection, use, and disclosure of their individually identifiable health information.
Collection, Use, and Disclosure Limitation	Individually identifiable health information should be collected, used, and/or disclosed only to the extent necessary to accomplish a specified purpose(s) and never to discriminate inappropriately.
Data Quality and Integrity	Persons and entities should take reasonable steps to ensure that individually identifiable health information is complete, accurate, and up-to-date to the extent necessary for the person's or entity's intended purposes and has not been altered or destroyed in an unauthorized manner.
Safeguards	Individually identifiable health information should be protected with reasonable administrative, technical, and physical safeguards to ensure its confidentiality, integrity, and availability and to prevent unauthorized or inappropriate access, use, or disclosure.
Accountability	These principles should be implemented, and adherence assured, through appropriate monitoring and other means and methods should be in place to report and mitigate non-adherence and breaches.

Source: Office of the National Coordinator, Department of Health & Human Services.

Notes

1. HITECH Programs, Office of the National Coordinator for Health Information Technology. Available at: https://www.healthit.gov/providers-professionals/ehr-incentives-certification.
2. HIMSS 2011–2012 Public Policy Principles, December. Available at: http://www.himss.org/sites/himssorg/files/HIMSSorg/policy/d/PolicyPrinciples2011.pdf.
3. EHR Incentive Programs, CMS.gov. Available at: http://www.cms.gov/Regulations-and-Guidance/Legislation/EHRIncentivePrograms/index.html?redirect=/ehrincentiveprograms/; see also: http://www.cms.gov/Regulations-and-Guidance/Legislation/EHRIncentivePrograms/Eligible_Hospital_Information.html.
4. Electronic Health Records and Meaningful Use. Available at: https://www.healthit.gov/providers-professionals/benefits-electronic-health-records-ehrs; see also: https://healthit.gov/portal/server.pt?open=512&objID=2996&mode=2.
5. Electronic Health Records and Meaningful Use, Why Electronic Health Records? Available at: https://www.healthit.gov/providers-professionals/benefits-electronic-health-records-ehrs.
6. Hon. Kathleen Sebelius, Meaningful Use Press Conference, July 13, 2010. Available at: https://www.cms.gov/Newsroom/MediaReleaseDatabase/Press-releases/2010-Press-releases-items/2010-07-13.html; The New Momentum Behind Electronic Health Records, Kaiser Health News, August 26, 2010. Available at: http://www.kaiserhealthnews.org/Columns/2010/August/082610Sebelius.aspx.
7. McCormick D, Bor DH, Woolhandler S, Himmelstein DU. Giving Office-Based Physicians Electronic Access to Patients' Prior Imaging and Lab Results Did Not Deter Ordering of Tests. *Health Affairs*. 2012;31(3). Available at: http://content.healthaffairs.org/content/31/3.toc.
8. Abelson R, Creswell J, Palmer G. Medicare bills rise as records turn electronic. *The New York Times*. September 21, 2012. Available at: http://www.nytimes.com/2012/09/22/business/medicare-billing-rises-at-hospitals-with-electronic-records.html.
9. Ibid.
10. Ibid.
11. Jayanthi A, Ellison A. 8 Hospitals' Finances Hurt by EHR Costs. *Becker's Hospital CFO*, May 23, 2016. Available at: http://www.beckershospitalreview.com/finance/8-hospitals-finances-hurt-by-ehr-costs.html.
12. O'Neill T. Are Electronic Medical Records Worth the Costs of Implementation?, American Action Forum. Available at: https://www.americanactionforum.org/research/are-electronic-medical-records-worth-the-costs-of-implementation/.
13. 65 Fed. Reg. 82467 (Thursday, December 28, 2000), citing Harris Equifax, Health Information Privacy Study, 2, 33 (1993); Starr P. Health and the Right to Privacy. *American Journal of Law and Medicine*. 1999;25:193–201.

14. Peel D. The Changing Landscape: The Impact to Patients' Privacy. *ID Experts*. Available at: https://www2.idexpertscorp.com/blog/single/the-changing-landscape-the-impact-to-patients-privacy.
15. 2011 ITRC Breach Report, Identity Theft Resource Center. Available at: http://www.idtheftcenter.org/Data-Breaches/2015databreaches.html.
16. Breaches Affecting 500 or More Individuals, Health Information Privacy. HHS.gov. Available at: https://ocrportal.hhs.gov/ocr/breach/breach_report.jsf.
17. Breach Portal: Notice to the Secretary of HHS Breach of Unsecured Protected Health Information, U.S. Department of Health & Human Services Office of Civil Rights, page 9. Available at: https://ocrportal.hhs.gov/ocr/breach/breach_report.jsf.
18. Westin A. What Two Decades of Surveys Tell Us About Privacy and HIT Today, 1st International Summit on the Future of Health Privacy, June 13, 2011. Available at: http://patientprivacyrights.org/wp-content/uploads/2011/06/AFW-SUMMIT-6-13-11.pdf.
19. Health IT Policy Committee Recommendations, October 18, 2011. Available at: http://www.healthit.gov/sites/default/files/pdf/HITPC_Privacy_and_Security_Transmittal_Letter_10_18_11.pdf.
20. Health IT Policy Committee Recommendations, August 19, 2010. Available at: http://www.healthit.gov/sites/default/files/pdf/HITPC_Privacy_and_Security_Transmittal_Letter_10_18_11.pdf.
21. 65 Fed. Reg. 82467, December 28, 2000. Available at: https://www.gpo.gov/fdsys/pkg/FR-2000-12-28/pdf/FR-2000-12-28.pdf.
22. HIMSS 2014-2016 Public Policy Principles, June 27, 2014, p10. Available at: http://www.himss.org/file/1242536/download?token=76RZEMZD.
23. A healthcare provider may be a doctor, clinic, psychologist, dentist, chiropractor, nursing home, or pharmacy, but only if it transmits information in an electronic form related to a transaction that HHS has adopted as a standard. A health plan includes health insurance companies, HMOs, company health plans, or government programs that pay for healthcare (such as Medicare and Medicaid). A healthcare clearinghouse includes entities that process non-standard data into a standard electronic format, or vice versa. See Health Information Privacy—For Covered Entities. Available at: http://www.hhs.gov/ocr/privacy/hipaa/understanding/coveredentities/index.html.
24. Treatment is the provision, coordination, or management of healthcare and related services for an individual by one or more healthcare providers, including consultation between providers regarding a patient and referral of a patient by one provider to another. See 45 CFR §164.501.
25. Payment means the activities of (1) a health plan to obtain premiums or to determine or fulfill its responsibility for coverage and provision of benefits under the health plan; or (2) a healthcare provider or health plan to obtain or provide reimbursement for the provision of healthcare provided to a patient. See 45 CFR §164.501.
26. The definition of healthcare operations is broad, and includes activities like (1) conducting quality assessments and improvement activities; (2) reviewing the

competence or qualifications of healthcare professionals; (3) underwriting and other activities related to health insurance contracts; (4) conducting or arranging for medical reviews, legal, or financial audits; (5) business planning and developments; and (6) business management and general administrative activities. See 45 CFR §164.501.

27. Rethinking the Role of Consent in Protecting Health Information Privacy. Center for Democracy & Technology, January 2009, page 3. Available at: https://cdt.org/press/cdt-paper-rethinking-the-role-of-consent-in-protecting-health-information-privacy/.
28. Ibid, page 3.
29. Ibid, page 4.
30. Principles, patientprivacyrights.org. Available at: http://patientprivacyrights.org/principles/.
31. The Centre for Information Policy Leadership's Response to the Public Consultation on the Proposed Personal Data Protection Bill, Martin E. Abrams, Center for Information Policy Leadership, page 5. Available at: http://www.huntonprivacyblog.com/wp-content/uploads/2012/05/Centres-Comments-Ministry-of-Information-Communications-and-the-Arts-_April-27-2012_.pdf.
32. More Patient Privacy Principles. Available at: http://patientprivacyrights.org/principles.
33. Comments on 45 CFR Parts 160 and 164, Letter to Hon. Kathleen Sebelius, September 13, 2010, Coalition for Patient Privacy, pages 14, 17. Available at: http://patientprivacyrights.org/wp-content/uploads/2010/09/NPRM-Comments-FINAL-09-13-10.pdf.
34. Ibid., pages 2, 4, 17.
35. Ibid., page 4.
36. Ibid., pages 3–4.
37. Rethinking the Role of Consent in Protecting Health Information Privacy, Center for Democracy & Technology, January 2009, page 5. Available at: http://www.cdt.org/healthprivacy/20090126Consent.pdf.
38. 67 Fed. Reg. 59, 14779, March 27, 2002, Standards for Privacy of Individually Identifiable Health Information. Available at: https://www.hhs.gov/sites/default/files/ocr/privacy/hipaa/administrative/privacyrule/2002proposedmods.pdf.
39. Markle Common Framework, Notification and Consent When Using a Record Locator Service, page 8. Available at: www.markle.org/sites/default/files/Overview_Professionals.pdf. © 2006 Markle Foundation. This work was originally published as part of the Connecting for Health Common Framework: Resources for Implementing Private and Secure Health Information Exchange and is made available subject to the terms of a license. You may make copies of this work; however, by copying or exercising any other rights to the work, you accept and agree to be bound by the terms of the license. All copies of this work must reproduce this copyright information and notice.
40. Ibid.
41. Ibid.

42. Markle Common Framework, Policies in Practice, Consent: Implementing the Individual Participation and Control Fair Information Practice Principle in Health Information Sharing. Available at: http://www.markle.org/sites/default/files/Consent Final.pdf.

43. Ibid.

44. Ibid.

45. Rethinking the Role of Consent in Protecting Health Information Privacy. Center for Democracy & Technology, January 2009, pages 1–2. Available at: https://www.cdt.org/files/healthprivacy/20090126Consent.pdf.

46. Ibid, page 6. Available at: https://www.cdt.org/files/healthprivacy/20090126Consent.pdf.

47. Rethinking the Role of Consent in Protecting Health Information Privacy. Center for Democracy & Technology, January 2009, page 9. Available at: https://www.cdt.org/files/healthprivacy/20090126Consent.pdf.

48. HIMSS 2011–2012 Public Policy Principles, December 10, 2010, page 12. Available at: http://www.himss.org/sites/himssorg/files/HIMSSorg/policy/d/PolicyPrinciples2011.pdf.

49. Consumer Data Privacy in a Networked World: A Framework for Protecting Privacy and Promoting Innovation in the Global Digital Economy, February 2012. Available at: http://www.whitehouse.gov/sites/default/files/privacy-final.pdf.

50. Ibid.

51. Consumer Data Privacy in a Networked World: A Framework for Protecting Privacy and Promoting Innovation in the Global Digital Economy, February 2012. Available at: http://www.whitehouse.gov/sites/default/files/privacy-final.pdf.

52. The Precision Medicine Initiative, White House, available at: https://www.whitehouse.gov/precision-medicine.

53. Precision Medicine Initiative: Privacy and Trust Principles, available at: https://www.whitehouse.gov/sites/default/files/microsites/finalpmiprivacyandtrustprinciples.pdf.

54. Markle Common Framework, Notification and Consent When Using a Record Locator Service, page 8. Available at: https://www.markle.org/sites/default/files/Overview_Professionals.pdf. (hereinafter "Markel: Consent When Using an RLS").

55. Markle Common Framework, Policies in Practice, Consent: Implementing the Individual Participation and Control Fair Information Practice Principle in Health Information Sharing, page 2. Available at: https://www.markle.org/sites/default/files/Overview_Professionals.pdf.

56. The Nationwide Privacy and Security Framework for Electronic Exchange of Individually Identifiable Health Information (December 15, 2008). Available at: https://www.healthit.gov/sites/default/files/nationwide-ps-framework-5.pdf.

57. Markle Common Framework's nine FIPPs-based privacy principles, page 4. Available at: https://www.markle.org/sites/default/files/Overview_Professionals.pdf.

Chapter 7

Transparency

By Leslie Francis, PhD, JD

Contents

Transparency is one of the key concepts of privacy protection. Transparency means openness about data collection, use, and retention. Individuals need to know what information about them is being collected, how it is being collected, how it is to be used and shared, how it is protected, what has been learned from data use, how what has been learned might benefit them, and how they can seek correction or redress for security breaches or other unjustified uses or disclosures of data. This chapter begins with a highly salient recent example of transparency in action: the principled commitment to transparency in the precision medicine initiative (PMI) and the limited extent to which it has been developed in the initiative to date. The chapter then provides an overview of justifications for transparency and challenges inherent in providing consumers with understanding that is meaningful to them. The chapter then considers methods for achieving transparency through publication or notice and what is known about the success or failure of these methods. For example, privacy notices have grown bloated and legalistic; patients rarely read them and if they do, they do not understand them. The chapter concludes with a discussion of emerging solutions.

The Principle of Transparency in the Precision Medicine Initiative

The PMI is a highly ambitious effort to create a cohort of over a million volunteers who agree to contribute their health data over many years to further investigation of the molecular, environmental, and behavioral aspects of disease. Led by the National Institutes of Health (NIH), it aims to develop an understanding of important variations among patients that will enable targeting therapeutic or other interventions to maximize success in treatment and prevention of disease. It also aims to create new models for patient engagement not only in care, but also in research. And the plan is to try to maximize diversity within the cohort so that individuals of different types are not left behind in the advantages that the PMI may bring. The information collected about cohort participants will be vast and various: blood and possible other tissue samples, information from electronic health records (EHRs), a baseline physical exam, insurance claims, mobile health devices, participant surveys, and other sources. And cohort participants will be expected to agree to be re-contacted over time to participate in a variety of more specific research studies.[1]

As thus envisioned, the PMI presents difficult questions of transparency. Participants in the cohort will vary in location, age, language and culture, race, socioeconomic status, and many other factors. As individuals are enrolled in the cohort, there will be an overall promise of what it may achieve but no precise information about how the data will be used, how frequently individuals will be re-contacted, what studies will be of interest, how long the data will be valuable, whether other data will be needed and combined with the types of data sought initially, and what will ultimately be learned. Any consent at enrollment therefore must perforce be highly general, based on whatever parameters can reasonably be anticipated. But these parameters may change as more is learned. Transparency thus will involve not only information at a single time slice, but information over time as the uses of the cohort change and results emerge.

The initial White House announcement of privacy and trust principles for the PMI included transparency as a guiding principle necessary to building trust among participants in the program and more generally in society as well. The principle of transparency was fleshed out into five areas, as follows:

1. A dynamic information-sharing process should be developed to ensure all PMI participants remain adequately informed through all stages of participation. Communications should be culturally appropriate and use languages reflective of the diversity of the participants.
2. Information should be communicated to participants clearly and conspicuously concerning: how, when, and what information and specimens will be collected and stored; generally how their data will be used, accessed, and shared; types of studies for which the individual's data may be used; the goals, potential benefits, and risks of participation, including risks of inappropriate use or compromise of the information about participants; the privacy and security measures that are in place to protect participant data, including notification plans in the event of a breach; and the participant's ability to withdraw from the cohort at any time, with the understanding that consent for research use of data included in aggregate data sets or used in past studies and studies already begun cannot be withdrawn.
3. Information should be made publicly available concerning PMI data protections and use, and compliance with governance rules.
4. Participants should be notified promptly following discovery of a breach of their personal information. Notification should include, to the extent possible, a description of the types of information involved in the breach; steps individuals should take to protect themselves from potential harm, if any; and steps being taken to investigate the breach, mitigate losses, and protect against further breaches.
5. All users of PMI data should be expected to publish or publicly post a summary of their research findings, regardless of the outcomes, as a condition of data use. To enrich the public data resource, mechanisms for data users to integrate their research findings back into PMI should be developed.[2]

These are impressive transparency goals. Putting them into practice will not be easy. The NIH working group report on building the PMI cohort, for example, references transparency only three times, and one of these is to

mention the White House announcement. The other two references emphasize the return of their own data to participants; what this means is not further explained, but perhaps the goal is to highlight the patient engagement
aspects of the PMI. The references do not as yet elaborate other aspects of
transparency, such as how to communicate what is being done with information collected for the PMI or what investigators will be expected to do
in sharing research results with participants and the public more generally.
In the first reference to transparency, in the final sentence of the executive summary, the working group states that "Transparency regarding data
access and use will be emphasized, with return of information to participants, including aggregate data and return of participant's personal data as
desired."[3] And in second reference, in the discussion of data access, use,
and analysis, the working group notes, "In the spirit of transparency and
collaboration, individuals and organizations that provide data to the PMI
cohort should, as a general policy, have unrestricted rights of access to
their own submitted data. Individual participants will have varying levels of
health and science literacy, and will need assistance with interpretation of
their data."[4]

These references are the only elaborations of transparency by the NIH
working group. Clearly, much more will need to be said about transparency
as the PMI is developed. More needs to be said about transparency for other
emerging uses of information as well.

Transparency: Its Meaning, Justifications, and Means

Transparency has long been a cornerstone value in the management of
information about individuals. What are called Fair Information Practices
(FIPs) were first proposed in a 1973 report[5] of the then-Department of
Health, Education, and Welfare. The report "Records, Computers, and the
Rights of Citizens"[6] stipulated that there should be no data collection systems whose existence was secret. Many subsequent formulations of FIPs
have fleshed this out to include aspects of data collection: people should be
able to know what data about them are being collected, who (or what) is
collecting the data, how the data are being collected, and how the data are
being stored, disclosed, managed, and used. Understanding what the quite
abstract idea of transparency means in different data contexts is challenging,
however, and turning briefly to justifications for transparency is useful in
this regard.

Justifications for transparency may be rooted in the obligations of the entity collecting the data, the rights of individuals, or contracts between the data collector and the individual. Myriad types of entities today are involved in data collection activities: with respect to health data, these include international organizations, such as the World Health Organization, governments (i.e., public health agencies), healthcare organizations, Internet search providers, newspapers, data brokers, other commercial entities, and most recently in the United States, the PMI—to name just a few. These data collectors may have very different rights and obligations. Governments—at least, democratic governments—are generally thought to have ethical obligations to their citizens to be open about what they are doing and about what they are learning, unless there are overriding reasons for information protection.[7] These obligations may be especially strong if matters of public interest or public safety are involved, and may be overridden in exceptional cases, such as individual privacy, law enforcement or national security, or commercial secrecy. Freedom of information laws and their exceptions reflect these commitments.[8] Commercial entities that assemble and market databases may assert intellectual property rights through copyright[9] or trade secrets law to these assets, as appears to be happening increasingly in the wake of court decisions limiting patent rights of genetic testing companies.[10] However, these intellectual property rights may be limited or overridden by public interests, such as public health or safety.[11]

Although understood in multiple forms, the individual right to privacy has been legally recognized for more than 100 years.[12] This right has been interpreted as rights to control access to the person, as rights to protection against intrusion into secluded space, as rights to control information, and as rights to make decisions about important or intimate matters, among other conceptualizations. The right to privacy also has been distinguished from the right to confidentiality: the right to control access to and disclosure of information about oneself.[13] Data collection, use, or disclosure may implicate both privacy and confidentiality as thus understood.

Many values have been asserted in support of these multiple understandings of privacy and confidentiality rights. These values include autonomy and choice, political liberty, physical security, intimacy, dignity, identity, equality, and justice. Some of these values relate directly to the individual, such as the ability to make choices about one's life. Understanding what information is being collected can help individuals make choices about what information to share, whom to trust with that information, and whether to rely upon their expectations about what will happen to their information.

Knowing what information has been collected, who has done the collecting, and whether the information has been disclosed to others can also help individuals to be aware of, and thus hopefully protect themselves against, information disclosures, such as those that might occur through a security breach. Some of these values may also be asserted on the level of a group: information about group members or about the group itself may lead to the group being targeted for attack (even genocide), may alter conceptions of group identity, may stigmatize, or may result in discrimination against members of the group.

Transparency may also be useful for the data collector. People may be more willing to share information—thus contributing to more robust data collection possibilities if they believe they can trust data collectors.[14] Notorious examples highlight how mistrust about data collection and use can harm data collection abilities. In Texas[15] and in Minnesota,[16] failures to inform the public about retention and subsequent uses of blood spots obtained in newborn screening programs resulted in public outcry and the eventual destruction of valuable public health resources and the data they contained. Arizona State University settled with the Havasupai tribe after researchers had used genetic data obtained in a study of diabetes and then de-identified it for research studies of mental illness and migration patterns.[17] Multiple studies sound the theme that consumer concerns about the privacy of their health information may generate reluctance to use patient portals, health information exchanges (HIEs), or personal health record (PHR) systems.[18] Although searching for health information is a common Internet activity,[19] recent data also indicates that willingness to share information depends on perceived trade-offs between risks and what is to be gained.[20]

Most generally, transparency refers to openness about what is being done. In contemporary statements of FIPs, this general idea of transparency has taken two importantly different forms: general publication and direct-to-consumer notice. As an example of the former, the U.S. Privacy Act requires that federal agencies publish notice in the *Federal Register* of the existence and character of the systems of records they maintain.[21] Another example of general publication would be the suggestion of the Federal Trade Commission (FTC) to data brokers—entities that collect and aggregate data for resale—to develop a website register of data collection activities for marketing purposes to allow consumers to understand what they are doing, know their access and choice rights, and opt out of uses of information about them.[22]

A second type of effort to ensure transparency is giving direct notice to the consumer. This has taken many different forms. Early in their development, FIPs were interpreted to require direct notice to individuals about specific disclosures. For example, the U.S. Privacy Act requires that federal agencies make reasonable efforts to provide notice of disclosures made under compulsory legal process when the disclosure will become a matter of public record.[23] Notification of security breaches of protected health information (PHI) is required by the Health Information Technology for Economic and Clinical Health (HITECH) Act amendments[24] to the Health Insurance Portability and Accountability Act (HIPAA) for covered entities and their business associates, and for vendors of PHRs.[25] Following California's lead in 2002, most states have also enacted breach notification statutes, although the majority of these do not include health information.[26]

The idea of a notice of privacy practices—either published on a website for readers to use or given in paper form to individuals—is a more recent development. As early as 1995, the European Union's Directive 95/46 on the protection of individuals with regard to the processing of personal data required member states to enact notice standards.[27] Under EU law, directives give member states flexibility in meeting minimum standards while regulations set out requirements for all to meet. In 2016, Directive 95/46 was replaced by the General Data Protection Regulation, which incorporates and strengthens the requirements of the Directive.[28] Any collection of personal data requires notice, including the identity and contact details of the data controller and data protection officer, the purposes of the data collection, the legal basis for the collection, the recipients or categories of recipients of the data, and any intent of the data controller to transfer data outside of the EU.[29] Similar information must be provided where personal data have not been obtained from the data subject.[30] All of this information must be provided "in a concise, transparent, intelligible and easily accessible form, using clear and plain language . . . ."[31] Further information "necessary to ensure fair and transparent processing is also required, including the length of data storage, the right to request rectification or erasure of the data, whether the data will be used in profiling and any envisioned consequences of this, and whether the data subject is required to provide the data along with the consequences of refusal."[32]

One major innovation of the Regulation is incorporation of the so-called "right to be forgotten," a right to have data erased under specified circumstances, including that there are no longer overriding legitimate grounds for maintaining the data.[33] A major motivation for the overhaul of EU data protection was the judgment that enforcement of standards for data transfer outside of the EU had become too lenient, especially for transfers to the

United States. In July, 2016, the EU and the United States finalized a Privacy Shield Framework so that data can be transferred back and forth between the two; the framework contains significantly stronger requirements and enforcement guarantees than the prior Safe Harbor arrangement.[34] Among the new requirements for Privacy Shield participants are compliance with EU notice and choice requirements and transparency regarding any enforcement actions against the participant.[35] The Privacy Shield Framework will likely result in increased transparency and stiffer notice requirements for companies seeking to transfer data from the EU.

Other federal and state laws also require privacy notices. Federally, the Financial Services Modernization Act of 1999 (otherwise known as Gramm-Leach-Bliley) requires financial institutions and insurance companies to send their customers conspicuous yearly notices explaining their policies with respect to information protection and disclosure.[36] Without the notice and information about how to opt out, these institutions may not disclose identifiable personal information to unrelated entities.[37] California state law requires a privacy notice to be included in a conspicuous manner on any commercial website collecting personally identifiable information about consumers.[38]

With respect to health information specifically, the HIPAA Privacy Rule requires covered entities to provide patients with a Notice of Privacy Practices (NPP). The HIPAA NPP must include prescribed language, in all capital letters, calling the reader's attention to what the notice concerns. Prescribed information includes a description of the types of uses and disclosures that are permitted without individual authorization, a statement that other uses and disclosures may occur with authorization, and separate statements about certain uses and disclosures, such as for fundraising. The NPP must also tell the individual about their rights of access to health information, rights to an accounting of uses and disclosures, and rights to request amendments.[39] The notice also requires contact information and information about how to file complaints. It is fair to say that the HIPAA regulation is prescriptive and complex and encourages lengthy and formalistic notices.

Over the past decade or more, privacy notices and statements of privacy policies have become a standard practice across the Internet. Many of these notices also feature a notice/choice format in which consumers are invited to make particular choices. Consumers may be asked to click "I agree," thus potentially becoming contractually bound to the contents of the notice. Or, they might be told that their data will be used in specified ways unless they opt out, and are offered a method for exercising this choice. For particularly controversial types of data use, such as marketing, consumers may be told that they must opt in to have their data used in this way and offered a "yes" button or some other mechanism of acceptance.

Understanding what these privacy notices should be like, what they should say, and what they can be expected to achieve has evolved as well. This chapter returns to these developments after reviewing widely understood challenges to successful transparency.

Transparency: Barriers to Achieving Successful Communication

Understood passively, transparency is not difficult to attain. Information about data collection activities can be published and individuals can be handed or mailed notices about these practices. If transparency is understood in terms of its justifications however, passive publication is not enough. Openness on the part of the government requires more than lists buried in the *Federal Register* or some other publicly accessible document; it requires education of and interaction with the public, so that at least a reasonable proportion has sufficient understanding to exercise any rights they might have and to participate in the political process with respect to information-gathering by their governments. A notice/choice model with respect to information uses and disclosures does not succeed in respecting individual autonomy unless individuals have sufficient understanding and opportunities to make meaningful choices. Thus understood, transparency requires at least some success in communicating. It is an ongoing process and its achievement is a matter of degree. But there are significant barriers to achieving transparency in this sense. The issues themselves are complex and answers are not easy.

First, individuals are not ideal recipients of communication, to say the least. In the background are variations in literacy, access to media, Internet familiarity, time and energy, cognitive biases, and cultural practices and attitudes. Commentators lament a "digital divide"[40] between those who have ready and skilled access to the Internet and those who do not, largely the poor, racial minorities, and rural populations, especially in the Southeast.[41] The advent of widespread smartphone use may be mitigating this divide, but in a manner that brings additional challenges associated with smartphone privacy, such as lack of password protection, lack of data encryption, or ease of loss. Demographically, at least in general, the elderly may have less familiarity with and understanding of technology and the Internet. Many Internet users are now very concerned about privacy but do not know a great deal about mechanisms they might use to protect it.[42] Also according to this study, people who are new to the Internet are more likely to need help to figure out how to use features of websites that enable them to protect information.[43]

With respect to privacy, social scientists have identified a so-called "privacy paradox."[44] Although individuals say that they value privacy, they do not act as though they do. Failure to search or to read privacy notices may exemplify this paradox.[45] Some economists and social commentators draw the conclusion that actions speak more loudly than words, and individuals' failures to protect their privacy may simply reveal that they do not value it very much and that privacy protection is therefore inefficient.[46] In a much-quoted remark, Scott McNealy, then-CEO of Sun Microsystems, opined: "You have zero privacy anyway. Get over it!"[47] On the other hand, there may be significant variations in the extent to which people value privacy, to some extent correlated with age cohort. People also may value privacy less if they believe that they will get important benefits from sharing their information—through social networking sites, such as Facebook, or through network sites that share information about health conditions, such as PatientsLikeMe®. Additionally, individuals may lack understanding of what privacy policies and law actually provide to them. One study suggests that misconceptions are widespread, especially in younger age cohorts; many people believe that having a privacy policy is the same as protecting privacy (it is not; a policy must simply state what protections exist, if any) and that they have rights to sue for damages if their privacy is violated (in general, they do not).[48] This confidence, based in misunderstanding, may explain why many people fail to read privacy notices. Other explanations include the length and difficulty of many privacy notices—as well as the fact that they may appear legalistic and boring.

Several studies have discerned cognitive biases as playing a major role in apparently paradoxical behavior about privacy, arguing that these biases can help explain what seems paradoxical. For example, increasing perceived control over publication of private information may increase willingness to disclose, even when the increase in perceived control is coupled with reduced protection of the information from access by others. This is a paradox of perceived control and risky behavior: the greater the perceived control, the greater the likelihood of risk-taking, with the perverse result of worse outcomes.[49] A further complexity is that differences in perceived relative risk—how much greater the risk of one alternative is in comparison to another—may be more influential on individual behavior in actual circumstances than differences in absolute risk.[50] Thus, a change in a privacy notice about a decreased level of protection may be more impactful on individual privacy behavior than lack of notice in the first place. Another illustration of this irrationality is the status quo bias and default settings: consumers are much less likely to change default privacy settings, even when they do not reflect their actual preferences. Policy makers are beginning to consider how to take these factors into account in designs of websites and their privacy policies, as a conference series at the U.S. FTC called PrivacyCon illustrates.[51]

Second, data collectors—whether public or private—may have legitimate reasons for caution about transparency requirements. Data collectors may be concerned that if they reveal the information that they have or what they are doing with it, they may be less able to protect it. They may find themselves overwhelmed with requests for the data—or worse, subject to criminally motivated attacks now that they have been identified as a likely target. They may be concerned that knowledge of their activities will lead to public objections or protest, or may generate litigation. Revealing the kinds of information they possess to competitors may diminish competitive advantages resulting from careful (and expensive) investments in data. Finally, transparency—at least of the sort designed to generate real understanding—takes time and may be expensive. For example, healthcare providers who work under significant time pressures may believe that the time they might spend on explaining a privacy notice could be far better spent on explaining patients' conditions or treatment alternatives.

On the other hand, both individuals and data collectors may act in ways that cannot be justified with respect to transparency. Individuals may be careless, lazy, or inattentive; they may not behave as responsible, rational consumers. Data collectors, too, may have problematic reasons for transparency reluctance. They may believe that consumers will be unwilling to share data if they become better informed about what will happen to it. They may wish to use data in ways that many people find objectionable—for example, for marketing. They may wish to use data in ways that violate individuals' moral—or even legal—rights (for example, to dismiss an employee in violation of anti-discrimination laws).

Efforts to achieve transparency must contend with both legitimate barriers and unjustifiable reasons for failure. The next section considers notice and choice as an instructive model for efforts to achieve transparency.

Notice as a Method for Achieving Transparency

As explained above, the idea of a privacy notice came into being relatively recently as a means for informing consumers about data collection activities. Privacy statements have become standard fare in the bottom margins of websites, waiting to be clicked on by interested consumers. These notices are frequently long, written in language that may appear reassuring, but actually convey little information to the average consumer, and designed to protect companies from liability.

The notice/choice model is rooted in a specific vision of autonomy. The idea is that if individuals are told what will happen to the data (given notice), they will then be able to make choices about what data they are willing to share, with whom, and for what purposes. In its most passive form, notice/choice simply tells a consumer that particular activities—use of a website, for example—constitute consent to the privacy practices. If people do not read notices, however, it is questionable whether their activities constitute genuine consent. Somewhat more active notice/choice models require individuals to signify agreement (an "I agree" or "I accept" hot button), possibly after actually opening a privacy notice. Although these models leave evidence of a statement of agreement and have been used in court to limit companies' contractual obligations to customers,[52] they do little to ensure that individuals actually read the notices or are informed about the content to which they are agreeing. Even so, they do remain available for consumers to examine at a later time. These notices also provide a statement of privacy practices that put a data collector on record about policies and establish rules for their employees.[53] Failure to adhere to a stated privacy policy is an unfair trade practice in that it may mislead the consumer and may subject the entity to an enforcement action by the FTC. Additional defenses of these limited notice/choice models could contend that individuals' failure to read notices signifies that privacy is not very salient to them or that individuals are responsible for what they allow to happen with information about them.

More granular notice/choice models permit or require individuals to agree to particular data practices. A privacy notice might offer individuals a menu of data uses, inviting them to opt out if they so wish. Such opt-out approaches leave data use or disclosure as the default, and there is evidence that many individuals leave default settings in place even if they do not reflect their preferences in fine-grained fashion.[54] Some notice/choice models, especially for sensitive data or controversial uses, require specific opt-in. Here, the default setting is that information will not be used or disclosed, and evidence suggests that some individuals do not opt in even when they would prefer the data practice in question. In the attempt to avoid such problems with default settings, another notice/choice model asks "yes/no" questions for particular types of uses or disclosures. These structures are more cumbersome, but it is arguable that they provide a better reflection of actual consumer preferences.

Designing notices to reflect actual choice raises a number of issues in addition to granularity. Explaining complex matters at a reading level most people can understand is one challenge. Another question is whether there should be a standardized format used by all notices to facilitate consumer comparison. Another is timing: whether the consumer should be presented actively with the notice at the particular point at which data are being used or disclosed, or whether it is sufficient to provide consumers with a notice only at the time of original collection.

Recognizing difficulties with respect to communicating through notices, the FTC has proposed "flexible" notice requirements.[55] In general, the FTC urges, privacy notices should be shorter, more clearly written, and more standardized to facilitate consumer understanding. Any notice and choice requirements should be tailored to the purpose and sensitivity of the transaction at hand. For some activities—for example, ordering commonly used consumer products over the Internet—notice may be very simple. If practices are consistent with the context of the transaction or the relationship between the company and the consumer, or if data collection is required by law, the FTC's judgment is that this simple notice and no further consumer choice is all that is required. For other transactions—for example, entering health information into a website designed for individuals with serious medical conditions—direct notice and choice at the time of entry are required. The FTC Report opts for an objective "context of the interaction" standard for consumer choice, in contrast to either a subjective standard of consumer expectations or a list of "commonly accepted" practices not requiring choice, in order to allow for innovation and the development of new business models. "First-party marketing"—such as follow-up service notifications from a dealership from which the customer has purchased an automobile—would not require consumer choice, but tracking across other websites would do so. "Data enhancement" activities—adding third-party data to data collected from the consumer—would also not require choice.

In reaching these conclusions about flexible notice requirements, the FTC assumes a background of what it calls "privacy by design." This means that appropriate levels of privacy protection are built into all data collection activities. For example, third parties that are the sources of data sets used for enrichment are assumed to have built appropriate privacy practices into their collection as well, so that all the data used for enrichment has been subject to whatever notice and consent is appropriate for that data and use. To the end of achieving privacy by design, the White House discussion draft of a consumer privacy bill of rights included industry-specific codes. Compliance with these codes, the discussion draft suggested, could serve as a safe harbor from FTC enforcement actions.[56] Whether such self-regulatory efforts are likely to achieve progress in transparency remains to be seen.[57]

Case Study: Office of the National Coordinator for Health Information Technology's Model Personal Health Record Privacy Notice and Beyond

PHRs, in many ways eclipsed today, are one vehicle for data collection in which the use of privacy notices has been explored extensively. PHRs allow individuals to create, develop, and control information about their health. At one point, they were thought to be an excellent way to involve consumers in their healthcare, although they appear to have been largely supplanted by other methods such as Internet apps or wearable devices. Evaluations suggested that PHRs were simply too complex for many intended users.[58] Many of the PHRs remaining in use are linked to EHRs maintained by healthcare providers; these PHRs are typically structured so that the information in them is protected by HIPAA and subject to HIPAA notice requirements. Some PHRs, however, are freestanding and may contain health information that has been uploaded by the patient or downloaded from HIPAA-protected entities, but the information in them is not subject to HIPAA because these freestanding PHRs are not HIPAA-covered entities. The vast explosion of Internet apps and wearable devices for collecting health information also has taken place largely outside of the realm of HIPAA protection, except for those devices that are directly linked to patients' medical records. The development of PHRs and later methods of health data collection thus provide an instructive case study for analyzing issues raised by reliance on notices as a method for achieving transparency.

In 2008, ONC began a process of developing a model PHR notice for PHR vendors to use, a process culminating in September 2011 with the release of a voluntary model notice. The project's goals were to increase consumer awareness and provide consumers with an easy method for comparing the practices of different PHR vendors.[59] The Office of the National Coordinator for Health Information Technology's (ONC's) background statement judged that the model notice should help vendors to be transparent about their privacy and security policies, generate trust in PHRs, and compete on the extent to which their policies protect consumers.[60] ONC's model notice was not designed to tell vendors what choices they should offer consumers or whether to provide additional information to meet legal requirements applicable in their jurisdictions. Instead, with transparency as the goal, the model notice was developed based on consumer testing and research involving cognitive usability and provided a standard template for insertion of "yes/no" answers into preset fields.

The template was titled "What are [company name] PHR data practices?"[61] It covered two topics: data release and security. "Release" questions asked whether data would be released for marketing and advertising, medical and pharmaceutical research, reporting about the company and customer activity, insurers and employers, and developing software applications—in each case as either personally identifiable or statistical forms. For "security," the questions were whether data are stored in the United States only and whether activity logs are kept for customer review. The template also encouraged vendors to add a "hot button" at the end for individuals to click on to access the vendor's complete privacy and security policies.

An earlier edition of this chapter reported significant problems with PHR privacy notices 10 months after ONC published its voluntary model privacy notice.[62] Notices were long and had an average reading level of 14.54, with a low of 12.44 and a high of 18.02, making it quite unlikely that the notices would be accessible by the many Americans without college degrees. By contrast, the National Cancer Institute recommends an eighth grade reading level for informed consent forms used for patients in research studies.[63] Several notices included explicit statements that the policy limited their liability to the consumer; these policies could be characterized as company protective rather than consumer informative. Many policies indicated that they would disclose information in response to requests by law enforcement or government agencies such as Homeland Security and only one indicated that the site would attempt to notify the consumer before disclosing the information. Because these disclosures might adversely affect consumers' legal rights, privacy advocates have been especially concerned that PHR vendors should at least inform consumers in order to give them an opportunity to object.[64] Many notices reserved the right to change privacy policies, in some cases without directly informing the consumer. A few indicated that consumers could delete information or terminate accounts, but others were silent about consumers' rights in this regard.

PHRs have been largely supplanted in the market by Internet apps for tracking various health measures such as diet or weight, and by wearable technologies such as fitness trackers. Because these mechanisms are outside of HIPAA protections, concerns about privacy protection have been significant. In 2016, ONC embarked on an update of its model privacy notice aimed at these mechanisms.[65] It solicited comments and received 13 comments representing broad coalitions of stakeholders. A search of these comments revealed frequent statements about the importance of transparency and a few suggestions of how that might be achieved. Table 7.1 summarizes these results:

Table 7.1 Comments to ONC on Revising Model Privacy Notice: References to Transparency

Comment Author	Mention of Transparency?	Content?
ACT/the App Association[66]	Yes	To inform consumers about planned commercial uses
AMA[67]	Yes	"clear privacy policies to ensure accuracy, transparency, and the appropriate level of consumer choice," citing lack of privacy policies in diabetes apps and noting that apps with sensitive health information should be moved toward the standards that apply to physicians
Center for Democracy and Technology	Yes	Created with the typical person in mind; disclosures should be clear, in a time and manner likely to be seen and acted upon; "concrete, digestible information about what entities actually do with user data, using written language and visual data flows whenever possible;" responsive to different languages and disabilities.
Comments on updates[68]	No	Does say that it is difficult for consumers to assess security risk levels and that it would be useful to know whether data will be aggregated
Consumer Partnership for eHealth[69]	Yes	Should also include disclosure of company's own uses
Consumer Technology Association[70]	Yes	Consumers want transparency about transfer to unaffiliated third parties; developers should have maximum flexibility
DirectTrust[71]	Yes	First principle for PHR notices; should include information about entities ownership, non-profit status, privacy policy

(*Continued*)

Table 7.1 (Continued) Comments to ONC on Revising Model Privacy Notice: References to Transparency

Comment Author	Mention of Transparency?	Content?
GetMyHealthData[72]	Yes	Explanation of choices in consumer-friendly language; distinction between HIPAA-covered and non-HIPAA-covered entities confusing; consumers should not be surprised by data uses
Humetrix[73]	No	Recommends explaining to consumer uses of de-identified information and aggregated information; should align with EU standards to the extent feasible
Linda Van Horn[74]	No	Lists information that consumers should have
NATE (National Association for Trusted Exchange)[75]	Yes	Concerned that without transparency consumers "will be lulled" into thinking that their providers and payers give better protection than exchanges
National Partnership for Women and Families[76]	No	Recommends sharing information about company's own uses, reporting for public health, and commercial uses
patientprivacyrights[77]	Yes	Most important information practice is transparency, as in accounting for disclosures. Should be "real-time online access, an available API, and notice anytime data drawn from the individual is used, even in de-identified form"

These results indicate a commitment to transparency, but less discussion of what transparency actually means or how it can be achieved. Perhaps the explanation is that the comments were submitted in response to ONC's request to answer other specific questions regarding updating model privacy notices for PHRs. Nonetheless, only two—CDT and patient privacy rights—refer to difficulties in achieving communication of data uses in real time to consumers. Many do indicate the importance of sharing types of uses with consumers, including the company's own planned uses and uses of de-identified information. All approve of ONC's plan to extend the voluntary model privacy notice to entities beyond PHR vendors; the AMA is perhaps the most forceful in stating that these entities should be moved toward the standards applicable to physicians because of the sensitivity of the health information they possess. Other commentators such as the Consumer Technology Association would give app developers a great deal of flexibility in how they communicate with consumers about what will be done with information. Achieving transparency for consumers over the life cycle of information use remains a challenge; this is a challenge that will surely need to be addressed as the PMI and other novel uses of large data sets evolve.

Beyond Posted Notices: Prescribed Product Labels and Other Techniques for Informing Consumers

This section considers several additional methods for attempting to achieve transparency. Product labels have become a common method of conveying information to consumers. They have the advantage of appearing every time the consumer purchases a product and, if they are noticeably affixed to the product, every time it is used. Nutritional labeling is one example. Statutory authority regarding nutrition labels is drawn from the Nutrition Labeling and Education Act of 1990,[78] thus enabling the FDA to prescribe their form and content by regulation. Current labels list information about calories, fat content, vitamins, and minerals as a percentage of daily requirements. The amounts are listed per serving, with an indication of how many servings are in a package; consumers reading only the amounts may fail to recognize that a package contains several servings. The United Kingdom by contrast uses a "traffic light" system that indicates by red, yellow, or green whether a food is "high," "medium," or "low" in comparison to recommended daily allowances. The Patient Protection and Affordable Care Act (ACA) requires restaurants with more than 20 locations nationally to provide calorie labels for standard menu items.[79] Another familiar product label required by statute is the gasoline miles per gallon (mpg) disclosure for automobiles.[80] Further illustrations can be found in the many disclosure requirements that apply to lending, securities transactions, insurance, and other financial transactions. This use of disclosure as a substitute for regulation gained traction in the Reagan administration and has been a standard proposal of critics of government regulation ever since.[81]

Some research has addressed the efficacy of nutrition labels and attempted to apply the model to privacy policies. A group at Carnegie Mellon found that although consumers would like more information in the labels, they might actually be confused by it.[82] The Carnegie Mellon group's research also indicated that nutrition labels do have a small effect on consumer behavior, especially for consumers who are already interested in the information because they are trying to control their weight.

Other research has explored methods for conveying the information in notices. A group at the Stanford Center for Internet and Society has explored presentation techniques for encouraging consumers to read notices and to make notices more vivid for them.[83] An experimental study on notice in the context of privacy by these researchers attempted to understand whether different formats achieved greater success in influencing people's actual privacy behavior. The researchers hypothesized that "visceral" notice strategies—notice strategies with apparent noncognitive appeal—would achieve superior success in influencing how much information people revealed deliberately or inadvertently.[84] The researchers constructed a website for a supposed new search engine and manipulated several different aspects of the website design: the formality of the website; whether the website revealed prior search history; whether the website featured interaction with a humanlike representation (such as an interface that includes an image of a human face); and whether the website revealed information about the user's current Internet location. The dependent variable of interest in this study was the extent to which participants revealed information about themselves when selecting questions for Internet searches. One conclusion was that informal website design increased the frequency of both direct and unwitting disclosure, probably because informality signaled to participants low levels of data collection by the website. Another conclusion was that participants were more likely to make unwitting disclosures under the notice conditions that prevail on websites today—a privacy policy containing standard notice conditions available for clicking at the bottom of the site. The presence on the website of a humanlike representation reduced the likelihood of disclosures. The research also concluded that there was no difference between traditional notices and simplified versions of these notices in the rates at which participants followed links to privacy policies on the website; users simply did not click on the link to the policy at all.

More research on the efficacy of forms of notice and their presentation is clearly needed, however, as is research on other forms of disclosure.[85] As a former administrator of the Office of Information and Regulatory Affairs at the Office of Management and Budget, Cass Sunstein called for further empirical research to assess the efficacy of different kinds of disclosure requirements.[86] As an example, Sunstein cites the mpg regulation. As originally structured, the notice told consumers only the estimated mpg of the vehicle under different driving conditions. This structure encouraged consumers to believe that the relationship between mpg and gasoline savings is linear, when it is not. Thus, consumers erroneously assumed that moving from a car burning 10 mpg to a car burning 15 mpg and moving from a car burning 25 mpg to a car burning 30 mpg produced equivalent savings. New labels now require additional information about gallons/100 miles driven and annual fuel costs that are intended to counter this consumer error, but Sunstein does not cite empirical evidence concerning the change.

An additional challenge is that these required statutory disclosures have major advantages over current model privacy notices. Their statutory foundation allows agencies to issue nonvoluntary regulations, specifying what is to be said and how it is to be presented. They are ubiquitous; consumers see them on the packages of any food, car, or menu and so become familiar with them over time. By comparison, use of PHRs never took widespread hold among consumers and there is no standardization and often little use of privacy notices among newer vehicles collecting health information. Consumers also see nutrition labels, menu labels, or mpg disclosures at times when they might be expected to be alert, nonthreatened, and interested in reading them: comparing the prices of food on grocery store shelves, shopping for cars, or sitting in a restaurant waiting for a server to take their order. And they view readily understandable information about familiar products.

These familiar notices also have advantages over HIPAA privacy notices. Although consumers do see HIPAA privacy notices more frequently and so may be more familiar with them, to date HHS has not used its regulatory authority to prescribe a common notice form like the nutrition label. In addition, consumers are given privacy notices when they access healthcare. Unlike shopping or eating in a restaurant, accessing healthcare may be a time of stress for patients and their attention is likely to be elsewhere than the privacy notice. Moreover, information from these devices and many other sources may be used in a wide variety of ways, including the PMI.

Conclusion

As described in this chapter, transparency is a goal for collectors and users of data to achieve. Transparency as openness about practices cannot be equated with notice and choice models for concluding that consumers have consented to data collection or use. Instead, transparency must be understood as a process of education, information communication, and, in appropriate circumstances, well-informed consumer choice. This process must continue over time and cannot simply be a one-off in a privacy notice that consumers may or may not pay attention to when they originally agree for their information to be collected. Transparency must also be set within a commitment to FIPs more generally. Ongoing study of consumer attitudes, communication barriers, and methods for effective information delivery remains imperative if individual choice is to be respected.

Notes

1. Precision Medicine Initiative Working Group. The Precision Medicine Initiative Cohort Program: Building a Research Foundation for 21st Century Medicine; September 17, 2015. Available at: https://www.nih.gov/sites/default/files/research-training/initiatives/pmi/pmi-working-group-report-20150917-2.pdf, Executive Summary, pp. 1–5.
2. White House. Precision Medicine Initiative: Privacy and Trust Principles; November 9, 2015. Available at: https://www.whitehouse.gov/sites/default/files/microsites/finalpmiprivacyandtrustprinciples.pdf, pp. 2–3.
3. Precision Medicine Initiative Working Group. The Precision Medicine Initiative Cohort Program: Building a Research Foundation for 21st Century Medicine; September 17, 2015. Available at: https://www.nih.gov/sites/default/files/research-training/initiatives/pmi/pmi-working-group-report-20150917-2.pdf, p. 79.
4. Precision Medicine Initiative Working Group. The Precision Medicine Initiative Cohort Program: Building a Research Foundation for 21st Century Medicine; September 17, 2015. Available at: https://www.nih.gov/sites/default/files/research-training/initiatives/pmi/pmi-working-group-report-20150917-2.pdf, p. 20.
5. For a very useful history of FIPs, see Gellman R. Fair Information Practices: A Basic History, version 2.16; June 17, 2016. Available at: http://bobgellman.com/rg-docs/rg-FIPShistory.pdf.
6. Report of the Secretary's Advisory Committee on Automated Personal Data Systems: Records, Computers and the Rights of Citizens; July 1973. Available at: http://aspe.hhs.gov/datacncl/1973privacy/tocprefacemembers.htm.
7. Pozen DE. Deep Secrecy. *Stanford Law Review.* 2010; 62:275–339.
8. The federal Freedom of Information Act is 5 U.S.C. § 552; 2016.

9. Asserting a copyright requires an element of creativity; mere listings of information such as material gathered from patient records would not be copyrightable, absent more. *Feist Publications, Inc. v. Rural Telephone Services Co.,* 499 U.S. 340; 1991 (telephone white pages listings not copyrightable). There has been considerable controversy regarding when databases are copyrightable, for example, Bitton M. A New Outlook on the Economic Dimension of the Database Protection Debate. *IDEA.* 2006; 47:93–169.

10. Trade secrets law requires the entity asserting this intellectual property right to make reasonable efforts to keep the information from being disclosed. Uniform Trade Secrets Act (1985) § 1(4)(ii). This law thus works very differently from patent law, which requires disclosure of the invention as a condition for asserting exclusivity. Companies with large data bases of patient information may claim these as trade secrets to gain competitive advantage—for example, a genetic testing company may have information about the significance of variants that is not generally available. See for example, Cook-Deegan R, Conley JM, Evans JP, Vorhaus D. The Next Controversy in Genetic Testing: Clinical Data as Trade Secrets? *Eur J Hum Genet.* 2013; 21(6):585–8.

11. Lyndon ML. Secrecy and Access in an Innovation Intensive Economy: Reordering Information Privileges in Environmental, Health, and Safety Law. *University of Colorado Law Review.* 2007; 78:465–531.

12. Warren S, Brandeis LD. The Right to Privacy. *Harvard Law Review.* 1890; 4(5):193–220; Prosser WL. Privacy. *California Law Review.* 1960; 48(3):383–423.

13. Francis LP. Privacy and Confidentiality: The Importance of Context. *Monist.* 2008; 91(1):52–67.

14. Froomkin AM. A New Legal Paradigm? The Death of Privacy? *Stanford Law Review.* 2000; 52:1461–1543.

15. Texas Department of State Health Services. Statement: Newborn Screening Settlement; December 22, 2009. Available at: http://www.dshs.state.tx.us/news/releases/20091222.shtm.

16. Minnesota Department of Health. Minnesota Department of Health to Begin Destroying Newborn Blood Spots in Order to Comply with Recent Minnesota Supreme Court Ruling; January 31, 2012. Available at: http://www.health.state.mn.us/news/pressrel/2012/newborn013112.html.

17. Harmon A. Indian Tribe Wins Fight to Limit Research of Its DNA. *The New York Times*; April 21, 2010. Available at: http://www.nytimes.com/2010/04/22/us/22dna.html?pagewanted=all.

18. For example: California HealthCare Foundation. *Achieving the Right Balance: Privacy and Security Policies to Support Electronic Health Information Exchange*; March 2012. Available at: http://www.chcf.org/publications/2012/06/achieving-right-balance.

19. The latest available data from the Pew Internet Project indicates that 87% of U.S. adults used the Internet in 2012, and that 72% of these Internet users had searched for health information during that year. Pew Research Center. Health Fact Sheet; Dec. 16, 2013. Available at: http://www.pewinternet.org/fact-sheets/health-fact-sheet/.

20. Rainie L, Duggan M. Privacy and Information Sharing; January 14, 2016. Available at: http://www.pewinternet.org/2016/01/14/privacy-and-information-sharing/.

21. 5 U.S.C. § 552a(e)(4);2016.

22. Federal Trade Commission. Protecting Consumer Privacy in an Era of Rapid Change: Recommendations for Business and Policymakers; March 2012; page 69. Available at: http://www.ftc.gov/os/2012/03/120326privacyreport.pdf. Although this suggestion was made in 2012, it does not appear to have been acted on as of 2016.

23. 5 U.S.C. § 552a(e)(8);2016.

24. HITECH Act §§ 13402, 13407.

25. HITECH Act § 13407.

26. Cal. Civ. Code §§ 1798.82, 1798.29(2016); National Conference of State Legislatures. Security Breach Notification Laws; January 24, 2016. Available at: http://www.ncsl.org/research/telecommunications-and-information-technology/security-breach-notification-laws.aspx.

27. Directive 95/46/EC of the European Parliament and of the Council, on the protection of individuals with regard to the processing of personal data and on the free movement of such data, Art. 10; *Official Journal of the European Communities.* no.281/31 (23.11.95). Available at: http://eur-lex.europa.eu/LexUriServ/LexUriServ.do?uri=CELEX:31995L0046:en:HTML.

28. Regulation (EU) 2016/679 of the European Parliament and of the Council of 27 April 2016 on the protection of natural persons with regard to the processing of personal data and on the free movement of such data, and repealing Directive 95/46/EC (General Data Protection Regulation); *Official Journal of the European Union* L119/1 (4.5.2016). Available at: http://eur-lex.europa.eu/legal-content/EN/TXT/PDF/?uri=CELEX:32016R0679&from=en.

29. Regulation (EU) 2016/679, Art. 13.

30. Regulation (EU) 2016/679, Art. 14.

31. Regulation (EU) 2016/679, Art. 12(1).

32. Regulation (EU) 2016/679, Art. 13(2), Art. 14(2).

33. Regulation (EU) 2016/679, Art. 17.

34. U.S. Department of Commerce, EU-U.S. Privacy Shield Program Overview; July 2016. Available at: https://www.privacyshield.gov/Program-Overview.

35. U.S. Department of Commerce, EU-U.S. Privacy Shield Framework: Key New Requirements of Participating Companies. Available at: https://www.privacyshield.gov/Key-New-Requirements.

36. 15 U.S.C. § 6803; 2016.

37. 15 U.S.C. § 6802; 2016.

38. Cal. Bus. & Prof. Code §22577; 2016.

39. 45 CFR §164.520; 2016.

40. Council of Economic Advisers Issue Brief. *Mapping the Digital Divide*; July 2015. Available at: https://www.whitehouse.gov/sites/default/files/wh_digital_divide_issue_brief.pdf.

41. Rainie L. Digital Divides 2016; July 14, 2016, slide 30. Available at: http://www.pewinternet.org/2016/07/14/digital-divides-2016/.

42. Rainie L. Digital Divides 2016; July 14, 2016, slide 41. Available at: http://www.pewinternet.org/2016/07/14/digital-divides-2016/.

43. Rainie L. Digital Divides 2016; July 14, 2016, slide 40. Available at: http://www.pewinternet.org/2016/07/14/digital-divides-2016/.

44. Nordberg PA, Horne DR, Horne DA. The Privacy Paradox: Personal Information Disclosure Intentions vs. Behaviors. *Journal of Consumer Affairs.* 2007; 41(1):100–126.

45. Groom V, Calo MR. Reversing the Privacy Paradox: An Experimental Study. Available at: http://ssrn.com/abstract=1993125.

46. Posner RA. The Right of Privacy. *Georgia Law Review.* 1978; 12(3):393–422.

47. Sprenger P. Sun on Privacy: 'Get Over It' *Wired*; January 26, 1999. Available at: http://www.wired.com/politics/law/news/1999/01/17538.

48. Hoofnagle C, King J, Li S, Turow J. How Different Are Young Adults from Older Adults When It Comes to Information Privacy Attitudes and Policies; April 14, 2010. Available at: http://ssrn.com/abstract=1589864.

49. Brandimarte L, Acquisti A, Loewenstein G. Misplaced Confidences: Privacy and the Control Paradox. *Social Psychological & Personality Science.* 2013; 4(3): 340–347.

50. Adjerid I, Peer E, Acquisti A. Beyond the Privacy Paradox: Objective versus Relative Risk in Privacy Decision Making; 2016. Available at: http://papers.ssrn.com/sol3/papers.cfm?abstract_id=2765097.

51. Federal Trade Commission. PrivacyCon. Available at: https://www.ftc.gov/news-events/events-calendar/2016/01/privacycon.

52. *Hill v. Gateway 2000*, 105 F.3d 1147 (7th Cir. 1997), cert den. 118 S.Ct. 47; 1997.

53. Statement of Robert Gellman, HIT Policy Committee, September 18, 2009. Available at: http://bobgellman.com/rg-docs/rg-HITPolicy-9-18-09.pdf.

54. Madden M, Lenhart A, Cortesi S, Gasser U, Duggan M, Smith A, Beaton M. Teens, Social Media, and Privacy, Part 2: Information Sharing, Friending, and Privacy Settings on Social Media; May 21, 2013. Available at: http://www.pewinternet.org/2013/05/21/part-2-information-sharing-friending-and-privacy-settings-on-social-media/. See also Thaler RH, Sunstein CR. *Nudge: Improving Decisions About Health, Wealth, and Happiness.* New Haven: Yale University Press, 2008; Trout JD. Paternalism and Cognitive Bias. *Law and Philosophy.* 2005; 24(4):393–434.

55. FTC. Protecting Consumer Privacy in an Era of Rapid Change: Recommendations for Businesses and Policymakers; March, 2012. Available at: http://www.ftc.gov/os/2012/03/120326privacyreport.pdf.

56. White House. Administration Discussion Draft: Consumer Privacy Bill of Rights Act of 2015 Title III. Available at: https://www.insideprivacy.com/wp-content/uploads/sites/6/2015/02/cpbr-act-of-2015-discussion-draft.pdf.

57. Bracy J. Will Industry Self-Regulation Be Privacy's Way Forward? *The Privacy Advisor*; June 24, 2014. Available at: https://iapp.org/news/a/will-industry-self-regulation-be-privacys-way-forward/.

58. NORC. Evaluation of the Personal Health Record Pilot for Medicare Fee-For Service Enrollees from South Carolina. Available at: https://aspe.hhs.gov/sites/default/files/pdf/75991/report.pdf.

59. ONC. Personal Health Record (PHR) Model Privacy Notice. Available at: https://www.healthit.gov/sites/default/files/phr-model-privacy-notice-final-2011.pdf.

60. ONC. About the PHR Model Privacy Notice: Background, Development Process, Key Points; September 2011. Available at: https://www.healthit.gov/sites/default/files/phr-model-privacy-notice-backgrounder-final.pdf.

61. https://www.healthit.gov/sites/default/files/phr-model-privacy-notice-implementation-guide-final.pdf.

62. Francis L. 2013. Transparency. In *Information Privacy in the Evolving Healthcare Environment*, ed. L. Koontz, 140–142. Chicago: Health Information and Management Systems Society.

63. National Cancer Institute. Simplification of Informed Consent Documents.

64. Center for Democracy and Technology. Building a Strong Privacy and Security Policy Framework for Personal Health Records; July 21, 2010. Available at: www.cdt.org/files/pdfs/Building_Strong_Privacy_Security_Policy_Framework_PHRs.pdf; The World Privacy Forum. Personal Health Records: Why Many PRHs Threaten Privacy; February 20, 2008. Available at: http://www.worldprivacyforum.org/wp-content/uploads/2012/04/WPF_PHR_02_20_2008fs.pdf.

65. ONC. Personal Health Record (PHR) Model Privacy Notice Project Updates. Available at: https://www.healthit.gov/policy-researchers-implementers/personal-health-record-phr-model-privacy-notice#comments.

66. ACT|The App Association. Comments of ACT|The App Association regarding the Office of the National Coordinator for Health Information Technology's Request for Information on Updates to the ONC Voluntary Personal Health Record Model Privacy Notice; April 15, 2016. Available at: https://www.healthit.gov/sites/default/files/ACT_Comments_MPN_041516.pdf.

67. AMA, Letter from James L. Madara to Karen DeSalvo; April 15, 2016. Available at: https://www.healthit.gov/sites/default/files/AMA_Comments_MPN_041516.pdf.

68. Comments on updates. Available at: https://www.healthit.gov/sites/default/files/Comments_on_Updates_MPN_041516.pdf.

69. Letter from Consumer Partnership for eHealth to Karen DeSalvo; April 15, 2016. Available at: https://www.healthit.gov/sites/default/files/Consumer_Partnership_for_eHealth_Comments_MPN_041516.pdf.

70. Consumer Technology Association. Comments of the Consumer Privacy Association; April 15, 2016. Available at: https://www.healthit.gov/sites/default/files/CTA_Comments_MPN_041516.pdf.

71. DirectTrust, Letter from Lucy Johns to Karen DeSalvo; April 15, 2016. Available at: https://www.healthit.gov/sites/default/files/DirectTrust_Comments_MPN_041516.pdf.

72. GetMyHealthData, Letter from Christine Bechtel to Karen DeSalvo; April 15, 2016. Available at: https://www.healthit.gov/sites/default/files/GetMyHealthData_Comments_MPN_041516.pdf.

73. Humetrix, Letter from Bettina Experton to Karen DeSalvo; April 15, 2016. Available at: https://www.healthit.gov/sites/default/files/Humetrix_Comments_MPN_041516.pdf.

74. Linda Van Horn. Request for Information on Updates to the ONC Voluntary Personal Health Record Model Privacy Notice. Available at: https://www.healthit.gov/sites/default/files/L_vanHorn_Comments_MPN_041516.pdf.

75. NATE, Letter from Aaron Seib to Karen DeSalvo; April 15, 2016. Available at: https://www.healthit.gov/sites/default/files/NATE_Comments_MPN_041516.pdf.

76. National Partnership for Women and Families. Letter from Mark Savage to Karen DeSalvo; April 15, 2016. Available at: https://www.healthit.gov/sites/default/files/National_Partnership_Comments_MPN_041516.pdf.

77. Patientprivacyrights. Model Privacy Notice Comments; April 15, 2016. Available at: https://www.healthit.gov/sites/default/files/PatientPrivacyRights_Comments_MPN_041516.pdf.

78. 21 U.S.C. § 343(q); 2016.

79. Patient Protection and Affordable Care Act § 4205(b).

80. 16 CFR § 259.2; 2016.

81. Dalley PJ. The Use and Misuse of Disclosure as a Regulatory System. *Florida State University Law Review.* 2007; 34:1089–1131.

82. Kelley PG, Bresee J, Cranor LF, Reeder RW. A 'Nutrition Label' for Privacy. Symposium on Usable Privacy and Security (SOUPS), July 15–17, 2009; Mountain View, CA; Kelley PG, Cesca L, Bresee J, Cranor LF. Standardizing Privacy Notices: An Online Study of the Nutrition Label Approach. CMUCyLab-09-014; January 12, 2010.

83. Groom V, Calo MR. Reversing the Privacy Paradox: An Experimental Study. TPRC Conference proceedings.

84. Groom V, Calo MR. Reversing the Privacy Paradox: An Experimental Study. TPRC Conference proceedings.

85. Szanyi JM. Brain Food: Bringing Psychological Insights to Bear on Modern Nutrition Labeling Efforts. *Food and Drug Law Journal.* 2010; 65:159–184.

86. Sunstein, C. Empirically Informed Regulation. *University of Chicago Law Review.* 2011; 78:1349–1429.

Chapter 8

Secondary Use of Protected Health Information

By John Mattison, MD, and Larry Ozeran, MD

Contents

In medicine, our healthcare system, and most of life, *balance is key*.

A major focus of this chapter is to emphasize why balance is necessary, because the risks of secondary use of health information are often publicly downplayed. Some commercial interests in secondary use of aggregated non-healthcare data are so significant that the public has been encouraged to believe that privacy has no value. "You have no privacy, get over it."[1,2] The authors touch briefly on this view and offer policy considerations to help organizations and our nation find balance between personal privacy and the use of individually identifiable health data for secondary purposes.

The philosopher Spinoza focused much of his work on the challenges of managing the trade-offs between competing virtues and values. Privacy is a celebrated virtue that cannot be isolated from all other virtues with which it sometimes conflicts. The need to balance the trade-offs between privacy and other competing virtues accounts for why there is so much controversy, both in our national debate on this issue and also beyond our borders. In the UK, Google has a contract to collect individually identifiable health data without express patient consent because the National Health Service (NHS) has deemed the use of the identifiable data to be for clinical treatment.[3] Does calling "data analytics" "treatment" make it so, or does redefining "treatment" in this way rob individuals of a say in how their individually identifiable health data is used?

The purpose of this chapter is to inspect these global tensions among virtues as they apply to the secondary use of health information. When sensitive data is collected for a "primary use" (i.e., direct patient care), and is subsequently reused for any other purpose, i.e., "secondary use" (e.g., research, quality control, or marketing), there is a need to actively evaluate these trade-offs in the context of each type of secondary use of those data.

For readability, we will use the phrase "secondary use" for the remainder of this chapter to mean "secondary use of protected health information (PHI)." The Health Insurance Portability and Accountability Act (HIPAA) defines PHI as any individually identifiable health information held or transmitted by a covered entity, which includes most providers, health plans, and health clearinghouses.

There is a direct trade-off between the virtues of protecting individual patient privacy and the value of secondary use, including payment, monitoring compliance, quality improvement, and clinical research. If it were possible to provide absolute privacy and enable all secondary uses, there would be no conflict and no need for this discussion. The only way to achieve absolute privacy is to lock down all information so tightly that no one could use it. Such an extreme approach impairs not only secondary use, but can impair the primary use for direct clinical care as well. It is precisely this conundrum that drives the deliberate consideration of how much privacy protection is required for a specific secondary use so that the benefits of the secondary use can be factored into determining the appropriate level of privacy protection. It would be convenient to simply say "all secondary use is OK if there is 100 percent protection of privacy of the individual," but the digital age has effectively invalidated the feasibility of such an approach. The technical capability to "re-identify" an individual from an array of "de-identified" data about that individual has risen to a point that "de-identification" is increasingly limited to preventing a *human* reader from re-identifying an individual, having much less impact on a computer with many databases and in-aggregate data analytical tools at its disposal.

As discussed later in this chapter, computer re-identification of de-identified data sets is an increasingly trivial pursuit for modern computational infrastructures. These considerations manifest with the following question: "How much privacy protection is practical and appropriate based on not only primary protection of the data, but also based on the benefit from the various types of secondary use?" For payment, even HIPAA recognizes that this use benefits the patient, but still permits the patient to keep health service information private when personally paid outside of insurance. For regulatory, auditing and quality management purposes, the benefit to the health system is generally considered to outweigh the risk to the individual. To reuse the data for research without explicit consent, the question is how low must the ratio of privacy risk to societal benefit be to advance the science and health of a population, including each specific individual.

When secondary use has an objective that benefits only a few (e.g., commercial monetization of information for marketing purposes), the balance must be considered very differently. The risk of re-identifying individuals must be much lower or the prospective data user must acquire explicit permission to avoid exploitation when an individual's data are used for secondary use objectives that offer no clear benefit (or very minimal benefit) to that individual or to a cohort that resembles that individual or to the broader population/society.

A continuum of secondary uses between these extremes challenges policy makers, who must create practical approaches to a broad array of known and as yet ill-defined future secondary uses. As our deepest secrets and our most personal health information become increasingly available in a digital form, finding the proper balance point on that continuum becomes increasingly critical. Much of these data are generated and contained within conventional secure boundaries, but wearable sensors and direct-to-consumer laboratory testing and genomics entities are increasingly generating similar data outside the traditional security perimeters. These new clinical arenas can place "the missing link to re-identification" in a relatively public and unprotected space.

In this chapter, the authors will discuss both the value and the financial, personal, and social costs (collectively referred to as "costs") of using health information for purposes other than those supporting direct patient care. Secondary use includes many legitimate, necessary, and desirable purposes, for example, billing, quality improvement, research, and postmarketing surveillance for side effects of new drugs. These secondary uses quickly become problematic when personal information is used to identify consumers to target them for advertising, violating a person's right to be left alone and their right to control their personal information, the definition of privacy.

There are also illegal secondary uses, such as exposing personal information about individuals with the intent of embarrassing them, for example, the celebrated and unfortunate disclosure of the mental health of Kitty Dukakis during the Presidential campaign of 1988. Beyond the primary purpose of direct patient care, there is a continuum of progressively controversial uses for which explicit authorization by individuals becomes increasingly important. The cost/benefit consideration for each level of authorization of the use of PHI yields spirited debates among privacy advocates, healthcare organizations, payers, researchers, and businesses about how to balance the overhead of various types of authorization with the potential benefit to the public good resulting from the free flow of information. For example, as we move to increasingly sensitive information, how do we decide when and where to require increasingly stringent access control and authentication (e.g., two or three factor identification or exclusive use of a blockchain-based identity controlled by each individual)? Should we be more transparent, explicit, and exclusive about who is (which roles are) permitted to access the data? We quickly collide with the age old philosophical question of when does the public good, however defined, take priority over the associated risks to individual rights to privacy? The authors will suggest a balance in areas where we have an opinion, as well as a process that organizations, policy makers, and patients may utilize to achieve a reasonable balance among some very thorny issues. There is no single "right" approach to authorization that is appropriate for each type of secondary use. The best we can do is to seek a balanced approach achieved through open debate founded on principles, which unfortunately often conflict. Further, there is a clear need for transparency into how balance is achieved so that consumers can understand exactly what benefits and risks were considered with each type of secondary use.

It can be all too easy to align one's perspectives with a single virtue to the exclusion of other virtues. The costs of this simplistic approach may be downplayed in order to support the benefit of choosing the "simplest" option. The battle over the secondary use of PHI has polar extremes of the debate represented by, on the one hand, a purist approach to privacy above all other considerations, and on the other extreme, a singular focus on quality of care and advancement of science for the benefit of the larger community. The privacy purists focus solely on privacy, insisting that each consumer must authorize each use of each element no matter what the purpose. The costs of this perspective (financial expenses, temporal delays, resources used, missed opportunities) may not be known to or valued as a key benefit by privacy purists. Conversely, the purists dedicated to advancing science for the good of all have alleged that it is "unethical" for consumers to deny use of their health information for any practice that might advance medical science for the benefit of an entire population. What must inform these debates is an understanding of *who benefits* (in what way—medically, financially—and by how much) from the sharing of data for secondary use and *who pays* (in what way—medically, socially, financially—and by how much).

We will only strike a reasonable balance if these polarized views that focus on a single virtue are moderated by an appreciation of the trade-offs of multiple virtues in varying circumstances. It is important to realize that these trade-offs exist even for primary use, but become more conspicuous and controversial across the range of secondary uses, as the data is repurposed in an endless series of digital migration, transformation, and re-aggregation.

Beyond the continuum of generally reasonable uses, there is another continuum of increasingly unreasonable uses, ranging from obtaining the pregnancy test results of an 18-year-old daughter without her permission, to collecting medical information in order to plot a "perfect" murder. There must be a mechanism for protecting individuals from secondary uses of their PHI that are generally not accepted as legitimate uses. The solution would be very simple if there were security mechanisms that provided 100 percent effective privacy without impairing the appropriate and permitted use of that information, but there will never be such "perfect solutions." Conversely, it would be convenient if we had perfect policy, detection, and punishment for all violations of privacy, so that the certainty of detection and punishment were so widely known that deterrence would be 100 percent effective. Unfortunately, neither of these options is possible. The end result is that both methods are necessary, i.e., security and preventive measures, plus policy for deterrence, detection, and punishment. Even in combination, these approaches will never be 100 percent effective. This is the challenge that drives our debate.

While payment and operations are commonly lumped together with treatment ("TPO" in HIPAA parlance), only treatment is a primary use of PHI. Patients do not need payment or operations for best care. In fact, some patients pay for certain care out of pocket, deliberately to avoid the threat to privacy associated with the HIPAA-permitted uses of those data for "payment and operations." The patient may not want a parent or spouse to know from the shared billing information what they had done. The value of secondary use may accrue to someone other than the patient or group of patients who provided the original data. The cost of this data sharing is borne by each patient who provided it in the form of the risk to them of exposing their personal and private health information to individuals other than those delivering their care. For example, a 21-year-old woman covered by her parents' insurance had a miscarriage revealed to her parents by their insurance company before she herself had an opportunity to discuss the pregnancy with them.[4] This caused a significant familial rift.

Some electronic health record (EHR) vendors collect and retain custody of large data sets of individually identifiable patient data for their provider clients. Some vendors, for example, Practice Fusion, have found ways to monetize these data. In what ways should this be permitted, if any, and in what ways should this be prohibited? Perhaps direct marketing to physicians is OK, but not within the EHR decision support systems. Secondary uses have the potential to negatively impact a patient's direct care if an ad for a drug is perceived to be a recommendation for the management of the viewed patient. Absent a notice that the recommendation was an advertisement rather than a clinically based recommendation, such advertisements masquerading as clinical decision support might inappropriately promote prescribing patterns that conflict with the best interests of both individual patients and their treating providers.

The remainder of this chapter will focus on the value and costs of secondary use in greater detail.

Secondary use has the potential to enable better care of entire populations through management of individual and grouped patients with specific disease processes:

■ by identifying at-risk patients for participation in ongoing research efforts;
■ by enabling inferences to be drawn about the likelihood of disease among others; and
■ from data mining in search of clinical patterns not previously known.

The costs of secondary use include the potential for identity theft for medical treatment purposes (one of the fastest growing forms of identity theft), release of sensitive or embarrassing information (e.g., exposing a positive HIV status or publicizing the pregnancy of someone who claims abstinence), loss of employment or altered treatment in the workplace (if an employer learns of a medical condition such as cancer), public release for political or personal gain by an opponent or adversary, or denial of life, long-term care or disability insurance as a result of genomic predispositions (not protected by the Genetic Information Nondiscrimination Act of 2008 [GINA] or HIPAA).

Privacy Rule Requirements for Secondary Use

As discussed in Chapter 4, the HIPAA Privacy Rule permits a range of secondary uses without patient authorization. The rule permits a covered entity to disclose PHI for the primary use of treatment and secondary uses of payment and healthcare operations. In addition, it permits secondary use and disclosure of PHI for a range of "public interest" purposes, including research, public health activities, and law enforcement purposes. (See Table 4.2 for a detailed description of these purposes.) All uses and disclosures not specifically permitted by the Privacy Rule require written authorization from the patient.

By contrast, the Privacy Rule places no restrictions on the use or disclosure of de-identified health information. De-identified health information is health information that does not, by itself, include enough information (often only in theory and in woefully outdated HIPAA language of safe harbors) to identify an individual or provide a reasonable basis for identification. Under the Privacy Rule, PHI is considered de-identified when either 18 specific identifiers are removed or a qualified professional provides an opinion that there is little risk that the information can be used to identify subject individuals. However, as the availability of data about each of us and mechanisms to aggregate those data have grown at a breathtaking rate, the hurdle for computer re-identification continues to shrink, and our assessment of the appropriate balance should be continuously reassessed.

The Value of Secondary Use

The value of secondary use is often in the eye of the user. If the user is selling celebrity health information, the value is cash to the seller; the cost of publicity, potential embarrassment, and loss of privacy are borne by the celebrity. If the user is a public health department using symptoms collected from all hospitals and medical offices in their region to detect a bioterrorist attack early in its evolution, or even a less concerning but serious flu outbreak, the entire community may benefit and the cost to the individual may be imperceptible. Public health aggregation of sentinel events early in a new challenge is unlikely to pose a significant privacy risk to individuals.

This balance between cost and value supports HIPAA-permitted secondary uses, including public health and law enforcement purposes. What types of secondary use are included in those categories?

HIPAA allows the release of PHI to law enforcement when subpoenaed in the investigation or for prosecution of a crime. The benefit of investigating and prosecuting criminal activity supports the fabric of society, an indirect benefit to everyone. While the rationale is generally supported by the "common good" argument, promoting a safe society directly supports the individual, even if that direct benefit is difficult to measure.

Similarly, public health agencies are authorized and in many cases mandated by various laws to collect PHI on various communicable diseases, like tuberculosis or HIV. Providers are legally compelled to report such information. As we move to population health management in the private sector, what additional data might benefit public health? Syndromic surveillance—the ability to monitor symptoms—as opposed to definitive diagnoses, may be able to provide an early warning system to the spread of an infectious agent, whether natural or nefarious. Similarly, identification of a toxic exposure in a community, or by consumers of a specific food or product, will more easily occur through secondary use of data. Further, the challenge to isolating the adverse impact of a particular chemical exposure amidst thousands of other chemical exposures is increasingly difficult without secondary use of very large data sets. Serious adverse drug reactions (ADRs) are frequently discovered only after the drug is released by the FDA for widespread use. Detection of ADRs is of high community value, but requires secondary use for discovery.

What secondary uses of PHI have clear value, yet are not explicitly addressed by HIPAA? The following are each secondary uses of PHI which may be of direct value to the individual patient:

- To identify potential candidates for clinical research trials.
- To recommend potentially beneficial medication, especially when based on new drugs or technologies applied to historical data that identifies individuals who might benefit.
- To group with other patients who share a similar, but uncommon disease.
- To connect patients who share a similar, but uncommon disease, with one another.
- To help individuals who share common genetic conditions understand what diseases and treatments are especially relevant to them.

To see the value of these uses, patients must provide explicit authorization. Generally speaking, any use for which a patient is willing to specifically authorize permission is permitted under HIPAA.

De-Identification

De-identification is the process of removing personal identifiers from data. It supports the use of personal information while concealing the identity of the source. In its simplest form, removal of traditional personal identifiers (e.g., first name, last name, and SSN) is mandatory. De-identification efforts must be as aggressive or comprehensive as needed based on the sensitivity of the data being shared. The goal is to prevent subsequent re-identification of the individual from the data. Computer re-identification is vastly more capable than human re-identification; for example, computer re-identification is possible with a single laboratory result with associated date and time if the user of that information has computer access to those same data elements in the source laboratory system. There will only be one person who has a serum potassium of 4.7 resulted at 6:45 am on February 12, 2017, in the Sacramento office of Nichols Laboratories. If the de-identified data reveals "potassium of 4.7 resulted at 6:45 from Nichols Lab in Sacramento," then finding that record and connecting it to the demographic identifiers attached to that lab result within the source system are possible. While this is a simple example deriving from a single result and the attached metadata, it illustrates a larger problem when more aggregated information can be triangulated for purposes of re-identification without necessarily having access to otherwise individually sequestered information sources.

The objective of de-identifying data is to allow for the secondary use of the data in the interest of advancing science and the health of a community without exposing the identity of any individual whose explicit or implicit rights or authorizations (legal or ethical) preclude such exposure. This ethical and legal objective poses several challenges in protecting the identity of individuals whose personal data has been collected and stored for one purpose, and then is repurposed for some other reasonable secondary use. There are two primary challenges in protecting the identity and hence privacy of any participating individual:

1. Human recognition of identity, i.e., human re-identification (this attempts to prevent a human from recognizing the identity of an individual by virtue of demographics, e.g., name, date of birth, phone number).
2. Computer recognition of identity, i.e., computer re-identification through sophisticated algorithms, the mosaic effect[5], and/or by matching a de-identified data signature with an identical data signature associated with an identity.[6]

The operational definitions of *de*-identification and *re*-identification should be considered in the context of the "human" and "computer" capacities to re-identify an individual from a data set. Many fascinating treatises address the distinctions between the computational abilities of the human brain versus those of the computer. The key distinction here relates to identity matching. Since computers are far superior at this task, we will first consider the computer capacity for re-identification, then the much lesser human capacity. This approach serves as a useful heuristic for exposing why the notion of de-identification (to prevent human re-identification in this taxonomy) is increasingly an obsolete consideration in the digital age.

Computers produce 100 percent reliability and reproducibility when applying statistical rules to identify the precise probability of a match between one set of data and another set of data. If either data set is attached to a specified human identity, then that identity can be applied to both sets of data and propagated across any pedigree of linked data. This matching process can apply across an infinite string of data sets with assignment of the probability of a match to each member of that "set of sets." This transitive property of identity is increasingly relevant in our increasingly connected world of "big data."

Precision and recall of the data element comparisons between sets in this computer re-identification process is not subject to error, so only the statistical algorithms and their effective implementation in a rule set can produce errors in the computer re-identification of a particular set of data. Once a specific probability of an "identity match" is assigned by a computer in this process, the onus is on the human reviewing the "computer calculations" to conclude that the calculated probability of a "match" is or is not sufficient to warrant subsequent actions based on that probabilistic identity.

The most widely known example of this process is the use of DNA for establishment of guilt or innocence in criminal trials based upon tissue samples and DNA sequencing assays. Many celebrated criminal cases have revealed how experts can disagree about interpretation of the statistical evidence. Recent advances in sequencing DNA from extremely small tissue samples is increasingly reducing the occurrence of these disputes among expert witnesses. The important observation about computer re-identification is that the larger the amount of and types of data within any of the two data sets undergoing an analysis for a match, the more accurately the probability of a match can be assigned.

There are numerous natural trends that affect the ability of the computer to re-identify individuals, and every one of these trends correlates positively with the capacity for computer re-identification:

- Improving tools for statistical analysis.
- Increasing quantity of digital data stored on each individual.
- Accessibility of digital data.
- Increasing storage capacity and decreasing cost.
- Increasing computational capacity and decreasing cost.
- Increasing "connectedness" and the capacity to link data across platforms.
- Increasing number of data signatures for any individual, both clinical (e.g., phenome, genome, microbiome) and nonclinical (e.g., geo-location, music preferences, purchasing habits, mobility, communication patterns).

Given that *all* of these trends increase the ability of computers to attach a human identity to any particular set of data, it is clear that there is a corresponding rise in the need for thoughtful policy, law, and enforcement to address the cultural values and individual right to privacy.

Health Information Exchange

During their lives, most patients will be treated by many different providers in different locations in different institutions. Very few patients will exclusively see the same providers in the same institutions over a lifetime. It is important that each individual receives the best possible care based upon everything that is relevant to their clinical health at any point in time. Maintaining a complete longitudinal record for any individual is effectively impossible without the ability to share information among healthcare providers, institutions, and EHR applications and platforms. Barriers to this sharing are shrinking as a result of legislative and regulatory action through such efforts as requiring EHRs to support Fast Healthcare Interoperability Resources Application Programming Interfaces (FHIR APIs) and rules against information blocking. While HIPAA is intended to address many aspects of privacy protection that apply to the exchange of information between providers, different states have independently created a hodge-podge of rules (legislative and regulatory) that directly or indirectly affect exchange of clinical data across any two state lines. For example, the laws in different states may impact what can be transmitted electronically with respect to sensitive diagnoses, such as HIV or hepatitis. There are four types of problems introduced by these interstate variations:

- Overlaps and conflicts between state privacy laws and federal HIPAA legislation.
- Lack of a coherent legal framework compounded by continual, and generally independent, evolution of both federal (HIPAA) and state legislation.
- Problems in creating consistent and coherent exchange of information between states with conflicting rules.
- Unintended consequences (e.g., double jeopardy, liability).

Several states, including California, Hawaii, and Kansas, have initiated efforts to reconcile state and federal rules, though these efforts are challenged by the continual evolution of both federal and state rules.

Healthcare providers that have a presence in multiple states struggle to accommodate interstate variations in how they exchange information between states to maintain a complete record for their patients who receive care in multiple states, even within that same health system.

There is a compelling and urgent opportunity to engage every state government to create a forum and a process for reconciling variations among states, and between the states and the federal government. Failure to develop a consistent process for managing this challenge will continue to complicate health information exchange. In many cases, these inconsistencies make clinical data exchange incomplete and delayed, leading to higher costs to support effective health information exchange and to provide optimal care.

There are some clear implications for secondary use of data in the context of these legal and regulatory dilemmas for health information exchange. Any information exchanged becomes part of the legal medical record at the recipient institution and must be maintained there to answer any future quality or legal questions about the clinical decisions made based on that information, when viewed retrospectively. As a result of storing the local medical record at the recipient institution, and absent the ability to distinguish which data were generated in that institution rather than acquired from other institutions through health information exchange, it is challenging to exclude those data from secondary uses that have been appropriately approved within the receiving institution. In most cases, the specific permissions authorized or exclusions requested by the patient and obtained by the sending institution do not travel with the data itself, so the receiving institution may not know that certain data is to be treated differently. While it is reasonable to expect that the origin of data elements would be retained in every record, if for no other reason than to verify purported revisions to the data from the originating institutions (e.g., an outside lab updates an inaccurate result), this is not routinely performed. If, in the future, atomic-level metadata are routinely maintained with respect to origin and chain of custody (i.e., atomic-level data provenance), then there will be a practical question about whether authorization for various secondary uses should be included with that metadata. Until such time as those origination metadata are routinely implemented, it may be a cost-prohibitive, and thus impractical, consideration. This is not an academic consideration, because origination metadata have been formally proposed as a key requirement in the President's Council of Advisors on Science and Technology (PCAST) report.[7] Recent advances such as Substitutable Medical Apps, Reusable Technology (SMART) on FHIR[8] provide more standardized and affordable solutions for tight binding of metadata as primary data is propagated to multiple destinations. Blockchain technology adds another dimension to enable individuals to manage the access to their PHI as a secure distributed ledger.

Big Data

Big data has become a buzzword that means different things to different people. For purposes of this discussion, big data refers to the aggregation of large quantities of data from a wide variety of sources (e.g., traditional textual health records, images, input from biomedical devices, and social networking activity). *Big data analytics* refers to many different analytical tools and processes which may be applied to these large aggregations of data.[9]

While *big data* and *big data analytics* have both become very *au courant* buzzwords, there is a nuanced distinction between them in terms of what is really new. The quantity and variety of data maintained in a single logical database have changed dramatically in recent years, but the qualitative changes have been less consequential. In contrast, big data analytics have experienced dramatic advances both quantitatively and qualitatively, including the ability to draw from multiple separate databases for a single analysis.

As mentioned in the section on de-identification, the quantity and array of data being captured and stored digitally are growing at exponential rates. A proliferation of data management tools is helping to normalize disparate data types to facilitate subsequent analysis. Finally, a proliferation of data analytics tools is operating on these exponentially growing quantities and types of data. There is a compound effect of all these developments with respect to privacy and identity management. Collectively, the ability to combine data from multiple sources and use powerful analytics to adjudicate and identify individuals from de-identified data is advancing at an astonishing pace.

Powerful business models from the financial industry, most notably those around identity and credit risk, have motivated vast investments in these technologies and capabilities. The impact of these advances was most poignantly described in a *Forbes* article about the father of a pregnant teenager who complained to Target about the advertisements they were sending, implying that she was pregnant. He subsequently apologized to Target because they had, in fact, correctly deduced from her apparently unrelated purchases that she was pregnant.[10]

The defense and intelligence industries are continuously enhancing these technologies for purposes of detecting and defeating both physical and virtual terrorist threats. Repurposing these tools for re-identification in healthcare is relatively straightforward. The ethical purposes in healthcare around research are quite transparent, but the undesirable uses of this cross-vertical application of big data analytics tools for secondary uses other than ethical research and advancing medical science are worrisome; their commercial value may put individuals at risk. Can and will the data collected for research be adequately protected from subsequent reuse, both accidentally and intentionally?

The capabilities for pursuing those commercially motivated goals are readily available and computationally trivial, so the evolution of big data analytics across vertical markets warrants specific attention in the healthcare vertical. This concern manifests in three ways, each involving "data mash-ups," i.e., aggregations of dissimilar data types or similar data from disparate sources.[11] Mashups have been created by merging data from non-healthcare sources (e.g., social media, food and beverage purchases, etc.) with data from healthcare sources:

1. For commercial healthcare purposes (e.g., determinations of insurability and coverage, or exclusion from either).
2. For commercial non-healthcare purposes (e.g., mass customized sales and marketing initiatives based on healthcare-sourced data, for insurability purposes [life, long-term care, and disability insurance are conspicuously missing from protection under GINA]).
3. To discover aspects of an individual's life that are not apparent from individual sources of data.

With respect to #3 above, these activities illustrate Solove's "harmful activity of aggregation" described in his taxonomy (as referenced in Chapter 1).[12]

> Aggregation is the gathering together of information about a person. A piece of information here or there is not very telling. But when combined together, bits and pieces of data begin to form a portrait of a person. The whole becomes greater than the parts. This occurs because combining information creates synergies. When analyzed, aggregated information can reveal new facts about a person that she did not expect would be known about her when the original, isolated data was collected."[13]

This process is now referred to as "the mosaic effect," as noted above.

Further complicating the inclusion of PHI and the aggregation associated with big data is the emergence of a new genre of unregulated commercial abuse of PHI. Recently, the company EazyDNA[14] began offering paternity testing based on simple oral swabs. This capability could allow individuals to take samples from unsuspecting persons (toothbrushes, dental floss, bandages, etc.) and submit them for genetic testing to resolve questions of paternity. Attempts to outlaw genomic testing without consent is largely a futile exercise, because the samples can be collected illegally and shipped to any of an abundance of offshore sequencing companies that are not subject to U.S. regulations. Hence, we can expect that this "unauthorized secondary use" of our most identifiable personal health information to proliferate despite any policy and regulatory interventions and sanctions. It will then be the frequency of successful policing and the strength of the punishment (whether incarceration, fines, or both) that ultimately determines the level of privacy protection that individuals can expect through the backstop of deterrence mechanisms.

The net effect of the emerging field of big data analytics and the cross-vertical application of these new tools brings greater urgency to advancing policy and legal frameworks to address potential abuses.

We need policy action now.

Genomic Data

A full genomic signature includes 3.2 billion key base pair sequences that identify an individual. Subsets of these signatures will become a regular fixture in every medical record, possibly within the next 5–10 years, and are already clinically invaluable for pharmacogenomics decision support, selection of best anti-cancer therapies, and microbiomic interventions. Since genomic information is inherently self-identifying and essentially resistant to de-identification procedures, the medical community will soon have to rethink the entire notion of de-identification as a credible exercise.[15] The ease of computer re-identification will force us to rely increasingly on policy and legal sanctions (with fines or lawsuits) as deterrents to unauthorized re-identification activities. There will need to be a broader public understanding of the distinction between controls preventing re-identification versus policy and legal sanctions against re-identification. When re-identification can no longer be prohibited by controls alone, policy will need to reflect the need for significant legal sanctions to provide the protection that these controls cannot.

It must also be noted that re-identification can be an incredibly valuable tool in appropriate circumstances. For example, after discovery of a complex combination of genetic attributes that significantly raise the risk of a serious adverse reaction to a common drug, we might want to notify all patients known to carry that complex of genetic attributes. Given the rapid pace of discovery in pharmacogenomics, and the lagging implementation of genomics-based decision support systems, it is likely that this exact scenario will play out repeatedly at an exponentially increasing rate associated with the rise of both genomic knowledge and genomic data in health records. As one simple example, there are many patients today taking cholesterol-lowering statins who are suffering from "subclinical" statin-induced myopathy, who could be notified to switch to a different statin with less risk to them of myopathy, or change drug class, or eliminate drug therapy altogether in favor of alternate methods.

It should be noted that genomics is the sentinel data set for a much larger and growing array of self-identifying personal signatures. In addition to genomics, one can include each of the following observable, individual variations: transcriptomics (regulation of genetic transcription), proteomics (proteins produced from genes), metabolomics (metabolism of proteins and related molecules), microbiomics (microbial colonization), exposomics (environmental exposures and influences), and other "omics," collectively referred to as "multi-omics." For the purposes of this chapter, we will restrict our comments to genomics, with full recognition that parallel issues apply to varying degrees to each of the members of this larger set of multi-omics.

Detailed Argument for the Practical Limitations of De-Identification Resulting from Genomics and Computer-Based Re-Identification

The following sections explore the issue of genomics with respect to secondary use (with parallels to the other "omics") by providing a detailed analysis of relevant base observations and assumptions, and identifying the resulting inferences and implications. The constraints of de-identification associated with the HIPAA definition of de-identification and the policy implications for those limitations are articulated thoroughly by McGraw.[16] This section builds on that *JAMIA* article and extends similar observations and concerns into the imminent world of pervasive multi-omics.

Observations

Observation 1: Current Status of Commercial Clinical Genomics

Several vendors of clinical decision support (CDS) systems (CDSS) now incorporate genomic information to guide both choice of drug and dosing parameters (which may soon become standard practice to guide therapeutic decisions for treating multiple common disease states, including depression, elevated cholesterol, and seizures). These CDS tools can help select the most effective drug therapies while minimizing risks of adverse reactions, whether toxic or idiosyncratic. Some companies are marketing genomic testing and dietary prescriptions based upon interpretation of individual genomic signatures. One example is Pathway Genomics, which focuses on genes responsible for variations in how different types of food are metabolized and processed at the level of an individual person, and then provides specific dietary recommendations based upon those individual genomic findings.[17] Several commercial enterprises have built their entire business models on the interpretation of very comprehensive data sets, including genomics, microbiomics, phenomics and extensive whole-body digital imaging.

Observation 2: Logarithmic Decline in Cost of Genomic Sequencing

The cost of sequencing the human genome, plotted over time, shows a logarithmic decline until very recently. The resumption of that rapid cost decline hinges on either new sequencing technology or cheaper reagents. During this period of relatively stable costs, new market entrants are either reducing the sequencing to targeted subsets or relying on various forms of secondary use for subsidizing the cost of sequencing, overtly reinforcing the core issues elaborated in this chapter.

Observation 3: Valid Genomic Signatures Are Always Self-Identifying

Genomic signatures are the ultimate "self-identifying" data set, and any deliberate attempts to de-identify these data are likely to render them useless at best and dangerously misleading at worst.

Observation 4: Legal Requirements for Providers to Retain Records

There is an enormous body of regulation that requires healthcare providers to maintain individual health records for specified periods of time. Substantial case law motivates providers to retain all information that supports every decision, recommendation, and intervention for each care encounter (whether face-to-face or virtual).

Observation 5: Consumer Rights to Retain a Copy of Their Records

HIPAA has ensured that consumers have the legal right to obtain copies of their own records. This right was extended to digital records with passage of the American Recovery and Reinvestment Act of 2009 (ARRA), under the Health Information Technology for Economic and Clinical Health (HITECH) Act.[18] Current policy, public discourse, and emerging technologies, for example, Blue Button, Open Notes, and FHIR APIs to download EHR data to patient-authorized apps, all increasingly support that right. This right neither conflicts with nor encroaches upon the requirement that providers retain subsets of that record relevant to their delivery of care to that individual. By the time you read this, several PHR offerings are expected, at least one of which is open source, that use blockchain technology to restore the ability of individuals to easily and securely retain access to their personal health information. The blockchain approach gives authority and agency to the individual person who manages those records, for the first time allowing what was previously unachievable, i.e., some direct control by individuals to decide what information to release to which provider under what conditions. This model is increasingly understood and embraced as a game-changing solution set that will disrupt many current models of data ownership and consent. The micro-consent models pioneered by Dixie Baker et al. in the Global Alliance for Genomics & Health (GA4GH) will complement the blockchain technology. The elegant work of John Wilbanks and Stephen Friend at Sagetrust.org has resulted in some archetypal consent profiles that have already proven invaluable for matching qualified researchers with willing research participants who have Parkinson's disease.[19]

Assumptions

Assumption 1: Affordability of Full Genomic Signature for Every Patient

The low cost of full genome sequencing may soon reach a price point at which every patient who consents to genetic testing will have a full genome in their health record. Genetics labs today frequently test for individual gene variations (e.g., markers for a risk of breast cancer or for inherited diseases like Huntington's chorea). Soon, the cost of the full genome will be essentially the same as a few of these single genetic tests, causing the "standard" genetic test to become the full genome, potentially making the market for targeted testing obsolete, unless a high volume of patients choose to authorize only targeted and more limited sequencing. That scenario seems much less likely than the scenario in which full sequencing is performed whenever DNA testing is done. Today, reduced costs and simplified process make it much more likely to get a full electrolyte panel rather than just potassium and creatinine levels. The same process change is likely to occur with DNA testing.

Assumption 2: Ubiquity of Full Genomic Signatures as Part of the Medical Record

The low cost of full genome sequencing and the rising value of that information is likely to result in a full genome being a core part of every medical record (with patient consent to the sequencing procedure). If you believe this to be unlikely, consider the probability of the opposite case: that people will not want a full sequence in their record. The explosion of new genomics knowledge continues to reveal:

- which genetic sequences are associated with higher risks of cancer (and hence the need for more frequent screening),
- the somatic marker screening for those cancers at increased risk or diseases in general when the assay costs decline, and
- which medication is most effective and safe for each disease.

As a result, personalized healthcare increasingly depends upon direct access to the full genome from an easily accessible linked source or directly from within each individual's health record.

Assumption 3: Genomic Signatures as a Prerequisite for Routine Medical Care

As millions of individuals are sequenced at low cost, the science that guides therapy for common diseases like diabetes and hypertension is likely to be increasingly founded on matching pharmacogenomic knowledge with personal genomic signatures (matching affected DNA sequences from research trials to individual patients).

Assumption 4: Necessity of Clinical Access to Full Genomic Signature

As genomic data is increasingly prevalent within health records, the utility of that information will also rise and become essential to guide treatment regimens. In the near future, every individual will benefit from having their genomic sequence in their medical record so that it can inform many medical decisions. Hence, the typical medical record of the future will contain a full genome for that individual and the typical CDSS will include tens of thousands of pharmacogenomics rules. As noted above, research evidence on the necessity of pharmacogenomics to inform direct clinical care is already impressive. Investment in pharmacogenomics research and application has created an abundance of information to guide prescription of the most effective and least toxic medications. However, aside from the utility in cancer and pharmacogenomics, the more pervasive opportunities to exploit genomic information, for example, early detection and monitoring of disease states, remain mostly untapped.

Assumption 5: Current Methods for Modifying Data to Protect Identity

One method to reduce the chance of re-identifying patient data is called "data perturbation." The data perturbation process makes subtle changes to the original data, such as changing a cholesterol result from 160 to 161, to reduce the chance of re-identification while not substantially altering the value of those data for secondary purposes, including clinical research. While these methods are clever and very useful to help protect the identity of individuals today, there is no apparent way to extend that perturbation model to genomic signatures. There are only four letters in the genomic alphabet (A, T, C, and G). Changing them changes their clinical significance, so at our current level of genetic understanding, perturbation is untenable with genetic information. A deliberate shift of a single-base pair in the genetic sequence may have profound implications for both clinical care and research. While we know that some base pair variations, which manifest as Simple Nucleotide Polymorphisms (SNPs), are inconsequential, others are the proximate cause of serious diseases (e.g., thalassemias). A complete understanding of the interaction of all genetic components represented in the 3.2 billion base pairs is, at best, a daunting task, if not impossible for the foreseeable future. We cannot assume that absence of evidence of an effect of a base pair perturbation constitutes evidence of absence. Further, even if we could perturb a known set of "inert" base pairs, the residual, "active" set of base pairs in a genomic signature are more than sufficient to be self-identifying. Hence, data perturbation strategies fail in their primary intent with genomic signatures. Adoption of computational methods to improve privacy, such as homomorphic encryption, may eventually replace perturbation methods and allow comparisons of data without decrypting it.[20,21]

Assumption 6: Community Standard to Use Digital Genomic Signatures

As a consequence of this evolving community standard, the human capacity of any physician to make common prescribing decisions will be increasingly dependent on this intersection of genomic knowledge with individual genomic signatures, and someday it may be considered below the standard of care to make many clinical decisions without access to both CDS and individual genomic signatures (except when prevented by lack of consent or authorization).

Assumption 7: Publishing Genomes of Cohorts for Clinical Research Will Become Routine

Clinical research is increasingly focused on the contributions of genomics to the outcomes of a specific intervention. It is likely that in the future every member of a research cohort will be tested for relevant genomic signatures and that those signatures will be directly relevant to the findings and conclusions of those studies. In those circumstances, disclosure of those underlying genomic signatures may become a standard convention so that (1) each specific conclusion of the study can be supported by the underlying data and genomic evidence, subject to validation by other researchers; and (2) meta-analysis of the data combined with data from other cohorts in other studies is possible. However, we may also create a new conundrum. Privacy policy may have a significant impact on (a) the value of the research if study participants are allowed to redact portions of their genome and (b) on study participation if publication of each study participant's entire genome is required.

Multi-omics will increasingly help to explain why a given intervention for a given disease produces different results in different individuals at different times. This is important to secondary use as research publications become fully digital and intimately associated with huge databases of the underlying multi-omics of the individuals comprising the study cohorts. The multi-omic data in these data sets contain varying levels of self-identifying information that in aggregate pose challenges to the prevention of re-identification. While this is not currently a major issue, it is likely to become a central issue in clinical research in the future. Insurers that sell products for long-term care, disability, and life insurance can legally seek this information to either redline individuals or price individuals out of the market because of these risk profiles. While this problem is not yet prevalent, if we fail to extend GINA beyond discrimination in employment and health insurance to also include long-term care, disability, and life insurance, it is simply a matter of time before market forces leave no alternative to these companies to remain competitive in their product offerings. As a society, we need to decide whether the purpose of insurance is to promote profit or share risk. Do we want the people most in need of insurance protection to be denied participation in the risk pool of the classic insurance model, allowing insurers to cherry-pick only those clients least likely to need services? Failure to prohibit cherry-picking will only guarantee these adverse outcomes.

Assumption 8: Strong Binding of Genomic Signatures to Health Record

The advance of genomic discoveries is on an exponential growth curve and many of these discoveries have direct relevance to medical care. The most prominent example is in knowing which medication is most effective and safest for an individual, (see "Observation 1"). The FDA currently recognizes over 100 pharmacogenomic associations.[22] Advanced CDSS will increasingly incorporate the growth of these genomics-based rules. After a brief pause for some consumer directed genomic entities (like 23andMe), individual consumers may increasingly obtain their genomic signatures. "Standard medical practice" may soon require that the world of genomic-based decision support be applied to each patient with a genomic signature at each encounter, and it may someday be malpractice to not provide that level of care to each patient. At that point, it will be imperative to tightly bind a patient's current clinical record to their genomic signature. The notion that the genomic signature (or, more specifically, the multi-omic signature) will be only occasionally relevant is a transitional artifact in this shifting paradigm. An individual's multi-omic signature may soon become an integral part of the fabric of how care is delivered. When that day comes, the genomic signature will be a critical component of each medical record for clinical, ethical, and legal reasons.

Assumption 9: "Weakest Link" Phenomenon for Computer Re-Identification

Given appropriate access and connectivity, computer re-identification can effectively link individual data sets derived from the same individual, even when those different data sets are distributed across multiple different data stores. If *any* one of those data sets links the de-identified data to demographic identifiers, then that linkage to an individual can be propagated across all data sets of that superset.

Inferences

If one accepts the above set of observations and assumptions, then there are several apparent and inescapable inferences with profound implications that each of us, our organizations, and policy makers should be considering.

Inference 1: Value Proposition for the Individual

When a large number of genomic associations have been definitively identified, it is likely that the individual value proposition, early identification of future risks, will overwhelmingly drive a decision to consent to genomic sequencing and authorize the use of that signature for direct clinical care. There will always be some risk-averse or anxious individuals for whom the full knowledge will be too scary to learn or the risk of disclosure will seem to be too great. Since the adoption curve for social change is consistently sigmoid, whether for adoption of a new technology like the Internet or an iPhone, or a new process like online banking or texting, it is likely that the adoption of widespread genomic testing will follow a similar adoption curve. It will probably follow the increasing depth of genomic understanding and disease association. Early adopters will move quickly, while most people will wait-and-see. Once the wait-and-see majority are satisfied with the stories of individuals who received significant benefit by virtue of their participation, they too will choose to be fully sequenced to support "the standard of care" and will view it as normal then as they do online banking today.

There may be substantial benefit directly to each individual not only to consent to sequencing one's entire genome, but also to authorizing its use for both clinical decisions and scientific research. Research that operates on a cohort that includes every individual's genomic signature is by definition more likely to yield scientific discoveries that will be specifically relevant to that individual. Increasingly, every individual will represent a "cohort of one" or "an N of one" (unless they have an identical twin). As a cohort of one, the broadest dissemination of their genomic signature into research databases will maximize their chances of participating in research targeted at genomic subsets that include them, and that will ultimately yield value in their treatment and maximizing their health outcomes in life. Public education on this point may motivate more people to voluntarily donate their health records for research purposes as long as the research organizations agree to share new knowledge with these individuals in return. For those who decline to do so while living, there should be a convenient option for donation upon death (e.g., with a designation on the driver's license that the driver is a "record donor" upon death). One of the fascinating dilemmas of such donations is that complete donation of a record, including multi-omics and family history, may constitute a disclosure of PHI of the donor's family members and social contacts. There is a need to develop tools that semi-automate a process of redaction to remove multi-omic information that risks exposing personally identifiable information about either genetic linkage or social contacts. This is a dilemma that warrants a rich and thoughtful discussion elsewhere.

Inference 2: Value Proposition for the Healthcare Provider

The value proposition for the provider, better care for their patients and reduced liability, may compel many to seek a complete genome on every patient prior to making many common clinical decisions, recommendations, and interventions. How widely this occurs may depend upon community practices and the fear that some providers express about having large volumes of information for which they are now responsible, but they do not feel that they can practically synthesize with the patient's other, more common data, like blood pressure or allergies, and are thus unsure how to manage. Further, the legal system for defending clinical decisions in court, if subsequently challenged, will encourage many to retain those data used in the context of every decision so that they can be produced in defense of that decision in a court of law. It may become nearly impossible to intelligently restrict the set of data retained that justifies each decision. Most notably, in the near future, a mature CDSS may contain many tens of thousands of genomic-based rules. This adds another layer of complexity to storing the complete genomic signature containing 3.2 billion base pairs. The complex intersection of the rule set extant at that moment with the genomic signature of that individual will render any attempt to identify subcomponents that are "irrelevant or unnecessary" wholly impractical. The implication is that providers will be compelled to retain the full signature both for future care of that patient, as well as for defending past care under legal challenge. The simple question of "What did you know and when did you know it?" becomes a very onerous burden of proof absent a complete retention of those elements in the "legal medical record." This legal question is further complicated by the fact that interpretation of genetic variants is subject to diverse opinion and conflicting evidence, which evolves over time. While numerous definitions of the "legal medical record" exist, the simple functional definition might best be stated as "whatever is potentially relevant and accessible to the provider in delivering the optimal care to that individual at that moment."

Inference 3: Decreasing Effectiveness of De-Identification in the Traditional Sense

If we accept the equation of de-identification with prevention of human re-identification, then nothing has really changed with the advent of ubiquitous genomic signatures, because the human capacity to compare genetic sequences is limited. However, as computer re-identification becomes faster, more accurate, and less expensive every year, and deliberate data perturbation is unacceptable for the genomic signature, then the focus on protecting privacy shifts dramatically to the prevention of computer re-identification because of its extraordinary superiority to human re-identification.

Inference 4: Implications for Policy, Law, and Enforcement

If we accept the above assumptions that:

- A legal medical record must be capable of containing full genomes;
- those genomes are immutably self-identifying; and
- the weakest-link problem will expose any de-identified subset of that record to simple computer re-identification;

then one can infer that a technical strategy to prevent computer re-identification will be extremely difficult, if not effectively impossible to implement. As a consequence, **the full burden of protecting privacy will increasingly fall on policy, law, and enforcement of those laws and policies to detect, deter, and prosecute breaches of re-identification policies**. This represents an inconvenient but compelling truth about the future we are now inescapably entering. There are some substantial efforts around encryption to offset some of these risks, but as with any encryption process, these are not foolproof and are subject to decryption as computer technologies evolve.

Inference 5: Implications for Public Dialogue

If one accepts Inference 3, then there is an urgent need to foster an open discussion about how to address the future of privacy vis-à-vis healthcare in the evolving digital world with rapid advancement in the multi-omic sciences. Unfortunately, the current political climate of polarized views reflects how each camp seizes on one virtue to the exclusion of the other (e.g., privacy vs. quality of care). The philosopher Spinoza focused on how essential it is to consider the trade-offs inherent in reconciling across multiple virtues and values. We desperately need to support a framework for discussion of this topic that reflects a deep understanding of these complexities. This generalized polarization of political discourse is already fully represented in the public discourse around privacy and consumer rights. It represents one of the greatest challenges for our cultural adaptation to the inexorable course of digital healthcare in the era of pervasive genomics, as their respective capabilities clash with the perceptions and realities of their risks.

Policy Considerations

Several key policy considerations support how we revise and extend existing policy and regulations to thoughtfully balance the benefits and risks of secondary use in different contexts of use. Federal policy on secondary use is primarily defined by HIPAA, the Common Rule, and GINA (for genomics) and applies to every state.[23] Federal policy makers should be weighing the individual risks of broad data sharing against the public benefits of research, especially from growing data stores of individual clinical and genomic data. We should not ban access to these data for secondary use outright, such as by requiring specific authorizations for each secondary use, purpose, and event. Instead, we need a multitiered approach to providing reasonable levels of security and de-identification, complemented by detection of and punishment for unauthorized actions. Based on our genomics discussion, de-identification is still useful to prevent human re-identification, but is increasingly obsolete to prevent computer re-identification. The imperative consequence of this evolving reality is that while we continue to focus on securing PHI, we must expand the policy and sanctions associated with unauthorized or prohibited secondary uses. Further, we must support better capabilities for detecting violations and pursue more effective means of deterring these events through the penalties imposed for all detected violations.

The Precision Medicine Initiative creates new challenges even as it creates new opportunities. With the goal of more accurately managing patients as they are, considering who they are (genomically) and where they are (socioeconomically and geographically), there will be even more binding between clinical and nonclinical data. While it seems clear that the research effort undertaken to recruit one million individuals and their genomic data will create new clinical insights, it is less clear how to protect the individuals who provide that data and who may see new risks from these expanding data linkages.

The authors support a balanced approach to privacy policy. We encourage federal policy makers to continuously reassess the individual risk compared to the public benefit and seek to find ways that individual risk can be reduced or otherwise limited. This is especially true as re-identification becomes increasingly trivial. Because federal policy impacts the largest cohort of Americans, one of the authors (Ozeran) suggests that federal policy favor the protection of the individual, yet permit different levels of experimentation at the state level to better discover and characterize the real individual risks and public benefit on a smaller scale.

We have also described the problems associated with the variations in privacy laws between states and the adverse unintended consequences of impeding information exchange even for the primary purpose of direct patient care. Efforts to reconcile and minimize these variations assume increasing importance in support of maintaining longitudinal records for each individual.

Conversely, we support efforts to allow states to experiment with new models of regulation, detection, sanctions, and enforcement, so that we can permit some level of innovation for this very challenging set of issues. At the risk of perpetuating or extending some of the existing state variations, the alternative of consolidating all progress and innovation in this space under a single federal roof would likely result in the higher cost of slower, inflexible, and monolithic solutions that do not foster the appropriate evolution of our capacity to manage these complex issues.

States must also weigh the personal risks against the public benefit, but should be able to try different balance points between a preferential focus on privacy for an individual and the preference of supporting legitimate secondary use that benefits the general population, consistent with the desire of the majority of that state's voters or representatives. Consideration might be given to having automatic reconsideration of these provisions every 2–3 years to ensure that their effectiveness and safety is reassessed periodically, perhaps through a sun-setting process. Given how much change lies ahead in the era of big data and genomics, it is likely that we will sail many uncharted waters in the years and decades ahead. These future opportunities for discovery should compel us to explicitly institutionalize periodic and deliberate review of all major policy in this space. We should create low thresholds for rewriting aspects of this policy and legal framework, so that it can evolve with our better understanding of the values at risk and the impact of evolving technologies and commercial trends on how those values are reflected and/or impacted. We are at a stage of development in a rapidly changing environment that benefits from multiple approaches, but we also need a national process that explicitly and regularly reviews the status of these varied approaches and ensures that best practices are identified by consensus and then propagated.

Organizations must abide by state and federal rules, but can gain access to large data stores of personally identifiable information, both data they have collected and data they have purchased. Organizational governance and process in managing individual privacy can be a divisive topic. Even the authors of this chapter see this issue differently (e.g., around the obligation of organizations to ensure that patients are fully informed about each and every secondary use that is contemplated which is not explicitly covered by a state or federal exemption). As a result, there is an option to either preclude all secondary use without specific re-authorization for each event or deploy a systematic approach to engage patients in understanding the benefits of ethical secondary use that is contemplated but not covered by a state or federal exemption. As a result, once authorized, patient data would be freely available for research use as new research methods and opportunities become available.

EHR vendors offering their products to providers as an application service provider (ASP) or software as a service (SaaS) are collecting large amounts of patient data. One of the largest of these vendors claims over 100,000 providers and millions of patient records. Ensuring that the privacy of these patients is appropriately monitored and maintained must be a priority.

Summary

In this chapter we have covered a very wide path. The key points to consider are:

- Primary use of data is using clinical and related data only for the purpose of treating the patient and promoting the patient's health and wellness.
- Secondary use of data is all other uses, whether beneficial or harmful to the patient or others.

Secondary uses of PHI can benefit the patient and society as a whole, but permission for those uses must be balanced against the attendant risk to privacy of the individuals whose data contributed to those uses.

Secondary uses for other purposes that benefit a small number of individuals should require explicit patient permission.

We must continue efforts to secure PHI to prevent both unauthorized access and unauthorized secondary use. However, security alone is becoming increasingly insufficient. Increasing numbers of legitimate and authorized secondary uses result in more instances of de-identified PHI that can be collated and computer re-identified with increasing ease.

De-identification for human readers of these data is still valid, but computer re-identification of data has become so sophisticated that de-identification is increasingly insufficient to prevent computer re-identification.

Our definition of what constitutes adequate de-identification must be continuously reassessed as computer re-identification becomes increasingly trivial.

We must support further policy development that includes thoughtful consideration of these complex trade-offs between benefits and costs of each specific secondary use.

We must support the creation of better tools to detect unauthorized uses of PHI, associated with appropriate penalties and consistent implementation of those penalties as a credible deterrent to abuse.

We need to widely deploy methods for preserving atomic-level data provenance, pursuant to the PCAST recommendations, so that assignment of culpability for inappropriate exposure of PHI can become practical and enforceable. As this data provenance becomes common, we must explore attaching patient authorization on the atomic level.

We must recognize that the complexity of these issues will continue to rise for many years, as digital commerce and digital health records become more sophisticated and pervasive. As a result, we must institutionalize frequent review and revision processes so that we do not institutionalize specific perspectives that either have unintended consequences or become obsolete as our experience with digital privacy and security issues evolve.

Notes

1. http://www.marketplace.org/2009/07/07/world/eric-schmidt-interview-transcript.
2. http://www.alternet.org/story/155479/
   the_terrifying_ways_google_is_destroying_your_privacy.

3. Revealed: Google AI has access to huge haul of NHS patient data" New Scientist, accessed 12/31/16 https://www.newscientist.com/article/2086454-revealed-google-ai-has-access-to-huge-haul-of-nhs-patient-data/

4. Insurance Dependents Can Face Special Challenges on Privacy. *Kaiser Health News*. 2012. Available at: http://www.kaiserhealthnews.org/Features/Insuring-Your-Health/2012/under-26-insurance-privacy-michelle-andrews-100212.aspx.

5. https://www.whitehouse.gov/sites/default/files/docs/big_data_privacy_report_may_1_2014.pdf page 19.

6. Hill K. How Target Figured Out a Teen Girl Was Pregnant Before Her Father Did. *Forbes*. February 16, 2012. Available at: http://www.forbes.com/sites/kashmirhill/2012/02/16/how-target-figured-out-a-teen-girl-was-pregnant-before-her-father-did/.

7. President's Council of Advisors on Science and Technology. December 2010. Available at: http://www.whitehouse.gov/sites/default/files/microsites/ostp/pcast-health-it-report.pdf.

8. http://smarthealthit.org/smart-on-fhir/.

9. McLeod PS. Aetna, Humana, Kaiser, United Health Put Five Billion Medical Claims into Database for Healthcare Cost, Utilization Research. *Dark Daily*. October 28, 2011. Available at: http://www.darkdaily.com/aetna-humana-kaiser unitedhealth-put-five-billion-medical-claims-into-database-for-healthcare-cost-utilization-research-102811. In what may turn out to be a positive development for clinical laboratories and pathology group practices, four of the nation's five biggest health insurance companies will collaborate and put their medical claims data for billions of transactions into a single database. Researchers say this database will give them an unprecedented ability to assess utilization trends and the clinical care delivered to patients covered by private health insurance.

   The four health insurance companies that will provide data are

   ■ UnitedHealth (NYSE: UNH)
   ■ Kaiser Foundation
   ■ Aetna (NYSE: AET)
   ■ Humana (NYSE:HUM)

   The data provided by each of these health insurers will be submitted to the newly created Health Care Cost Institute (HCCI—www.healthcostinstitute.org) This data will consist of more than five billion medical claims dating back to 2000. These claims represent more than $1 trillion in spending. The health insurers are also providing the financing required to launch HCCI.

10. Hill, op. cit.

11. See: http://en.wikipedia.org/wiki/Mashup_(web_application_hybrid).

12. Solove DJ. A Taxonomy of Privacy. *University of Pennsylvania Law Review*. January 2006; 154(3):477; GWU Law School Public Law Research Paper No. 129. Available at: http://ssrn.com/abstract=667622.

13. Hill, op. cit.

14. See: http://www.easy-dna.com.

15. See: http://www.modernhealthcare.com/article/20110221/BLOGS02/302219938/privacy-and-genses.
16. McGraw D. Building Public Trust in Uses of Health Insurance Portability and Accountability Act De-identified Data. *J Am Med Inform Assoc.* doi:10.1136/amianjl-2012-000936.
17. See: http://www.pathwaygenomics.com and http://en.wikipedia.org/wiki/Pathway_Genomics.
18. http://library.ahima.org/doc?oid=98645.
19. https://www.michaeljfox.org/foundation/publication-detail.html?id=562&category=.
20. https://crypto.stanford.edu/craig/craig-thesis.pdf.
21. https://www.wired.com/2014/11/hacker-lexicon-homomorphic-encryption/
22. http://www.fda.gov/Drugs/ScienceResearch/ResearchAreas/Pharmacogenetics/ucm083378.htm.
23. See: http://www.genome.gov/24519851 and http://en.wikipedia.org/wiki/Genetic_ Information_Nondiscrimination_Act.

Chapter 9

The Past, Present, and Future of Healthcare Privacy

By Kimberly S. Gray, Esq., CIPP/US

Contents

Absent the gift of psychic awareness, it's hard for anyone to accurately predict the future, even with the benefits of knowledge, education, and intuition.

Nonetheless, this chapter will take a look backward to the development of healthcare privacy law, a look at where privacy is in the healthcare field today (and how the healthcare industry itself has changed), and a stab at figuring out where healthcare privacy may land in the future.

The Globalization of Privacy

Just a few short years ago, more than 50 of the world's data protection authorities (those who are in roles of privacy ombudsmen or data protection regulators, and who generally oversee privacy protections for their various countries) who were meeting in Madrid at the 31st International Conference of Data Protection and Privacy Commissioners agreed to the "Madrid Resolution" on international privacy standards. The Madrid Resolution states that the right to privacy is a fundamental value in society and that development of communication and information systems must be controlled in order to prevent uses of personal data that threaten this right. It brought together the various approaches, from across the globe, for protecting privacy; it respects both different national traditions and the need for a common standard. The Madrid Resolution was also supported by 10 large multinational companies (e.g., Procter & Gamble, Microsoft, Google, General Electric, IBM, and others).[1] It was seen as the basis for a future universally binding agreement on a consistent set of privacy principles.

While many privacy professionals and others dismissed the Madrid Resolution as merely pie-in-the-sky yearning for data protection consistency, we have witnessed a continuation of the collegiality between and among data protection authorities and regulators worldwide, and collaboration and support for one another while drafting regulations and enforcing laws. It's no longer unusual to see U.S. regulators attend Data Protection Authority conferences abroad, and it is no longer unusual to see regulators from Canada, Europe and elsewhere in attendance at U.S. regulatory roundtables.

The past few years also have seen a broader range of countries enter the data privacy world. We are seeing more and more countries develop data protection legal models where none existed (e.g., Turkey, Singapore, Peru, Columbia, South Africa, and others). In developing their new data protection models, many countries have taken the EU data protection model[2] as the basis for creating their own data protection regimes (with the EU itself revising its overall approach in the General Data Protection Regulation [GDPR], being implemented between now and 2018).[3] These new laws and regulations are robust, focusing on addressing increasing risks and increasing use of personal data. While many of these laws apply across the board to personal information, most also create special categories of "sensitive" information that typically include healthcare information.

At the same time, we also have seen new international tensions. When the European Court of Justice struck down the EU–U.S. Safe Harbor Agreement (a data transfer mechanism for personal data moving between the EU and the United States),[4] after more than a decade of relatively uncontroversial transfers, the decision sent shockwaves through the data protection area, affecting companies in virtually all industries. While the EU and U.S. governments continue to struggle with developing an appropriate data transfer mechanism (settling recently on the "Privacy Shield" program as a replacement to Safe Harbor),[5] we have seen increased focus on a different kind of "consistent" approach, through the broadening scope of Binding Corporate Rules (BCRs) as a means for appropriate data transfer (with the parallel development of principles for Cross-Border Privacy Rules [CBPR] in Asia).

While the legal structure has not yet developed appropriate consistency across the world, there is also an increased recognition that personal data moves on a global basis, and that there is a need to facilitate these transfers for a wide range of appropriate purposes. We have seen a more concentrated focus on certain key principles of privacy protection in most areas—including accountability, individual engagement, industry codes of conduct and reasonable but appropriate enforcement. These developments coincide with an increased recognition that some advancing technologies (e.g., cloud computing—delivering hosted services over the Internet as opposed to using company servers at a particular physical location) have removed geographic borders and have allowed data to flow quickly around the world. There is an increased recognition of the benefits of data research and overall de-identification of personal data on a global basis as a means of facilitating important public benefits. At the same time, nonetheless, regulations exist globally that are related to these geographic borders and the data that would pass through them. Addressing cross-border transfers of personal information in these new technological scenarios will also push regulators globally to work together to find common ground.

Will we ever see the Madrid Resolution and its progeny be put into practice? Is it possible to have a global privacy regime that is based on a common set of information practice principles? Obviously, there is no clear answer, but, at the same time, we are seeing increased efforts to create a similar overall approach to data protection, reflecting a combination of laws, regulations, industry codes of conduct, best practices and other common themes for creating an appropriate data protection environment.

With so many countries already embracing principles that are very similar, it's likely that a global data protection and privacy regime could be put into place at the principles level. For this to work in practice, however, implementation would need to be flexible and enforcement (through compliance monitoring) would have to be as consistent as possible, while allowing for obvious country differences.

The global trend toward basing data protection and privacy on information practice principles models that are relatively consistent will likely encourage (or coerce) the United States into moving toward a more comprehensive regime. This could take the form of more regulation in industry sectors that aren't now regulated in the way that healthcare and financial services are (e.g., retail) or it could take the form of a sector-agnostic, across-the-board regime (perhaps with carve-outs for those sectors that already have privacy regulatory frameworks).

If the United States wishes to continue to engage in global commerce as a world leader, it may need to broaden its viewpoint as to appropriate privacy and data protection management. There is a reasonable debate as to whether the overall mix of privacy and data security laws in the United States provides more or less protection than more straightforward approaches in other countries. However, as new data protection laws are enacted in countries that didn't have them in the past, they are tending to model the EU framework that dictates primarily a "one size fits all data" approach. The United States does not today have any such generally applicable privacy law—and may need to consider one in the future, both for purposes of global consistency and to reflect some realities (as discussed below) about the changing nature of personal data and the difficulties in defining categories of data and specific industry sectors.[6]

If this more comprehensive regime requires laws, rules, or regulations (beyond accountability) in order to comply with a global architecture, there is an excellent model for a more comprehensive U.S. regime. The financial and healthcare industries may have complained bitterly when the Gramm-Leach-Bliley Act and the Health Insurance Portability and Accountability Act of 1996 (HIPAA) came along, but they probably would now agree that the data their industries handle is well protected, that overall compliance, while not at all easy, has been manageable, and that the industries can display their practices as models for both an accountability and legal framework.

The Healthcare Industry

While the world of privacy changes regularly, the healthcare industry is changing equally as fast. In the United States, over the past decade, we have seen an enormous variety of new healthcare programs overseen by the federal government, including the implementation of the Medicare prescription drug program, substantial changes to the Medicare Advantage program (Medicare managed care), expansion of Medicaid managed care and, of course, the creation and implementation of the Affordable Care Act, providing a broader range of health insurance options for a variety of individuals who previously were provided with few or no choices.

In addition, we are seeing new goals for the healthcare system related to transparency and patient engagement. There is increasing recognition that providing the means for individuals to become more directly engaged in their own healthcare provides important benefits for both those individuals and for the system at large. Wellness programs provide incentives and guidance on improving individual health. "Wearables" are providing means for individuals to track their own health status, focusing on particular controllable events. Mobile applications provide an enormous range of health data opportunities. Personal health records provide a means to collect and store important health information. And, at the same time, the federal government and others are seeking important new means of making healthcare data available on a far broader level for research and public health purposes, while still providing appropriate protections for personal privacy.

There also is a broader recognition for the need for healthcare data to be shared across a broader range of audiences, consistent with appropriate privacy and security protections, to both improve health and make the overall healthcare system more effective and efficient. Data sharing is a goal of this system, consistent with appropriate privacy practices. Healthcare data is needed beyond the traditional (and now somewhat old-fashioned) doctor–patient relationship. There are the readily apparent viewers, such as health insurers, pharmacies, nursing homes, etc., and then there are the not-so-readily apparent viewers: life and casualty insurers;

gyms and spas; schools (vaccination records, medications, etc.); state government (e.g., driver's licensing departments, Medicaid program, vital statistics department); federal government (e.g., Medicare program); medical transcription organizations; healthcare equipment monitoring companies; employers; and so on. These entities often have reasonable needs for healthcare information—for the benefit of both patients and others—and consistent and appropriate practices are being designed to make this data sharing work.

The Role of the Patient in Data Sharing

Patient engagement clearly is an important and useful goal of the healthcare system. More engaged patients typically have better health, to the benefit of themselves and the system as a whole. At a broad level, then, patients need to participate in their own healthcare and in how their healthcare data is used. It makes perfect sense for patients to be partners with their healthcare providers by learning from their practitioner and by engaging in joint decision-making about their health with their practitioner. But at some point, it also makes sense for the patient to appreciate the suggestions of their practitioner and to yield some authority to the practitioner. At some point the patient must trust the surgeon to perform the surgery appropriately.

Likewise, at some point the patient must trust the data steward who is holding his or her data. It is unrealistic to expect patients to go through a consent exercise each time their data may be shared. Not only would it be difficult for the data handlers to oversee such a consent process, but it would be burdensome on the patients themselves. As patients, we must at some point rely upon others to take good care of our data. We must entrust others with our information, and we must entrust others—at some points—to make decisions about our data.

This takes us back to our discussions concerning accountability. Trust is necessary, but this trust can be enhanced by visible and appropriate practices and standards. Organizations that handle this patient information and are making decisions concerning it must be accountable in order to maintain patient trust. One should engage the patient early on and allow his or her participation as a fully informed partner, and then maintain the patient's trust by using good data protection practices.

There clearly is a long way to go in educating patients. Over the past few years, QuintilesIMS (a global healthcare data analytics company) has conducted surveys of U.S. voters to gauge consumer understanding of and support for various healthcare propositions. In each of several years, voters have shown surprisingly little knowledge about the healthcare industry and healthcare system generally.

At the same time, it also is critical for patients to understand the role that their personal information can play in important advances for the healthcare industry and society in general. However, without trust, patients may seek to shut down the sharing of their data. As also noted earlier, without the sharing of data, healthcare policies that would improve care for all and that would address current problems with the system (such as disparities in care for certain sectors of the population) will be stymied.

It would therefore behoove all of us to ensure we are better-educated healthcare consumers. With education and knowledge can come trust that will allow the use of healthcare data to benefit individuals and to benefit society.

In the future, look for more educational campaigns by both government and industry to ensure that our patients are making truly informed choices as to their healthcare information.

Consistent Information Privacy Principles

While we do not yet have consistent laws and regulations across countries or even across industries, there is an increasing recognition of the core set of principles that should govern the use and disclosure of personal information. A short review of the various principles that guide privacy and data protection around the world will produce more similarities than differences. One need only look at the United States (U.S.) Health Education and Welfare (HEW) Fair Information Principles (1973), Organisation for Economic Co-Operation and Development (OECD) guidelines (1980), the European Union Directive 95/46/EC (1995), the HIPAA privacy principles, Federal Trade Commission (FTC) Fair Information Practice Principles (1998), the Department of Health and Human Services (HHS) *Nationwide Privacy and Security Framework For Electronic Exchange of Individually Identifiable Health Information,*[7] and others to see commonalities.

Common to many regimes are principles of notice/awareness, choice/consent, access/participation, integrity/security, data minimization, and enforcement/redress. While these principles are put into effect in most laws and regulations, there also is an increasing debate about the relative importance of these principles. For example, in many situations, there is a concern about the realistic value of privacy notices, particularly in online or mobile settings where there may be little feasible means of reviewing detailed privacy notices. Privacy regulators and lawmakers continue to review how best to implement these principles, providing choices where appropriate but also providing the means for effective privacy controls that are implemented automatically, without the need for individuals to make specific choices to restrict the uses of their data.

As more and more countries and companies begin working together in a global economy, it only makes sense that they will seek out a data protection system that is interoperable and that allows the free flow of data while protecting privacy. To the extent that there is agreement as to what privacy means, protecting privacy by applying similar principles of confidentiality and data protection will ease the transfer of data and will improve transparency around what happens during the data life cycle.

In the future, we will likely see more seamlessness between principles-based data protection regimes. While there clearly will be country differences, there will be increasing similarities. The same principles applied to other data will be applied to health data (as many already are).

Industry Codes of Conduct/Practice

Lately we have been witnessing a sharp uptick in the development of industry codes of practice or industry codes of conduct (Codes) that set a consistent bar for data handling, extending beyond specific laws and which apply across geographic borders. These Codes primarily seem to be addressing real or perceived needs for better data-handling practices and better customer relations. They are also key factors in instilling a viable self-regulatory scheme that presumes accountability and leadership.

Codes are typically outcomes based. They don't tend to address how one gets from Point A to Point B to protect privacy, but they address the end result. For example, a Code might state that a company should have a data classification scheme for protecting sensitive data, but it would allow the company flexibility in determining the sensitivity levels of its data and how the different levels would best be protected. The effectiveness of this privacy protection might then measured by having a third-party review (and possibly certify) its data classification scheme.

Because the development of (and revisions to) Codes are driven by their members, there are usually comparisons of data-handling procedures of member organizations (a form of benchmarking or norm determination), which then leads to the development of best practices. As practices change over time, Codes are modified to reflect these changes in a form of continuous process improvement.

Most industry Codes drive self-policing. Companies have an incentive to abide by Codes to avoid public embarrassment and brand damage, and without the need for laws, rules, and regulations. Although laws, rules, and regulations may be necessary for dealing with malfeasance, they often aren't well suited to changing norms/best practices and changing technologies.

Additionally, as Codes become embraced more by various industry sectors, including healthcare, those adopting them will be well situated in the event of the enactment of new laws, rules, and regulations—and if the Codes are robust and well followed, the need for new laws, rules, and regulations may be minimized or erased.

Nonetheless, existing laws, rules, and regulations may still be used to ensure compliance with Codes. For example, in the United States, the FTC has indicated, in its report, "Protecting Consumer Privacy in an Era of Rapid Change,"[8] that it would support the efforts of the U.S. Department of Commerce to facilitate sector-specific codes of conduct. The FTC went on to indicate that these self-regulatory codes will be enforceable; the FTC will enforce the FTC Act against those companies that fail to abide by the self-regulatory codes that they join, using the unfair or deceptive practices rationale.

Look for the adoption of industry Codes to increase in the future, including adoption of healthcare codes of conduct that will have relevance globally as more and more healthcare companies operate worldwide. We also may see a broader use of company implementation of appropriate codes of conduct as part of a more enforceable set of privacy commitments, through the continued expansion (as a global data transfer device) of standards such as Binding Corporate Rules (BCRs) in the EU and CBPR in Asia.

Accountability

The accountability movement has been gaining momentum globally for several years. Accountability is becoming *de rigeur* in the handling of personal information, from both the perspective of those handling the data and the regulators. It is taking shape through many means, including:

- Performing Privacy Impact Assessments (business tools that support data governance activities related to the collection, use and storage of data; these address the privacy impact of any substantially revised or new information).
- Adopting and implementing Privacy by Design (privacy is proactively embedded into the design and architecture of IT systems and business practices as a default, throughout the data life cycle and in a transparent manner).
- Obtaining and implementing Binding Corporate Rules (a strict, intra-corporate global privacy policy that offers a means of complying with the EU Directive to legalize certain transfers of personal information; Binding Corporate Rules must be approved by the Data Protection Authority of the relevant EU member states before being implemented).
- Laws, rules and regulations have limited utility in privacy and data protection when technology and social media's explosive impact and availability of data are advancing so rapidly. It makes much more sense for organizations to be accountable and to practice good, safe data-handling practices that are transparent to the data subjects. It's about doing the right thing, and wise organizations can see the potential as a market differentiator.

Enforcement

Whereas in the EU and many other areas around the world, privacy is driven through principles, today in the United States it tends to be handled primarily through procedural requirements in theory, and often enforcement mechanisms in practicality. As privacy and data protection principles reach more common ground globally in the future, expect that privacy and data protection enforcement will also embrace more common ground.

Turning solely to the United States for a moment, however, we will take a quick peek into the crystal ball at the enforcement landscape for healthcare in the future.

In the U.S. healthcare sector, the HHS Office for Civil Rights (OCR) has regulatory enforcement oversight for those organizations and persons handling protected health information (PHI) as that term is defined under HIPAA. OCR initially only had enforcement authority over "covered entities"—healthcare providers, health plans, and clearinghouses. In recent years, following the passage of the Health Information Technology for Economic and Clinical Health (HITECH) Act, it also now has enforcement jurisdiction over "business associates"—service providers to those covered entities. OCR's overall approach to enforcement reflected some of the policy tensions in privacy regulation, particularly for the healthcare industry. OCR was concerned—when the HIPAA rules first went into effect—that healthcare providers and others would be nervous about sharing health information even in appropriate and beneficial situations, and therefore implemented an approach that was designed to educate, support, guide, and revise privacy-related activities rather than taking aggressive enforcement action. Because it was open and forthcoming about this approach, the healthcare industry quickly adapted to the HIPAA structure, and, in most situations, information that needed to be shared was shared.

Fast-forward a few years, to our current environment. HIPAA enforcement has increased, although not substantially. Most of the published enforcement actions have related to security problems, more than specific provisions of the privacy rules. Common themes for enforcement involve failures to conduct appropriate overall risk assessments and security problems related to mobile devices and other online activity. Now that the HIPAA breach notification rule (another HITECH Act innovation) is in full effect, reports of large security breaches have become a primary source of investigative leads for OCR in its enforcement activities. While many reported breaches do not end up leading to enforcement activity, these breaches trigger investigations that are guiding the overall OCR approach to enforcement. We can expect enforcement to continue to increase, although this increase likely will continue to be gradual.

The OCR approach to enforcement against business associates also will be important to watch. Business associates cover a wide range of entities—including one-person consulting firms and some of the biggest business firms in the world, along with everything in between. Beyond mere size, some business associates play a prominent role in the healthcare industry, while others may serve only one or two healthcare clients as part of a much broader kind of business activity (think an accounting or consulting firm that has clients in every industry with a modest portfolio in healthcare). In addition, some business associates are heavily involved in the use and disclosure of health information, while others may play a much more tangential role in any identifiable personal data. We will be watching how OCR draws these lines in enforcement activities down the road. While the overall enforcement approach still reflects a good understanding of reasonable efforts and an understanding of when companies are trying hard to get things right, we can expect to see ongoing pressure to engage in enforcement in appropriate settings.

Big Data and the Impact on Healthcare

The big data revolution affects every industry, but few can gain more from better uses of data than the healthcare industry.

Big data highlights some of the information opportunities for healthcare. Big data provides more opportunities to analyze a wider variety of data, and to make connections based on facts that never before were possible. In the United States, for example, the White House—led Precision Medicine Initiative is trying to harness the power of big data as a means of successfully creating individualized approaches to medicine through creation of a massive database of more than 1 million patients.

Big data also highlights how "non-healthcare data" can be used for many healthcare purposes. We are seeing in big data how information not typically thought of as "health" information can be used for healthcare purposes. We've seen recent news stories discussing how:

- "You may soon get a call from your doctor if you've let your gym membership lapse, made a habit of picking up candy bars at the check-out counter or begin shopping at plus-sized stores."[9]
- Health plan prediction models using consumer data from data brokers (e.g., income, marital status, number of cars), to predict emergency room use and urgent care.[10]
- Healthcare analytics companies can mine workers' medical claims, pharmacy claims, and search queries to figure out if an employee is trying to conceive or is already pregnant.[11]
- Employee wellness firms and insurers are working with companies to mine data about the prescription drugs workers use, how they shop and even whether they vote, to predict their individual health needs and recommend treatments.[12]

These big data projects show both opportunity and potential for concern related to the healthcare industry and how it uses big data. The recent White House Report on Big Data[13] indicated that:

- A significant finding of this report is that big data analytics have the potential to eclipse longstanding civil rights protections in how personal information is used in housing, credit, employment, health, education, and the marketplace.
- The privacy frameworks that currently cover information now used in healthcare may not be well suited to address these developments or facilitate the research that drives them.

At the same time, the report also noted that "Modernizing the health care data privacy framework will require careful negotiation between the many parties involved in delivering health care and insurance to Americans, but the potential economic and health benefits make it well worth the effort."

Big data also highlights how much new "non-HIPAA" healthcare data is being collected by websites and other new technologies that gather and distribute healthcare information without the involvement of a covered entity, including a broad range of commercial and patient support websites, personal health records, mobile applications, and wearables. Many of these new technologies—which can provide important benefits to both patients and the healthcare system—are outside the scope of HIPAA and potentially outside the scope of any current regulation. As former FTC Commissioner Julie Brill has noted,

> Then the question becomes, though, if we do have a law that protects health information but only in certain contexts, and then the same type of information or something very close to it is flowing outside of those silos that were created a long time ago, what does that mean? Are we comfortable with it? And should we be breaking down the legal silos to better protect that same health information when it is generated elsewhere.[14]

These developments highlight the current gap in the legal structure for protecting healthcare privacy, based on the language and history of the HIPAA law itself, which focused on the "portability" of health insurance coverage and "administrative simplification" involving standardized transactions for certain core healthcare transactions (such as submission of a claim), rather than any specific principles about privacy.

For those organizations handling healthcare data outside of HIPAA's reach, the FTC will attempt to fill in some of the enforcement gaps, but its ability to regulate data practices is limited by its current statutory authority to regulate only "unfair and deceptive" trade practices. Moreover, any efforts by the FTC to develop enforcement approaches for "non-HIPAA" healthcare data may lead to (1) continuing differentiation in healthcare data based on the originating source of the data (HIPAA rules for healthcare providers and health plans, some other principle for other entities). In addition, the current sectoral approach to privacy also creates real concerns as "big data" and increasingly sophisticated data analytics tools also lead to innovative uses of "non-healthcare data" (e.g., income levels, marital status, number of cars) as means of predicting health-related behavior.

All of these developments point in the same direction—more and more information is being gathered about the health of individuals and other data that may lead to judgments about the health of these individuals (and the broader possibility of more societal learning about health), and there is an increasingly complicated array of laws and practices that may provide better or worse protection for this information, depending on who is gathering and holding it. Under the current approach, particularly under U.S. law, there will continue to be differences in principle and practice based on these regulatory and legal quirks. We can expect to see continuing pressure—from a variety of interested audiences—to "fix" this existing problem and fill these regulatory gaps, but there currently is no consensus whatsoever on how best to do this.

Use of De-Identified Information

An essential goal of data protection is to prevent physical, financial, and social harm to individuals and society as a result of inaccurate, incomplete, lost, stolen, or otherwise compromised personal information. It is prudent to attempt to prevent harm from occurring by taking reasonable steps to protect personal information, bearing in mind the sensitivity of the data, the likelihood that its compromise could result in harm, and the significance and severity of any resulting harm. Because properly protected de-identified information is not linked to a particular individual, de-identification supports this objective. Risk of harm is greatly reduced when information has been stripped of identifiers.

Therefore, one potential solution to one of the key challenges in the healthcare system is to take advantage of improved "de-identification" techniques. The goal of de-identification is to remove individual identifiers in a way that protects individual privacy interests while still permitting data to be utilized for a broad variety of public and private purposes, including public health, research, and benchmarking.

Companies involved in the "Big Data" process will want to pay close attention to both the regulatory developments and the related technological innovations connected to de-identification, as appropriate de-identification remains an important element in the overall goal of benefiting from data without creating undue privacy risks. Because of the volume of data generated by many companies, and the public and private opportunities that can arise from appropriate use of this data, smart de-identification has become a critical component of most companies' overall data strategy.

At the same time, our legal structure is still evolving in connection with de-identification standards. On a broad basis, it is clear that:

- There is a broad recognition of the public and private benefits of using de-identified data.
- There are varying legal frameworks, all pointing toward appropriate means of reducing privacy risks while maintaining value of data.
- Because of the broad and global flow of information, there is a need for harmonization and consistency across legal regimes and types of data.

When the HHS was considering the HIPAA Privacy Rule, HHS saw the need for an overall balance between privacy interests and the overall operation of the healthcare system. The overall "use and disclosure" principles of HIPAA reflect this balance. The de-identification principles reflect another component of this balance—the protection of privacy interests through appropriate de-identification while still permitting uses and disclosures of data that benefit patients and the healthcare system. De-identification is a vital tool and means to engage in privacy protective data stewardship when conducting data analytics that are fundamental to improving patient care.

The HIPAA Privacy Rule creates the most robust de-identification standard that currently exists in law—and is often called the "gold standard" for de-identification. Under HIPAA, individually identifiable health information (known as "PHI") has restrictions on its access, use and disclosure. However, if the identifiers are removed consistent with appropriate procedures, PHI is no longer subject to the regulation because it is no longer "individually identifiable." According to HHS, the "Privacy Rule permits a covered entity to de-identify protected health information so that such information may be used and disclosed freely, without being subject to the Privacy Rule's protections. Health information is de-identified, or not individually identifiable, under the Privacy Rule if it does not identify an individual and if the covered entity has no reasonable basis to believe that the information can be used to identify an individual.[15]

This regulatory standard does not mean that there is 0% risk of re-identification (virtually nothing that we do in life carries with it no risk). Instead, the regulation sets the threshold at that of a very low risk. In drafting the regulation, HHS recognized that "perfect" de-identification would result in little usable data with only small privacy benefits. In fact, when evaluating the alternative, release of only anonymous information (i.e., zero risk approaches vs. very small risk approaches), HHS officials made clear that a "stronger" de-identification standard would provide no more than a marginal boost in privacy protections with the much higher costs of reducing beneficial uses and disclosures of this de-identified information. Further, any "zero risk" standard precluded many laudable and valuable uses of data and would impose too great a burden on less sophisticated covered entities to be justified by the small decrease in an already small risk of re-identification.

Specifically, in proposing the de-identification sections of the Privacy Rule, HHS stated that "We agree with the comments that said that records of information about individuals cannot be truly de-identified, if that means that the probability of attribution to an individual must be absolutely zero. However, the statutory standard does not allow us to take such a position, but envisions a reasonable balance between risk of identification and usefulness of the information."[16]

Beneficial Uses of De-Identified Data

The HIPAA Privacy Rule anticipates the beneficial uses of de-identified data to advance healthcare in such forms as expanding medical research and improving public health. Healthcare data that has been properly de-identified can be used for such purposes as:

- Quality improvement and outcomes research analysis
- Treatment protocol improvements and new therapies
- Reduction of medical errors and improved patient safety
- Healthcare cost management
- Provider quality transparency to patients
- Early disease outbreak detection and geographic tendencies
- Bio-surveillance and homeland security
- Healthcare fraud monitoring and control

- Reduction in disparities of care
- Public health improvement through disease tracking
- Addressing orphan disease and developing orphan drugs

More recently, in issuing guidance on these de-identification provisions, HHS stated that "The increasing adoption of health information technologies in the United States accelerates their potential to facilitate beneficial studies that combine large, complex data sets from multiple sources. The process of de-identification, by which identifiers are removed from the health information, mitigates privacy risks to individuals and thereby supports the secondary use of data for comparative effectiveness studies, policy assessment, life sciences research, and other endeavors."[17] By meeting these secondary purposes through the use of de-identified data, the healthcare system reduces the flow of individually identifiable data and resultant risks of data compromise.

De-Identification Process (HIPAA)

There are two means by which one can de-identify data under HIPAA. The first is by removing the 18 identifiers noted in the HIPAA Privacy Rule.[18] Many healthcare organizations only have familiarity with this first method, and have therefore not embraced de-identification. There is concern that with this "safe harbor" method of de-identifying, most (and maybe all) data utility is gone.

The second method, however, offers the best of both worlds—data utility and privacy protections. Under the "expert determination" method of HIPAA (set out at 45 C.F.R. § 164.514[b]), an entity subject to the HIPAA rules may determine that health information is not individually identifiable health information only if:

A person with appropriate knowledge of and experience with generally accepted statistical and scientific principles and methods for rendering information not individually identifiable;

i. Applying such principles and methods determines that the risk is very small that the information could be used, alone or in combination with other reasonably available information, by an anticipated recipient to identify an individual who is a subject of the information; and

ii. Documents the methods and results of the analysis that justify such determination.

This process (1) relies on appropriate experts; (2) adjusts with changes in technology and the evolution of available data; and (3) permits a context-based evaluation that allows consideration of contractual and security controls along with other elements, to provide a reasonable basis for a de-identification conclusion.

The FTC applies a similar approach in its own evaluations on this topic. In its March 2012 report entitled "Protecting Consumer Privacy in an Era of Rapid Change: Recommendations for Businesses and Policymakers,"[19] the FTC states that personal data has been de-identified when an entity de-identifying the data can meet a three-part test. This test involves the following steps:

- the company must take reasonable measures to ensure that the data is de-identified. This means that the company must achieve a reasonable level of justified confidence that the data cannot reasonably be used to infer information about, or otherwise be linked to, a particular consumer, computer, or other device;
- a company must publicly commit to maintain and use the data in a de-identified fashion, and not to attempt to re-identify the data. Thus, if a company does take steps to re-identify such data, its conduct could be actionable under Section 5 of the FTC Act; and
- if a company makes such de-identified data available to other companies—whether service providers or other third parties—it should contractually prohibit such entities from attempting to re-identify the data.

Although the HIPAA de-identification framework is not the only de-identification approach that is available (in the United States and elsewhere), it provides a useful model for analysis and discussion because it is more detailed and comprehensive than other applicable approaches. It is the gold standard for de-identification and adapts well to changing data sources and changing technology; in fact, the HIPAA framework incorporates technological change as a component of its overall analysis. It strives to balance the need to protect individuals' identities with the need to allow de-identified databases to be useful.

While much has changed in the healthcare landscape since HIPAA's inception, including greater availability and use of data, concerns about the sufficiency of the HIPAA de-identification methodologies are largely unfounded. HIPAA de-identification methodologies are holistic, risk-based, and readily adaptable to changes in the healthcare environment.

Practical De-Identification

To meet the overall standard set forth in the HIPAA Privacy Rule (particularly using the "expert determination" method), effective de-identification is a combination of removing, generalizing, and disguising patient identifiers, imposing privacy and security safeguards (i.e., administrative, technical, and physical safeguards, including contractual limitations), and a mindfulness as to the value of research data and appropriate protection of privacy.

This means that any entity pursuing de-identification—whether using the HIPAA standard or otherwise—should follow certain key steps:

- First, re-identification risk thresholds should be determined, considering the context of the data, data recipients, potential re-identification attacks and controls. If the measured risk is below the threshold, then the data will be considered to be de-identified.
- Next, there must be a way to objectively measure the risk of re-identification in a repeatable and objective manner; therefore, metrics must be defined that are consistent with the kinds of threats that could be directed against the data (including deliberate attempts to re-identify or other external hacks against the data) that have been identified and the nature of the data.
- Then, direct identifiers are removed, and indirect identifiers are evaluated (and possibly removed); special attention should be paid to dates and geo-locators.
- The methodology must also consider potential adversaries' interest in re-identifying the data.
- At this point the organization will transform the data to de-identify it (e.g., via suppression, pseudonymization, generalization, perturbation, substitution, elimination of small cell counts, k-anonymity, etc.).
- Lastly, auditable controls to manage residual risk must be put in place, and data utility must be considered.

An Overall Approach to De-Identification: The HITRUST Framework

In order to provide entities both in and out of the HIPAA regime with appropriate guidance on de-identification, the Health Information Trust Alliance (HITRUST) undertook an exercise to develop standards and controls that provide guidance on how to determine when data is de-identified and how to protect it once it is in that form. The HITRUST De-Identification Framework was developed to offer a solution to the challenges facing the healthcare community regarding de-identification. Developed in collaboration with healthcare, information security, and de-identification professionals, the HITRUST De-Identification Framework provides a consistent, managed methodology for the de-identification of data and the sharing of compliance and risk information among entities and their key stakeholders.

For its key elements, the HITRUST De-Identification Framework

- provides an overall, integrated approach to de-identification;
- incorporates a broad range of existing legal frameworks;
- provides guidance on the development of repeatable and consistent best practices for de-identification; and
- identifies and evaluates additional means of protection for de-identified data.

After a review of multiple de-identification programs and methods, including those propounded by agencies in the United States, Canada, and the United Kingdom, the HITRUST De-Identification Working Group (DIWG) believed that no one method is appropriate for all organizations. Instead, the DIWG has identified 12 criteria for a successful de-identification program and methodology that can be scaled for use with any organization. These 12 characteristics are further divided into two general areas:

- The first set of characteristics represents those for the program and the administrative controls that an organization should have in place to govern de-identification.
- The second set represents how the organization can actually arrive at a de-identified data set, either on an ad hoc basis or by instituting a process that will deliver de-identified data sets.

Therefore, for any entity pursuing an appropriate de-identification program, it is critical to ensure that the program meets the following elements:

Program Components

- Overall Governance
- Documentation

- Explicit Identification of the Data Custodian and Recipients
- External or Independent Scrutiny

De-Identification Methodology

- Re-Identification Risk Thresholds
- Measurement of Actual Re-Identification Risks
- Identification and Management of Direct Identifiers and Quasi-Identifiers
- Identification of Plausible Adversaries and Attacks
- Identification of Specific Data Transformation Methods and How They Reduce the Risks
- Process and Template for the Implementation of Re-Identification Risk Assessment and De-Identification
- Mitigating Controls to Manage Residual Risk
- Data Utility

Protecting De-Identified Data

Even beyond these "programmatic" elements, there also are critically important protections that can be put into place to ensure both that de-identified information is useful and that any resulting risks of re-identification remain law. A means of ensuring that this risk of re-identification remains low is to put data protections in place that are similar to those used for fully identifiable data. Using administrative, technical and physical safeguards to protect even de-identified information is prudent. This helps ensure that the risk of re-identification will remain very low—even if these protections are not formally required by law. It's just good practice, for any business.

It's also a good idea to ensure contractually that others receiving the de-identified data also treat it with due care. Information security protections similar to that of the original data source should be passed along as requirements for any downstream recipient of the data. Also included in the contract terms should be a prohibition against any attempts to re-identify the data. There are legislative proposals and regulatory provisions that may require these contractual prohibitions in some circumstances—and even the possibility of future law prohibiting re-identification—but businesses should implement these protections wherever possible.

Another best practice for an entity disclosing de-identified data is to reserve the right to audit the de-identified data recipient's data stewardship practices for compliance with contract terms and legal requirements.

If organizations do not willingly embrace these best practices and do not practice good stewardship of de-identified data (i.e., practice accountability), look for legislators and regulators to address the need to protect the data in the form of laws, rules and regulations. Even if these practices are adopted, it is still likely that regulations will be promulgated that will directly prohibit re-identification of de-identified data.

Summary

In short, look for the following three themes in the future:

1. There will be a globalization of privacy, in which information practice principles are relatively consistent across the world, there is more accountability, and enforcement increases. Further, expect that healthcare data will be part of this globalization as healthcare companies expand their borders and any geographic lines blur.
2. Expect an open information economy in which geographic borders are permeated, data are viewed by increasing numbers of people, and in which greater transparency and better education of healthcare consumers will be necessary to maintain patient trust.
3. De-identified data will take on a more prominent role as a protector of patient privacy that allows the free flow of data for innovation and research. Look for more healthcare organizations to embrace the expert determination method of de-identification and to recognize its appropriate use for applications in which PHI may be used today, to the benefit of both individuals and the healthcare system.

Notes

1. http://www.gov.im/lib/docs/odps//madridresolutionpressreleasenov0.pdf.
2. *See generally* http://ec.europa.eu/justice/data-protection/index_en.htm.
3. *See generally* http://eur-lex.europa.eu/legal-content/EN/TXT/?uri=uriserv:O J.L_.2016.119.01.0001.01.ENG&toc=OJ:L:2016:119:TOC.
4. *Schrems v. Data Protection Commissioner*, Case C-362/14 (Sept. 23, 2015), available at http://curia.europa.eu/juris/document/document.jsf;jsessionid=9ea7 d2dc30dd477423966d15418b92bee2c0f3a80e1d.e34KaxiLc3qMb40Rch0SaxuTbx r0?text=&docid=168421&pageIndex=0&doclang=en&mode=req&dir=&occ=first &part=1&cid=421417.

5. *See generally* http://europa.eu/rapid/press-release_IP-16-2461_en.htm?utm_content=buffer73ba4&utm_medium=social&utm_source=twitter.com&utm_campaign=buffer.

6. *See* Nahra, Is the Sectoral Approach to Privacy Dead in the U.S.?, Bloomberg BNA Privacy and Security Law Report (April 4, 2016), available at http://www.wileyrein.com/media/publication/197_Is-the-Sectoral-Approach-to-Privacy-Dead-in-the-US.pdf).

7. https://www.healthit.gov/policy-researchers-implementers/nationwide-privacy-and-security-framework-electronic-exchange.

8. http://ftc.gov/os/2012/03/120326privacyreport.pdf.

9. *See* Pettypiece and Robertson, Hospitals Soon See Donuts-to-Cigarette Charges for Health, (Bloomberg.com, June 26, 2014), available at http://www.bloomberg.com/news/2014-06-26/hospitals-soon-see-donuts-to-cigarette-charges-for-health.html.

10. *See* Singer, When a Health Plan Knows How You Shop, (*New York Times*, June 28, 2014), available at http://www.nytimes.com/2014/06/29/technology/when-a-health-plan-knows-how-you-shop.html?_r=0.

11. Zarya, Employers Are Quietly Using Big Data to Track Employee Pregnancies, (Feb. 17, 2016), available at http://fortune.com/2016/02/17/castlight-pregnancy-data/.

12. Silverman, Bosses Tap Outside Firms to Predict Which Workers Might Get Sick, Wall Street Journal (Feb. 17, 2016), available at http://www.wsj.com/articles/bosses-harness-big-data-to-predict-which-workers-might-get-sick-1455664940.

13. Executive Office of the President, Big Data: Seizing Opportunities, Preserving Values, (May 2014), available at https://www.whitehouse.gov/sites/default/files/docs/big_data_privacy_report_may_1_2014.pdf.

14. Quoted in Dolan, In-Depth: Consumer health and data privacy issues beyond HIPAA, (May 23, 2014), available at http://mobihealthnews.com/33393/in-depth-consumer-health-and-data-privacy-issues-beyond-hipaa.

15. 67 Fed. Reg. 53181, 53232 (Aug. 14, 2002).

16. 65 Fed. Reg. 82462, 82708 (Dec. 28, 2000).

17. *See* HHS Office for Civil Rights, Guidance Regarding Methods for De-identification of Protected Health Information in Accordance with the Health Insurance Portability and Accountability Act (HIPAA) Privacy Rule, (Nov. 26, 2012) at 5, available at http://www.hhs.gov/sites/default/files/ocr/privacy/hipaa/understanding/coveredentities/De-identification/hhs_deid_guidance.pdf.

18. 45 CFR 164.514 (b)(2)(i)(ii)

19. Available at https://www.ftc.gov/sites/default/files/documents/reports/federal-trade-commission-report-protecting-consumer-privacy-era-rapid-change-recommendations/120326privacyreport.pdf.

Index

Printed in the United States
by Baker & Taylor Publisher Services